AF732697

PRIMARY

GREAT **WORSHIP** FOR KIDS

HE IS POWERFUL

STANDARD PUBLISHING
Cincinnati, Ohio

Writers

Anita Kohl, Sessions 1-6, 9
Kathleen A. Underwood, Sessions 7, 8
Kathryn McKee, Sessions 10-17
Diana Crawford, Sessions 18-26

Artists

Dan Grossmann—Page 8, Activity Page 2B
Sandy Wimmer—All Other Inside Art

Scripture quotations are from the following versions:

The *International Children's Bible, New Century Version*, copyright ©1983, 1986, 1988 by Word Publishing, Dallas, Texas 75039. Used by permission. (Sometimes identified as ICB.)

The Holy Bible, New International Version, copyright ©1973, 1978, 1984 by the International Bible Society. Used by permission of Zondervan Bible Publishers. (Sometimes identified as NIV.)

Library of Congress Cataloging-in-Publication Data

(Revised for volume 2)

Great worship for kids. Primary.

Contents: [1] He is Lord — [2] He is powerful.
1. Worship (Religious education)
BV1522.G67 1991 268'.432 91-8431
ISBN 0-87403-922-3 (v. 2)

Table of Contents

What Is Great Worship for Kids?

Welcome to 26 weeks of great worship sessions for your Primaries. What makes the worship a great experience for your kids? What is *Great Worship for Kids*? To determine what great worship is, we must first determine what it is not.

Great Worship for Kids is **not** a second Sunday-school hour. The emphasis in Sunday school is on instruction. The emphasis in worship is on worship.

Great Worship for Kids is **not** a mini-adult worship service. Primaries do not think like adults. Great worship for kids enables them to worship on their level of understanding and development.

Great Worship for Kids is **not** a service designed simply to keep children occupied while adults are in worship. The children's worship is as important and meaningful as the adult worship.

What **is** *Great Worship for Kids*? It is a program in which your Primaries truly worship God with understanding and have the opportunity to participate actively in worship. Primaries take part both in preparation and in actual worship.

Each session provides six small-group activity choices. In the small groups, children prepare to lead the call to worship, Scripture, prayer, special music, devotional, offering, Lord's Supper, or personal praise. As Primaries learn about God—who He is and what He has done, they are given opportunity to respond in praise and thanksgiving. Thus, Primaries are led to worship God.

When children participate in this worship program, they

KNOW Biblical concepts and basic skills of worship.

FEEL positive attitudes toward worship.

DO actively participate in worship.

When children prepare and lead the worship time, they learn that worship is giving, not receiving. Worship is active, not passive. Worship is each person's responsibility, not the responsibility of the person in front of the church.

Worship cannot be forced on anyone. But when children know who God is and what He has done, they can respond in love, praise, and thanks. Their response is true worship.

How to Use This Material

How Is This Material Organized?

This book contains 26 sessions. The sessions are divided into six units of four or five sessions each. The units explore ways to worship God. Worship God by: learning to tell about Jesus, telling about Jesus, telling about Jesus when it is difficult, choosing to do right, choosing to do right even when it is hard, choosing to do what God says is right. The sessions are based on Scriptures taken from Standard Publishing's Primary Sunday-school curriculum.

The sessions are planned so that children work in small groups to prepare the elements of the worship time (call to worship, Scripture, special music, devotional, and so on). The elements the small groups have prepared are then incorporated into the worship time.

Each weekly session is designed to last 80-95 minutes. This includes the time between the end of Sunday school and the beginning of adult worship.

The sessions are organized into six segments.

Worship Focus
Transition Time (10-15 minutes)
Launching the Theme (10 minutes)
Building the Theme (30 minutes)
Sharing in Worship (20-25 minutes)
Closing Moments (10-15 minutes)

Within each segment, suggested talk by the teacher is printed in **bold type**.

What Happens in Each Segment?

Worship Focus

This section gives a way to worship God. Worship God by telling about Him, by obeying Him, by choosing to do what He says is right. Every activity in the session centers on the worship focus.

Transition Time
(10-15 minutes)

Transition Time is the flexible time between Sunday school and children's worship. This is a casual time for relaxation and conversation. It includes a rest-room and drink break, as well as a game which allows the children to move around freely. This freedom is important after they have been sitting during the Sunday-school hour.

Involving the children in organized activity as soon as they arrive also avoids confusion and eliminates the moments you spend gathering children from the halls when you are ready to begin the worship time.

Launching the Theme
(10 minutes)

During *Launching the Theme*, the leader introduces the theme of the session to the pupils. The leader may tell a Bible story or modern-day story, use puppets, present an object lesson, present a skit, or ask children to role play. Involving children during this section is a priority.

The leader also explains the small-group choices and allows children to choose in which group to participate. The leader guides the children to choose groups they are interested in. Depending upon the maturity level and group dynamics of the children, the leader may assign groups rather than letting children choose.

Building the Theme
(30 minutes)

During this time, children work in their groups to prepare the elements of the worship time: call to worship, prayer, Scripture, special music, group singing, Lord's Supper, offering, personal praise, or devotional. During *Sharing in Worship*, the children present what they prepared in their groups.

Sharing in Worship
(20-25 minutes)

The large group gathers for the worship time. The leader directs this time and integrates the small-group activities into the worship time. Thus, the children participate in worship.

Closing Moments
(10-15 minutes)

Closing Moments is the flexible time between the end of Primary worship and the end of adult worship. This section lists a variety of activities, but each one can be dropped quickly and easily when the adult service is over.

What Other Materials Will I Need?

Activity Pages

Following each worship session are two reproducible activity pages. The pages are used in a variety of ways—an introductory game, a cut-out craft, words to a song, a cut and fold book, and so on.

Worship Songs

The final section of this book contains worship songs which are incorporated into the worship sessions. You may wish to pull out the song section and place it in a looseleaf notebook for easy reference. Add song sections from each **Great Worship for Kids** to your notebook to make your own worship song book.

Classroom Supplies

See the Suggested Supplies on this page for a list of supplies you should have available every week. At the beginning of each activity is a list of materials you will need. Read the session early in the week and make a list of any special items or supplies you will need to gather ahead of time.

How Many Leaders Do We Need?

A coordinating leader is responsible to plan *Transition Time, Launching the Theme, Sharing in Worship,* and *Closing Moments.* You will need as many other leaders as you have small groups during *Building the Theme.*

What If We Have Only One Leader?

Shorten *Launching the Theme*, and lengthen *Building the Theme*. Choose two or three small-group activities to complete with your group. The devotional includes a leader talk which can be completed without a group presentation, so you would not need to complete that activity.

Some activities can be completed without adult guidance. Write or tape record the instructions for a self-explanatory activity. Choose older or more mature children to complete the activity. Choose an activity that you can lead the rest of the group in completing at the same time as the self-explanatory activity. If you have time, choose another activity to complete as a large group.

During *Sharing in Worship*, omit sections if you did not offer the corresponding activity. The Lord's Supper, Offering, and Devotional may always be completed without the group presentations.

What If We Worship First and Have an Activity Time Second?

Use the activity in *Launching the Theme* to introduce the worship time. Then proceed with worship, using the leader talk provided with each section and the devotional talk to tie in the worship to the theme of the day. During the activity time, choose group activities from *Building the Theme* which reinforce the concepts discussed in worship. If you have time, children may share what they have learned in their small groups at the end of the session rather than completing the activity in *Closing Moments*.

What If One Small Group Finishes Early?

If you have not chosen to do the self-explanatory activity for that session, have the materials available. Children who finish early can complete that activity. A challenge activity is often included in the session. This activity is for gifted or older pupils and will take longer to complete. If you have children who are consistently finished early, assign them to this activity. You may also wish to use one of the reproducible activity pages in each session as an optional activity to be completed by pupils who finish early.

Suggested Supplies

index cards
Bibles
markers
pencils
pens
crayons
tape recorder
blank cassette tape
paper fasteners
yarn or string
chalkboard and chalk
stapler and staples
push pins
old magazines
newspapers
scissors
glue
cellophane tape
Plasti-Tak
paper hole punch
plain paper
writing paper
construction paper
newsprint paper
poster board
paper towels
tissues

Primary
Worship

Worship
Path

Worship Plan Sheet

Session ____ Date __________
Unit Title ______________________________
Session Title ______________________________
Worship Focus ______________________________

Transition Time

Leader ______________________

Materials: ______________________________

____

Preparation: ______________________________

____

Procedure: ______________________________

____

____

Launching the Theme

Leader ______________________

Materials: ______________________________

____

Preparation: ______________________________

____

Procedure: ______________________________

____

____

Building the Theme

Group 1. ____________________ Leader ______________________

Materials: ______________________________

____

Preparation: ______________________________

____

Procedure: ______________________________

____

____

Group 2. ____________________ Leader ______________________

Materials: ______________________________

____

Preparation: ______________________________

____

Procedure: ______________________________

____

____

Group 3. ____________________ Leader ______________________

Materials: ______________________________

____

Preparation: ______________________________

____

Procedure: ____________________

Group 4. ____________ Leader ____________

Materials: ____________________

Preparation: ____________________

Procedure: ____________________

Group 5. ____________ Leader ____________

Materials: ____________________

Preparation: ____________________

Procedure: ____________________

Group 6. ____________ Leader ____________

Materials: ____________________

Preparation: ____________________

Procedure: ____________________

Sharing in Worship

Leader ____________

Closing Moments

Leader ____________

Materials: ____________________

Preparation: ____________________

Procedure: ____________________

Activities for Special Days

Invitation

Purpose: Child will tell about Jesus by inviting another child to come with him.

Materials: A copy of page 15 for each child, crayons or markers, and pencils.

Distribute the copies of page 15. Give the children the following instructions. Be prepared to help the children fill in the blanks on the cards. Have a sample card prepared to show the children.

1. Color the cross.
2. Cut out the card.
3. Fold the card where it says Fold 1 and Fold 2.
4. Write the information your teacher tells you in the blanks on the card.
5. Write your name at the bottom of the page.
6. Take the card home with you. Choose someone to invite to come with you next week. Give that person the invitation.

Cross Bookmark

Purpose: Child will make a bookmark to remind him to celebrate Jesus' death and resurrection.

Materials: A copy of the cross on page 12 made on construction paper or felt material, scissors, glue, paper hole punch, yarn, markers, rickrack, narrow ribbon, cross or Easter stickers, and so on to use to decorate the cross. If desired, also use the pattern to make crosses on poster board. Cut these out ahead of time for the children. The construction paper or felt cross can be glued to this for added strength.

Distribute the materials. Give the children the following instructions.

1. Cut out the cross pattern.
2. Punch a hole in the top of the cross.
3. Tie yarn through the hole.
4. Decorate the cross. Use the materials to make a nice cross bookmark. It will remind you to celebrate Jesus' death and resurrection.

(Optional: 5. Glue your bookmark to a poster board cross.)

Be certain the crosses are completely dry before the children put them in their Bibles.

Do Right Wheel

Purpose: Child will make a reminder for him to choose to do right wherever he is.

Materials: A copy of pages 13 and 14 for each child, scissors, crayons or markers, paper fastener for each child.

Distribute the copies of pages 13 and 14. Give the children the following instructions.

1. Color the pictures in the circle. Color in the outlines of the letters.
2. Cut out the blank wheel on the other paper. Be sure you cut the wedge out of it too.
3. Color the blank wheel if you want.
4. Place the blank wheel on top of the circle with pictures.

5. Match the dot on the wheel with the dot on the circle.
6. Use a paper fastener to attach the wheel to the page with the circle.
7. Turn the wheel to see places where you will choose to do what is right. Tell how you will do what is right in that place.
8. Hang your picture in your room at home to remind you to choose to do what is right.

Cross Bookmark Pattern

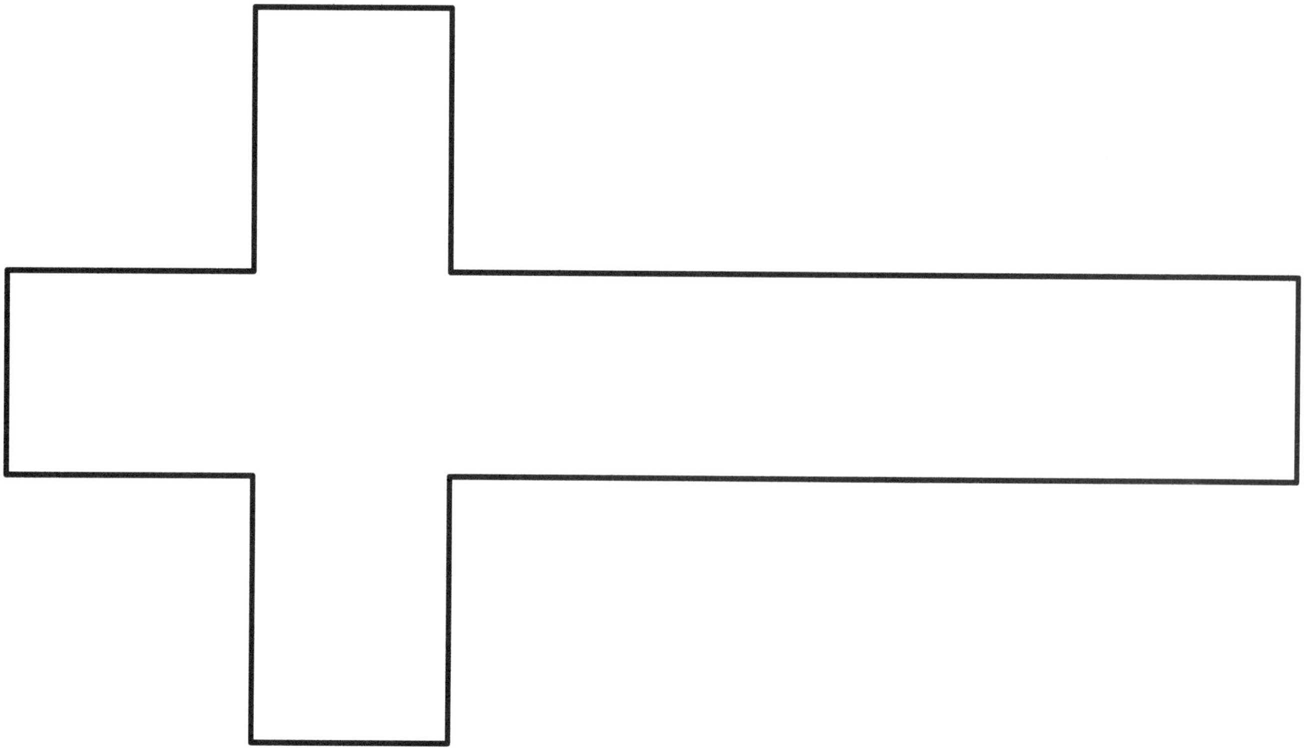

I WILL CHOOSE TO DO WHAT IS RIGHT!

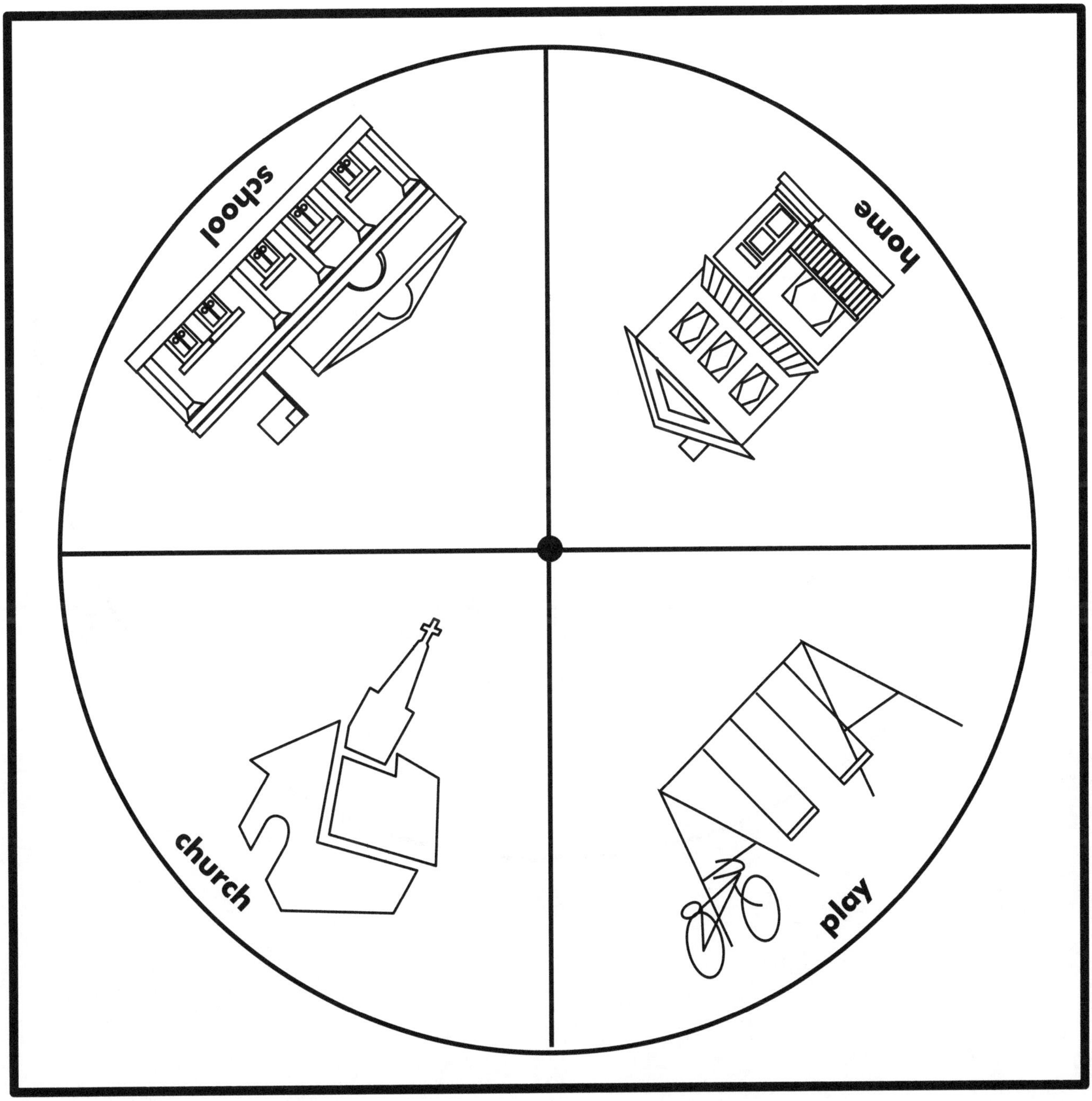

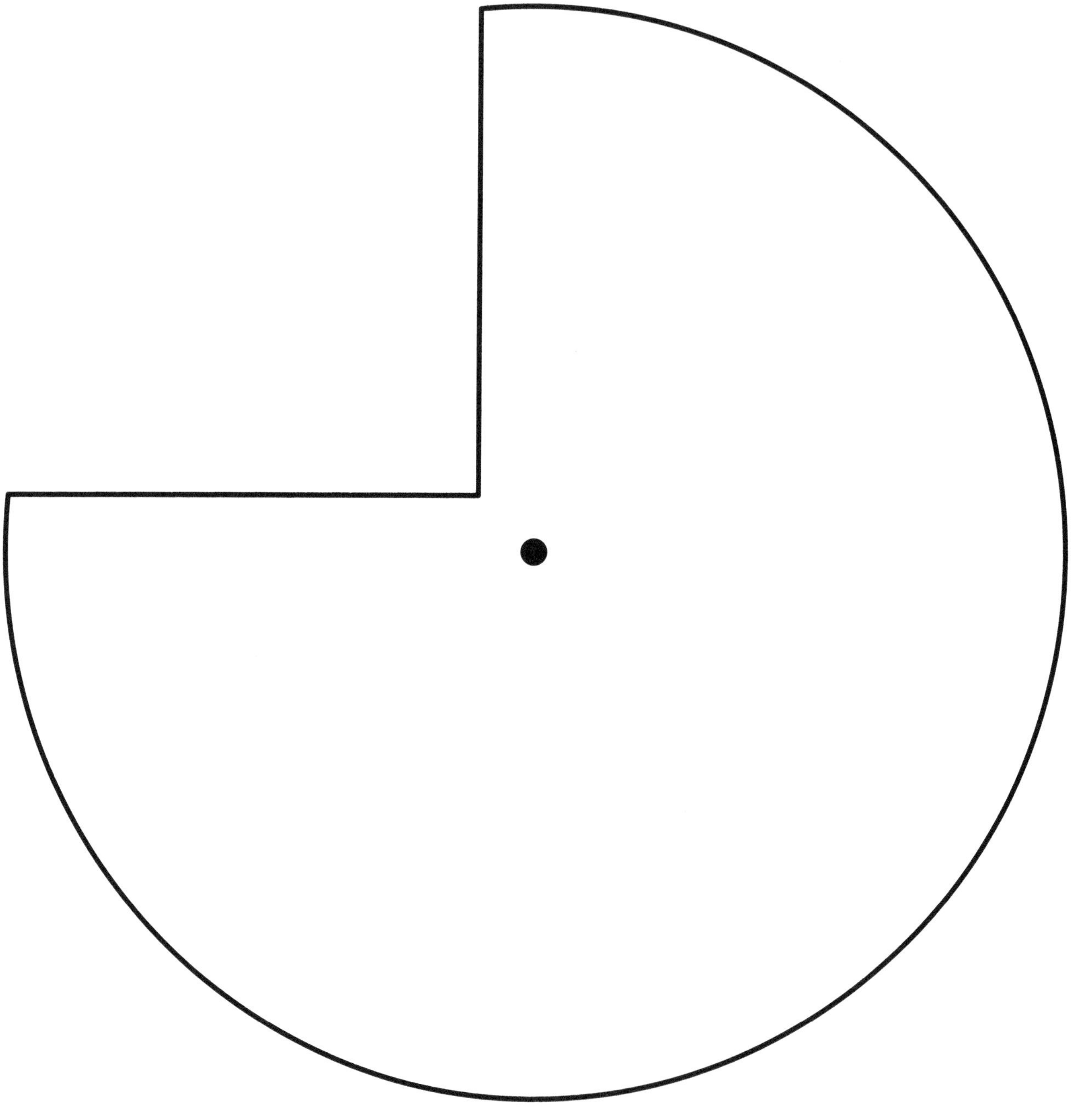

fold 2

You are invited!

Please come with me to worship Jesus.

Sunday, ______________________
(date)

at ______________________
(time)

to ______________________.
(place)

____
(your name)

fold 1

Mobile Pattern

Session 17

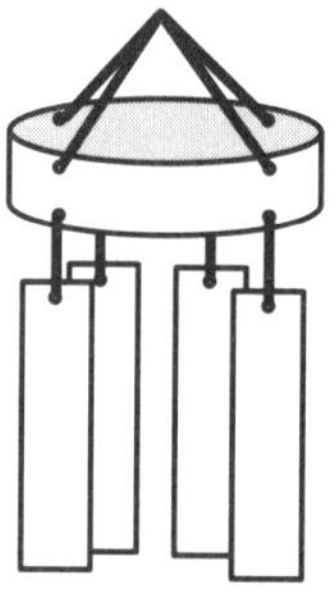

LOVE 1

LOVE

WORSHIP 2

WORSHIP

SERVE 3

SERVE

OBEY 4

OBEY

THE ONE TRUE GOD 1 2 3 4

THE ONE TRUE GOD

Jesus Stops a Storm

Worship Focus

We worship Jesus because we have faith in Him and we can trust Him.

Transition Time

(10-15 minutes)

Encourage the children to use the rest room and get drinks as they come to the room. Choose two student helpers and give each of them a badge.

(Prior to class, make badges for your helpers. Make two photocopies of the badge on page 26. Color, if desired, glue to poster board, cut out, and glue a safety pin on back. Cover with clear, adhesive-backed paper if desired.) Use these badges each week or make new ones to allow children to take them home. Alternate student helpers so every child takes a turn.

Drop the Sail. (Materials needed are a piece of cloth for the sail.) **We are going to play a game about ships at sea. As new people come, make room for them in the ship.** Have the children form a circle. Call this the ship. Designate an area outside the circle as the ocean. Choose a captain to carry the sail around the ship and give it to a sailor. The sailor and the captain move (run, walk, or crawl, depending on the size of the activity area) in opposite directions around the circle. The first one back to the empty space is the captain, and the loser goes to the ocean. The teacher can control the time of the game and the size of the ship by rescuing those in the ocean by saying, "Jesus will save you!" Those in the ocean may then return to the ship. As new people come, have the student helpers get them into the game.

Creative Drawing. (Materials needed are paper and crayons or markers.) **In Sunday school you learned about a storm. Think about storm sounds and draw a picture of what you think you would see, hear, smell, and feel in a storm. When you are done, write as many words as you can think of that would tell about your picture.** Play a record or tape recording of storm sounds if possible. Check your local library for such a recording. Display the completed pictures. Use them in *Sharing in Worship*.

Banner. (Materials needed are butcher paper approximately four feet long, markers or crayons, and letter stencils if desired.) Have the children decorate and/or color in letters of a banner reading "We Worship Jesus Because. . . ." Use this banner to start a display of the weekly *Worship Focus* in Unit One. This week's *Worship Focus* will be added during *Building the Theme*, so only complete banner title now.

Launching the Theme

(10 minutes)

Assemble the group by playing "It's Time to Praise the Lord." (Use live music or a tape recording.)

We are getting ready to worship Jesus because we have faith in Him and we trust Him. Listen while I tell you about a time when Jesus taught the disciples about faith and trust.

Choose from these option to illustrate the story. Draw with markers or colored chalk as you tell the story (or have a previously drawn picture). Or use flannelboard figures on a flannelboard. (For variety, attach magnets to figures and use a metal cookie sheet as a display board.)

Divide the children into two groups (half representing the disciples and half representing Jesus) to participate in the storytelling.

Act out the story as I tell it to you. Think about how the people in this story might have felt as things happened.

It had been a busy day for Jesus. All day long, He had been teaching the people by the Sea of Galilee. The crowd had been so large that Jesus had to get into a boat and move a short distance off shore so everyone could see and hear. He had told them parables about a sower, a lamp on a stand, and a mustard seed. Now it was getting dark. Jesus

knew that if the people could see Him, they would not leave; so He told the disciples to sail the boat to a place on the other side of the water.

Jesus was very tired. Did you ever think about Jesus' getting tired or hungry? As the boat moved away from shore, the sounds of the crowd faded away, and it got very quiet. Show me how you would feel if you were Jesus. It is quiet, you have been teaching all day, and the boat is gently rocking. You would get sleepy, and that is what happened to Jesus. He went to sleep. What would the disciples be doing? (They would be rowing, sailing the ship, sleeping.)

But suddenly a storm came up! This happens quite often on the Sea of Galilee. Remember that some of Jesus' disciples were fishermen. Probably they had been caught in one of these storms before, and they knew they were dangerous.

Jesus is still sleeping, but, Disciples, show me how you would be feeling. The wind is getting stronger. The waves are getting higher. Lightning is flashing! Thunder is crashing!

Disciples! What are you going to do? (Wake Jesus.)

You people who are tired, peacefully sleeping with Jesus, how do you think Jesus felt? Did He get angry? Did He get scared? No. He got up, and He spoke to the wind and the waves.

You people who are pretending to be Jesus, listen to what Jesus said, and then you say it the way you think Jesus would have spoken. He said, "Quiet! Be Still!" (Choose several to give their interpretations.) **And the sea became calm and the wind stopped blowing.**

Disciples, show me how you would feel (amazed, relieved).

Jesus must have been disappointed in the disciples because He asked them two questions: "Why are you so afraid?" and "Do you still have no faith?"

Why could Jesus calm the storm? (He is the Son of God.) **Why do you think Jesus was disappointed in the disciples?** (They still did not show that they had faith and trusted in Him.) **How can we show that we have faith in Jesus and know we can trust Him?** (We can: ask Him for help, trust that He will help us, worship Him.)

Let's divide into groups and prepare some things to help us worship Jesus and thank Him that we can trust Him to take care of us. (Explain the six small groups activities to the children. Use the months of their birthdays to divide the children into groups.)

Building the Theme

(30 minutes)

1. Song. This group will make and decorate a song chart for "It's Time to Praise the Lord." You will need poster board and markers. Provide the words to the song for the children to copy. This chart will be reused each week to teach newcomers the words.

We can praise the Lord at any time of the day. In fact, it is important to praise God, even when things seem to be going wrong. One way that we can praise God is through our singing. Let's make a song chart to help us lead the song "It's Time to Praise the Lord" during our worship time.

Help the children learn the song so they can teach it to the group. For a challenge activity, have the children develop motions to teach to the group.

2. Banner Addition. Have the children make and decorate an addition to the banner display. (See *Transition Time* description of the banner.) The addition should read, "We have faith and trust in Him to take care of us." You will need butcher paper and markers or crayons.

What are some ways we can show that we have faith and trust in Jesus? (Pray to Him, obey His commands.) **What are some ways that we trust Jesus to take care of us every day?** (Know that parents will care for us, trust that daytime and nighttime will continue, have faith that we will have food to eat and water to drink, and so on.) **After we have written our *Worship Focus* on our banner, let's write the words or draw pictures of ways that we trust Jesus and ways that we show that trust.**

Help the children hang the addition to the banner when they are finished.

3. Scripture. We are going to find and practice reading the Scripture that will be used as our Call to Worship.

Have the group find and learn to read Hebrews 11:6 and Proverbs 3:5. Encourage the pupils to read from their own Bibles. If possible, the children should use the *New International Version* for this activity. Provide enough extra Bibles for the children to have the same version. Practice reading the verses aloud together. Use bookmarks to help the children locate these verses easily during *Sharing in Worship.*

Complete the activity by having the children draw something to illustrate the verse. Choose one or two to use in the Call to Worship. You will need drawing paper and markers or crayons for this activity.

If time allows, memorize one or both verses (or divide the group and assign each child one part of the verses to memorize) to recite for the group during *Sharing in Worship.*

4. Interview. You have all watched or read interviews with famous people. Let's do an interview having some of you being the disciples and one of you being a reporter. It is the day after Jesus calmed the storm. When the interview is over, we will write a newspaper story about the interview.

Have some volunteers pretend they are a few of the disciples and a reporter the day after the Scripture story happened. The rest of the group will listen as the volunteers act out an interview about the storm. Help as needed with questions or answers to draw out the complete story as well as imagined emotions.

Then the pupils will write a newspaper article based on the interview. They could work individually or as a group with you or an older student writing the story as the group dictates it. Choose one of the students to read the article during the Devotional.

5. Independent Story Review. You will need activity page 1A. (Reproduce enough for this group to use.) You will also need construction paper, scissors, glue, and crayons or markers. Make a chart of the following instructions for the children. (This activity needs minimal supervision. Post the chart in center where this activity will be.) Read Mark 4:35-41 in your Bible. Cut out the puzzle pieces. Read the captions on each piece. Place the pieces in the correct order to make a scene. Glue the puzzle to a piece of construction paper and color the scene. You will show your story review puzzle during the Devotional.

6. Offering Scriptures. Give each child in the group a photocopy of activity page 1B. Assign each child one verse to read aloud. (Some verses may be repeated.) After the children have read the verses (Psalm 103:2; Psalm 96:8; Matthew 10:8; and 2 Corinthians 9:7), focus the conversation on the meaning of the verse. **What are some of the kindnesses God shows us? What are His temple courtyards today? How can we help other people freely? How do we give happily? Why does God love the person who gives happily?**

After you have made sure that the children understand the verses, allow each child to illustrate his verse in the space at the bottom of the activity page. Some suggests for illustrations follow. *Verse 1:* Pictures of God's gifts. *Verse 2:* Church building, people going to church, or giving an offering in church. *Verse 3:* Pictures of things God has given us or of one helping another. *Verse 4:* A smiling face.

Before the Offering this group will read each Scripture in the order given and show the illustrations of each Scripture after it is read. Each verse should be read by only one child, but all children who illustrated that verse should show their illustrations.

Sharing in Worship

(20-25 minutes)

Omit any of the following sections if you did not offer the corresponding activity. The Devotional may be completed without the presentations of Groups 4 and 5.

Play the song "It's Time to Praise the Lord" to assemble the group.

Call to Worship (Groups 2 and 3)**: Look at the banner that Group 2 Prepared and listen as they read and explain what it says.** Have Group 2 stand and do so. **Now listen as Group 3 reads two Scriptures.** Have Group 3 stand, recite the verses, and show their illustrations. **Notice that these Scriptures talk about faith and trust, just as the banner did.**

Song (Group 1)**:** Group 1 will teach "It's Time to Praise the Lord" to the large group. **Group 1 will sing a worship song for us. Listen carefully so that all of us can sing it the second time.**

Thank Group 1; then lead the large group in singing two or three more songs.

Lord's Supper: In the Bible story Jesus taught the disciples a lesson about having faith and trusting. We know we can trust Jesus to take care of us if we have faith in Him. Let's remember this and thank Him for caring enough to die for us, so that our sins could be forgiven.

Offering (Group 6)**: Group 6 has some Scriptures which will help us understand better how we should give our offerings and why.** Have the student helpers receive the offering.

Devotional (Groups 4 and 5)**: Group 5 will review our Bible story for us.** Let them do so. **That was an amazing thing to happen. The people in Group 4 have written newspaper articles about the Bible story. Let's listen to what you might have read in a newspaper the day after the storm.** Have volunteers read their articles.

Throughout our time this morning, we have been talking about trusting. I am going to help you think about trusting. As you are listening to me, think about some adults you know who might be good examples of trusting people.

When you buy a can of food, why are you sure there is tomato soup or tuna inside? You trust the label. **When you step into an elevator, what are you trusting?** The elevator will operate correctly and not fall. **When you come to an intersection and the light is green, why do you feel it is safe to go on through?** You trust the people on the other street to stop.

What are you trusting each time? People and machines. **How long will you continue to trust them?** Until they show they are not trustworthy.

Who are people you trust? Parents, friends, policemen are a few. **How do you know they are trustworthy?** They have proven themselves to be trustworthy. **You trust your parents to come pick you up when they have taken you to Scouts or to a friend's house. You trust your friend not to tell your secret. You trust the doctor to give you the right medicine to make you well. You trust all of these people. Why?** You know them and see them all the time.

Do you believe the Bible is trustworthy? Why? You have faith. Read Hebrews 11:6; Proverbs 3:5, and John 20:30, 31. **What do these Bible verses tell us we should do?** Have faith, trust, and believe. **Can we be sure this is the right thing to do? Why?** The Bible teaches this.

Prayer: Let's pray about this. Lord, help us learn to have faith in You and to trust you always, even though we do not see You. In Jesus' name, amen.

Closing Moments

(10-15 minutes)

Make a door poster to illustrate trust reading, "Nothing will happen today that You and I can't handle, Lord."

Materials needed for the poster include large sheets of construction paper, copies of coloring book pages showing someone or an animal being trusting, tape or glue, scissors, markers or crayons. Scraps of material or decorative trim and stickers could also be used to make the poster attractive.

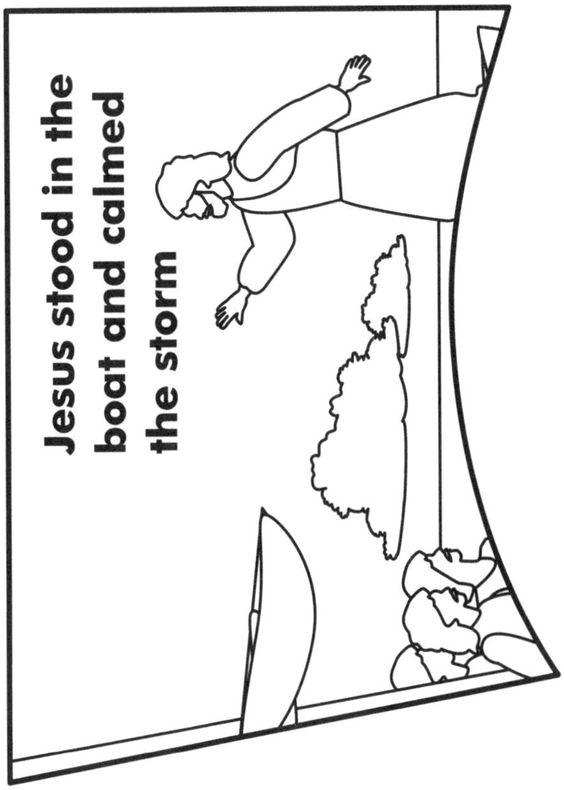

What you do:

- cut out the puzzle pieces
- read the captions on each piece
- place the pieces in correct order to make a scene
- glue to construction paper and add color

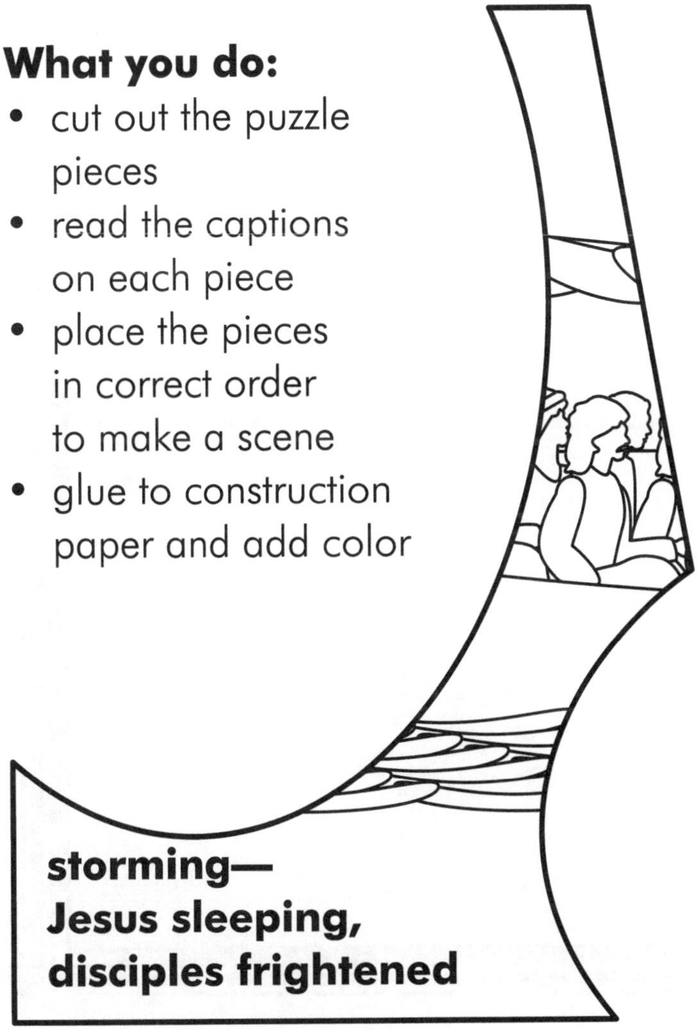

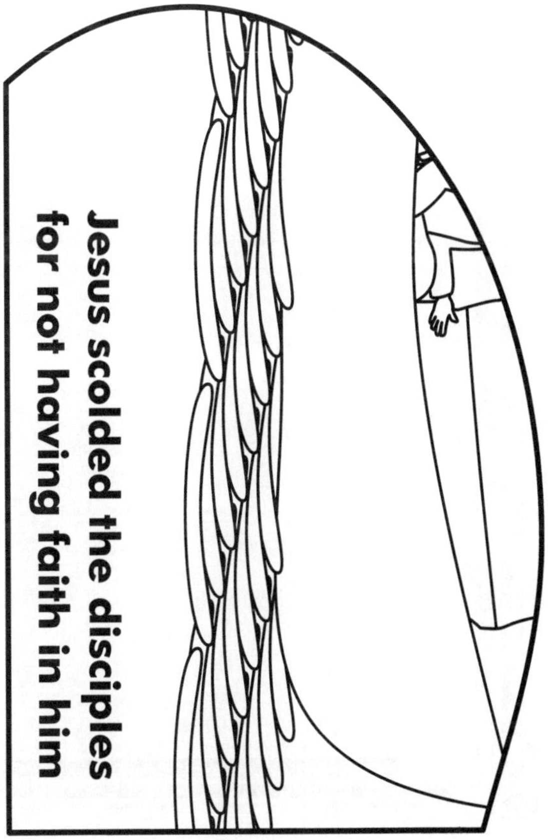

"My whole being, praise the Lord. Do not forget all his kindnesses" (Psalm 103:2, *ICB*).

"Praise the glory of the Lord's name. Bring an offering and come into his Temple courtyards" (Psalm 96:8, *ICB*).

"I give you these powers freely. So help other people freely" (Matthew 10:8, *ICB*).

"God loves the person who gives happily" (2 Corinthians 9:7, *ICB*).

Jesus Heals a Man Who Is Deaf

Worship Focus

We worship Jesus because He can do wonderful things.

Transition Time

(10-15 minutes)

Encourage the children to use the rest rooms and get drinks as they come to the room. Choose two students helpers and give them badges.

(Prior to class, make badges for your helpers. Make two photocopies of the badge on page 26. Color, if desired, glue to poster board, cut out, and glue a safety pin on back. Cover with clear, adhesive-backed paper if desired.) Use these badges each week or make new ones to allow children to take them home. Alternate student helpers so every child takes a turn.

Walk to the music. Materials you will need are newspapers, live music or tape-recorded music and tape player (lively music is best), and tape. Prior to the session mark a path around the room using sheets of newspaper secured to the floor with tape. Leave several large areas where there is no newspaper.

The children must keep moving forward as long as the music is playing. When the music stops, each child must stop and then take one more full step. If this takes him off the paper, he must sit down. The last one or two remaining are the winners.

Isn't it wonderful to be able to hear? You could not have played this game if you could not hear the music. Jesus did a wonderful thing when He made a deaf man hear.

Hearing Impaired Display. Before this session, write for information about hearing impairment or use information from your library. (Addresses for information are in *Suggested Resources* at end of this session.) Set up a center using these materials. If possible, have a hearing-impaired representative present to answer questions.

Banner Addition. Make and color the addition to the *Worship Focus* banner begun last week. (If you did not do this activity, see page 17 for instructions.) Materials you will need are butcher paper (about four feet long), markers or crayons, and letter stencils. This week's addition is "He can heal a deaf man." Add the banner to last week's display.

Launching the Theme

(10 minutes)

An interview. Before the session photocopy activity page 2A for two people. Choose two of your best readers to be a reporter and the deaf man whom Jesus healed. Allow them to practice during *Transition Time*.

Deaf Man Hears

Reporter: What was wrong with you, sir?

Man: I could not hear or speak.

Reporter: How did that make you feel?

Man: Lonely—and sad. I didn't know what people were saying. I could not answer them. I couldn't hear music. I could see the birds, but I couldn't hear their songs.

Reporter: What did Jesus do for you?

Man: He took me aside, away from the crowd. And He put His fingers into my ears. Then He spit and touched my tongue. He looked up to Heaven and said something. Later they told me that He said, "Be opened."

Reporter: And what happened?

Man: My ears were opened! I could hear! I could speak!

Reporter: That is wonderful! You surely do talk plainly today. And you heard everything I said. How do you feel now?

Man: How do you think I feel? Happy! So happy! And so grateful to Jesus for doing this wonderful thing for me.

Reporter: How do you think it was possible for Jesus to do this miracle?

Man: Because He is the Son of God. Jesus can do wonderful things because He is the Son of God.

Jesus made a deaf man hear and speak. Let's listen to an interview with someone pretending to be that man. Listen carefully to the interview. I want all of you with blue eyes to be ready afterward to tell me how the man felt before Jesus made him hear. Those of you with brown eyes be ready to tell me what Jesus did. Those with green eyes can tell me how the man felt after Jesus made him hear.

Let the reporter interview the deaf man. After it is over, allow the children to talk about the man's feelings and what Jesus did.

Explain the six activity choices. Use the vowel sounds in the children's names to dismiss them to the group of their choice (long a, short a, long e, and so on).

Building the Theme

(30 minutes)

1. Signing a song. Even though hearing impaired people cannot hear or speak well, they still can have choirs. They learn to sign a song in rhythm. Let's learn some motions for the words of "Isn't He Wonderful?" and then practice doing them as a choir. We will hum the tune as we do our word motions.

The following are some suggested motions for the song. HE—point up; WONDERFUL—clap, clap, clap; JESUS—point to nail holes in each palm; MY—point to self; LORD—both hands over head to make crown; EYES—point to eyes; HAVE SEEN—pretend to hold binoculars to eyes; EARS—point to ears; HAVE HEARD—cup hands by ears; IT'S RECORDED—pretend to write; GOD'S—point up; WORD—hold hands like open book.

The children will begin the song time in *Sharing in Worship* with this song.

2. Scripture Song. In the story about the deaf man, Jesus did a wonderful thing. We need to tell other people about Jesus and the wonderful things He has done. Please find Mark 16:15 in your Bibles. Allow time for the children to do this. **Listen and follow along while I read this verse.** Ask for a volunteer who will read this verse during *Sharing in Worship* and allow him to read it once also. Teach the children the song "Go Everywhere!" Let the children make a song chart with the words to the song so they can teach the large group "Go Everywhere!" Provide chart paper or poster board and markers for this activity.

3. Speaking With Hands. Before class, photocopy activity page 2B for the children in the group. Let the children experiment with the sign language alphabet. (If you had a hearing-impaired person in the room for *Transition Time,* ask him to help the children learn the alphabet.)

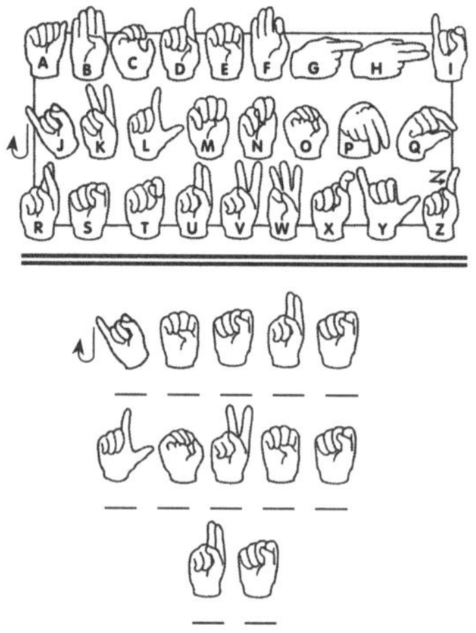

Let's learn how to spell with our fingers. Look at the top part of the page. It has the manual alphabet for spelling with your fingers. Deaf people use this alphabet as well as other signs that they make with their hands. First locate the letters that are in your name. Then try to spell your name. Next try to read someone else's name as he spells it. After you have practiced that a few times, we will practice a message that will be used during the Lord's Supper meditation. Allow the children time to practice. Work with them, spelling your name and reading theirs. Let the children decode the message on activity page 2B. They will write the letter on the line under the hand sign. The message is "Jesus loves us."

Jesus loves us very much. In fact, He loves us so much that He died on the cross for us. Today let's tell the other children that Jesus loves us. We will practice so that together we can spell the sentence, "Jesus loves us." After we have spelled the message, we will say together, "Jesus loves us."

Let the children practice spelling "Jesus loves us" with their fingers until they can do it smoothly and well.

4. Make-a-Sound Story. We have been talking about a world without sound, but what would a world without words be like? Let's review today's Bible story using ordinary sounds

Materials you will need are a tape recorder and a selection of objects for making a variety of sounds. (Don't forget that hands and feet can make several noises, too!) You will also need chart paper and markers for writing the review of today's Bible story.

If you have advanced students, let them write out the story, taking turns dictating and writing. Refer to Mark 7:31-37 to refresh memories or fill in details. If necessary, write the story yourself as the group dictates to you.

After the story is complete, assign sounds to the main characters and major verbs. Mark the sounds by the corresponding words throughout the story. Use symbols for the sounds if possible. Let each child choose a sound to make. (If necessary, let the children choose two sounds apiece. More than that would be confusing.)

Practice the story. Read the story yourself and allow the children to make the sounds at the appropriate time. (Omit saying the words that have sounds assigned for them.) The story will be read and "sounded" during the devotional portion of *Sharing in Worship.*

5. Montage. At the top of a large sheet of poster board, print "Wonderful Things to Hear." Cut out pictures from magazines, story papers, and so on, of wonderful things to hear. (Music, people's voices, birds, and so on). The pupils may select pictures, cut them out, and past them on the poster board to make a montage.

The pupils will display their montage during the Devotional.

If you could not hear at all, probably any sound would seem wonderful even though not all of them might be beautiful. Find some pictures of things making sounds.

When the montage is complete, let the children practice taking turns explaining the sounds that are represented.

6. TELL Time. Prayer is time for telling things to God. What do we want to tell Him today?

Make a list on a chalkboard or chart. Suggestions: we love Him; we are glad He sent Jesus His Son; we thank Him that we can hear; we want to tell others about Jesus.

Have the pupils print in a large letters each letter of the word *tell* on a separate square of cardboard (approximately five inches square). Fasten a dowel stick to the bottom of each card. The pupils will hold up their cards as the leader introduces the prayer time during *Sharing in Worship.* Volunteers from this group will tell the suggestions from their list.

Sharing in Worship

(20-25 minutes)

Omit any of the following sections if you did not offer the corresponding activity. The Lord's Supper and devotional may be done without the contribution of Groups 3 and 4.

Call to Worship (Group 2): Have the volunteer from Group 2 read Mark 16:15. Then all of Group 2 will sing "Go Everywhere!" Display the song chart so the larger group can sing along the second time.

Song (Group 1): Group 1 will hum and pantomime "Isn't He Wonderful." Let a volunteer from Group 1 lead the large group in another song.

Lord's Supper (Group 3): **Death makes us sad. We are sad when our grandparents or aunts or uncles or friends die. There was one death that mattered more than any other—Jesus' death. Jesus died on the cross. He died for us because He loves us. Remembering Jesus' death makes us sad. But remembering why He died and that He came back to life makes us happy. The Lord's Supper is a time for remembering what Jesus did. Group 3 will use sign language to give us a message to think about during the Lord's Supper.** Let Group 3 sign and tell their message.

Offering: Have the student helpers receive the offering.

Devotional (Groups 4 and 5): Pupils in Group 5 will display their montage "Wonderful Things to Hear." **These pictures illustrate some of the things we can hear.** Allow Group 5 to explain the montage.

Group 4 has prepared a review of our Bible story using sounds that we often hear. After Group 4 has presented the story, continue. **Isn't it wonderful to be able to hear these sounds? Hearing is something we often take for granted. People who use sign language cannot hear all of these wonderful things. One of the wonderful things Jesus did was to make the man who was deaf able to hear and to make his tongue able to speak. That man probably told everyone he met about Jesus.**

We need to tell people about Jesus too. We need to let them know that Jesus is God's Son, and that He does wonderful things.

Prayer (Group 6): Let Group 6 hold their cards up so the large group can see the word *tell.* **Prayer is the time for telling things to God. Some of the pupils in Group 4 will suggest some things that we can tell God when we prayer to Him today.**

Have a time of silent prayer closed by a leader or one of the pupils.

Closing Moments

(10-15 minutes)

Until parents come to pick up the children, play "I Can't Hear You!" Before the session prepare small strips of paper on which you have written statements, such as "I want a drink." "Where is the telephone?" "The sun is too bright!" and as many and varied ideas as you can think of. Try to have at least as many statements as you expect to have children in your session. Place these strips of paper in a basket or box so children can reach in and take one.

Most people who are deaf also have a problem speaking. What would it be like if you couldn't speak? Let's try this game to see what it might be like. The children will take turns taking a paper strip out of the basket and pantomiming the statement. The rest of the children will guess until they have figured out what the child is trying to "say." Let each child who wishes to play have a turn before allowing anyone to pantomime twice.

Suggested Resources

The following organizations will send catalogs, brochures, and other information, such as addresses and phone numbers of local organizations.

TJ Publishers, Inc.
917 Silver Springs Avenue.,
Suite 206
Silver Springs, MD 20910
(310) 585-4440

National Association of the Deaf
814 Thayer Avenue
Silver Springs, MD 20910

Gallaudet University Press
800 Florida Avenue, NE
Washington, D. C. 20002-3695
(202) 651-5488 (Voice/TDD)
(800) 451-1073 (Voice/TDD)

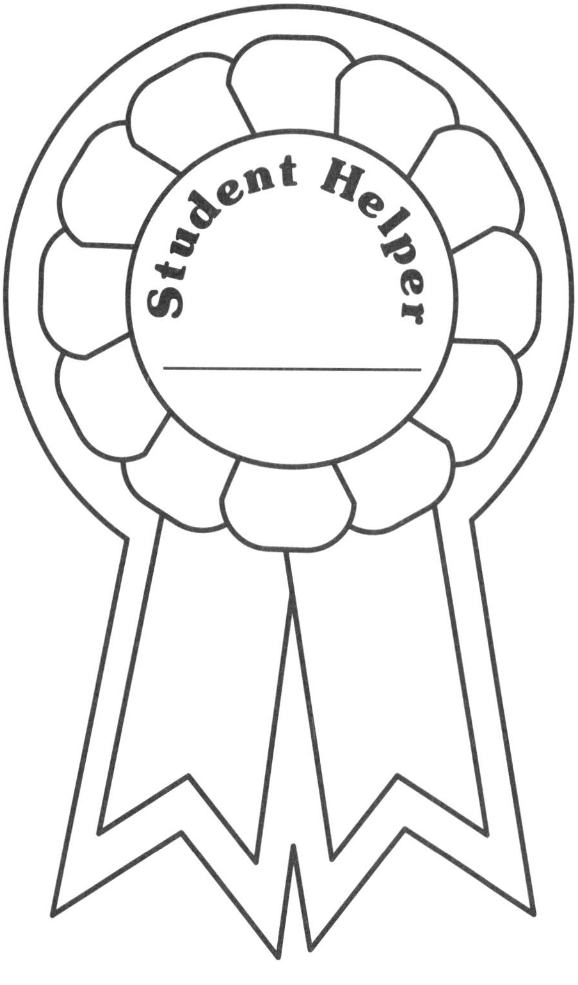

Deaf Man Hears

Reporter: What was wrong with you, sir?

Man: I could not hear or speak.

Reporter: How did that make you feel?

Man: Lonely—and sad. I didn't know what people were saying. I could not answer them. I couldn't hear music. I could see the birds, but I couldn't hear their songs.

Reporter: What did Jesus do for you?

Man: He took me aside, away from the crowd. And He put His fingers into my ears. Then He spit and touched my tongue. He looked up to Heaven and said something. Later they told me that He said, "Be opened."

Reporter: And what happened?

Man: My ears were opened! I could hear! I could speak!

Reporter: That is wonderful! You surely do talk plainly today. And you heard everything I said. How do you feel now?

Man: How do you think I feel? Happy! So happy! And so grateful to Jesus for doing this wonderful thing for me.

Reporter: How do you think it was possible for Jesus to do this miracle?

Man: Because He is the Son of God. Jesus can do wonderful things because He is the Son of God.

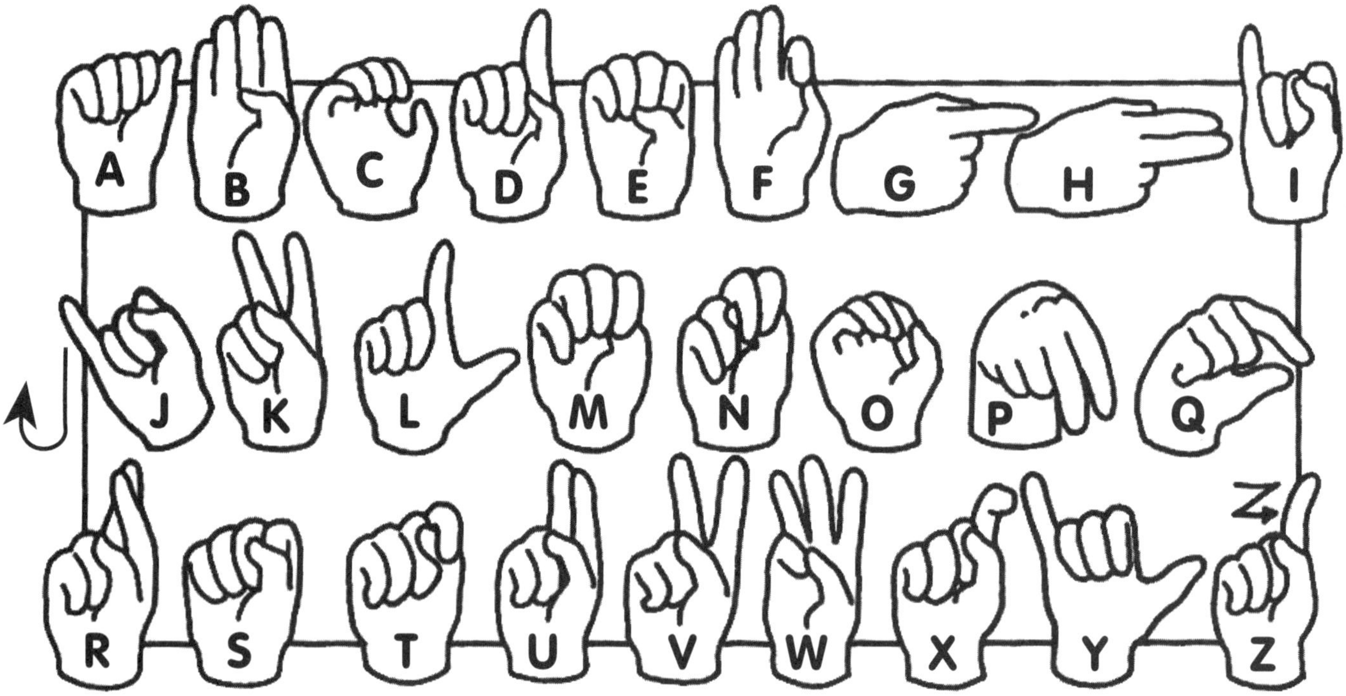
A B C D E F G H I
J K L M N O P Q
R S T U V W X Y Z

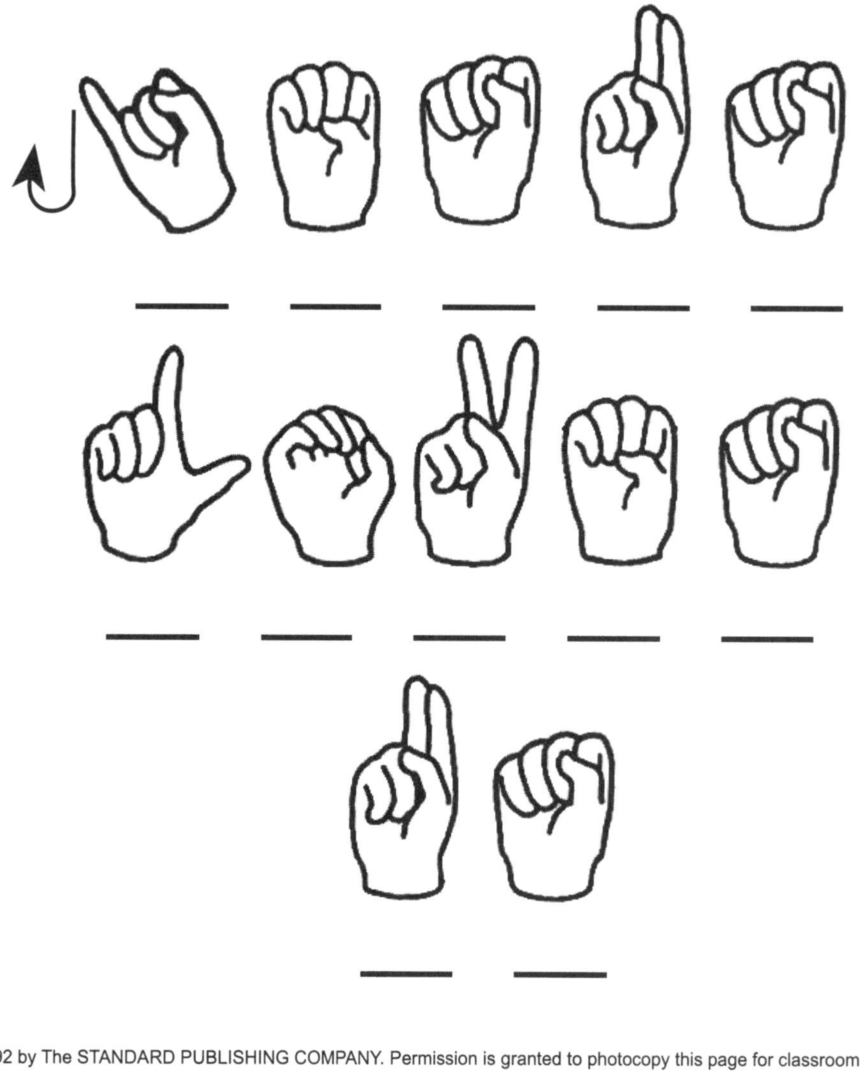

Jesus Heals a Man Who Is Blind

Worship Focus

We worship Jesus by telling others about Him.

Transition Time

(10-15 minutes)

(Prior to class, make badges for your helpers. Make two photocopies of the badge on page 26. Color, if desired, glue to poster board, cut out, and glue a safety pin on back. Cover with clear, adhesive-backed paper if desired.) Use these badges each week or make new ones to allow children to take them home. Alternate student helpers so every child takes a turn.

Prior to the session make enough blindfolds or gather enough handkerchiefs or strips of cloth to cover the eyes of the pupils. If any pupil is reluctant to wear one, don't push him to do so. Also set up a maze using chairs and boxes. Put written directions, such as "sit down," "crawl through," "step over" at several locations along the maze.

Encourage the children to use the rest room and get drinks as they come to the room. Choose two student helpers and give each of them a badge.

Trust Me. As the children return to the room, put them in pairs. One partner will be blindfolded, and the other will guide him through the maze holding his arm. The guide will read the written directions and assist his partner through the maze. If time permits, let pupils reverse roles and repeat the maze. Have them go to the assembly area as they finish the maze.

If you have no room for the maze or have extra time, use this quiet activity. You will need blindfolds, paper, and writing or drawing utensils. Before the session draw a simple shape. Label your drawing with lengths and shapes so you can give directions easily.

Give each child materials and a blindfold. Have the children locate the edges of their paper and their drawing equipment. The leader will give directions for drawing. Use "finger-width" and "pencil-length" to define distances. Tell the children not to lift their marker (pencil, crayon) until you go to the next direction so they will not lose their place on the page. When the activity is complete, have the children compare their drawings with your original.

Launching the Theme

(10 minutes)

Before the session, have cards with the Braille alphabet. Addresses of some information sources are at the end of this session. Check in your area for associations for the blind. If you are unable to obtain cards, use a photocopy of the top portion of activity page 3A and make a sample Braille alphabet by putting dots of glue on the printed dots to form each letter. If you use colored glue (or add powdered tempera paint to your glue), the children will be able to see as well as feel the alphabet.

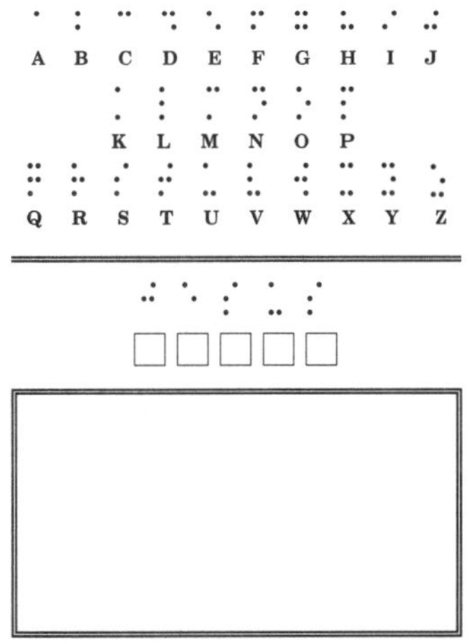

In the activity we have just done, you needed to trust someone else to give you directions. Then you needed to what you were told to do. If you didn't follow directions, you had problems.

Listen to this morning's story and be thinking about these three questions: Why did Jesus heal the blind man? What might have happened if the blind man had not followed Jesus' instructions? and What did the blind man do after he was healed? Write these questions on the board. Read John 9:1-11. Allow the children to answer the questions (to show God's power; he would not have been healed; he told about Jesus).

The blind man in this story was healed, but blind people today are not so lucky. They must learn to get along in the world without sight. One of the important things they must learn to do is read. Many years ago a blind man named Louis Braille developed an alphabet that blind people could read with their fingers. Pass out Braille cards or display your Braille alphabet.

Each letter of the alphabet is made with raised dots. By feeling the dots, a blind person can read the dots just as we read printed letters. The next time you are in an elevator, look to see whether there are dots by the numbers of the floors. These are the Braille symbols for the numbers and letters. The Bible has been written in Braille, so blind people can read about Jesus.

There are also people who tape record whole books so a blind person can listen as a book is read to him. The Bible on cassette tapes is a way blind people can learn about Jesus also.

Since blind people cannot use their eyes to find out about things, they learn to use their other senses, especially hearing and touch. We are going to divide into groups now. Take your blindfolds with you. Divide the large group into six small groups using eye color and whether or not the children wear glasses.

Building the Theme

(30 minutes)

1. **Choral Reading. Let's find out some of the problems with learning Scripture when you cannot see. Put on your blindfolds please. Turn in your Bibles to Psalm 9:1, 2. What? You can't see to find it? Well, then listen while I read it to you. You will have to listen carefully because you must recite these verses as our Call to Worship during *Sharing in Worship*.** Read the verses two or three times using the ICB. Then divide the children into four groups and assign each group one phrase of the Scripture as shown below.

"I will praise you, Lord, with all my heart."

"I will tell all the miracles you have done."

"I will be happy because of you."

"God Most High, I will sing praises to your name."

Practice until the children are comfortable with reciting the verses. If time allows, talk about some of the miracles Jesus did. Also talk about how different it is not to be able to see. Allow the children to remove the blindfolds when they become uncomfortable wearing them, but encourage them to keep them on until it is time to assemble in the large group.

2. **Song. Please put on your blindfolds. Sometimes we use song charts to help us learn the songs we sing in worship. But if you are blind, how can you see the words to the song? It would be awkward for all of you to try to read a big Braille song chart with your hands on the exact same letters and words at the exact same time, wouldn't it? Instead, you will need to listen carefully while I teach you our special music for today. The tune is familiar, but there are new words to it. Listen.**

Sing the following words to the tune of "Jesus Loves Me." Sing only one stanza two times and then encourage the children to sing along. When they feel comfortable with that, sing the second stanza for them to learn. Practice both stanzas together. After each stanza sing the original chorus of "Jesus Loves Me." If time allows, encourage the children to talk about how it feels not to be able to see. Also talk about other miracles Jesus did. The children may wish to make up more stanzas to the song.

I love You, Jesus, love You so.
You're the Son of God, I know.
Since You are I'll worship You,
And tell others all You do.

I love You, Jesus, love You so.
You're the Son of God, I know.
You can make a blind man see.
And I know you care for me.

Allow the children to remove the blindfolds when they become uncomfortable wearing them, but encourage them to keep them on until it is time to assemble in the large group. If you wish, have them sing the song blindfolded and then remove the blindfolds when they sing, "You can make a blind man see." This will be the special music during *Sharing in Worship*.

3. **Writing Braille.** You will need a copy of activity page 3A for each child in this group and also several bottles of glue. **When blind people are writing in Braille, they usually use a special typewriter or an instrument called a stylus to make the raised dots. We are going to use glue to make the dots, so we will need to work very carefully and neatly. On the top part of your page is the Braille alphabet. Carefully put a dot of glue on each dot in the letters. Do not touch these dots, they must dry first. Also make sure you don't make the dots too big because they will take too long to dry.**

In the middle of the page, a word is spelled out. What word is that? Jesus. **Put glue on each of the dots of those letters. At the**

bottom of the page, choose a word, such as obey or tell or good news, to write in Braille. First use a pencil to make dots to spell the word. Then I will check the word. Then you can put the glue on. During *Sharing in Worship* we will allow the other children to read the Braille we have written.

4. Memory verse in action. Help the pupils find and read today's memory verse: "Christ . . . gave me the work of preaching the Good News" (1 Corinthians 1:17, ICB). **Paul wrote these words in the book of Corinthians. What people might say these words today?** Make a list: preacher, Sunday-school teacher, missionary, you, and me. **What kind of people do they tell the good news?** Encourage the children to think about everyone—all races and nationalities, all economic groups, all levels of education, all handicaps and all without handicaps.

Ask for volunteers to take the parts of a preacher, a teacher, a missionary, and a child of today. Use props if you wish. The preacher can hold a Bible (and stand behind a speaker's stand). The teacher can hold a Sunday-school book. The missionary can carry a piece of luggage and/or a map. The child can hold a story paper. Each pupil identifies himself and then says the memory verse, "I am a (preacher). Christ gave me the work of preaching the Good News."

The other children in the group can represent people who need to hear the good news. They may also have props: rags for poor, a cane for a lame person, a foreign language dictionary for someone from another country, and, of course, a blindfold for a blind person. Each of these children can identify himself and say, "I am (blind). I need to hear the good news of Christ."

We will present the verse in this way as the Scripture reading during *Sharing in Worship.*

5. Skit. You will need enough copies of the skit on activity page 3B for each child in this group. This skit will introduce the Devotional during *Sharing in Worship*. **Let's imagine what would happen if the blind man hadn't obeyed Jesus.**

Assign the parts and read through the skit. Discuss how the blind man's obedience was important in his healing. **It is important for us to obey Jesus also. Part of what He has told us to do is to tell other people about Him. How can we do that? What happens when we don't tell other people about Jesus?** Allow time for brief discussion, especially about the importance of telling other people about Jesus so they can go to Heaven too. Then rehearse the skit until the children are comfortable with it. If possible, have the blind man wear his blindfold.

6. Texture Picture. You will need paper and glue for each child. You will also need either sandpaper (for option a) or salt or sand (for option b). For both options, you will need cardboard templates of a cross, circle, square, and rectangle.

Usually pictures are something we look at. We are going to make a picture that we can feel and that a blind person could enjoy.

Option a. Have the pupils use the templates to cut out sandpaper shapes. Have them arrange the shapes on the paper and use the scraps to complete the picture and add the word "tell." Glue the sandpaper to the paper.

Option b. Have the pupils use templates to outline shapes on paper. Use crayons or markers to complete the picture and add the word "tell." Fill in the shapes and outline "tell" with a moderate amount of glue. Sprinkle with salt or sand to add texture. Allow to dry.

The children will present their work during offering time. This will be a representation of giving their talents to tell others about Jesus.

Sharing in Worship

(20-25 minutes)

Omit any of the following sections if you did not offer the corresponding activity. Assemble the group by playing "It's Time to Praise the Lord."

Call to Worship (Group 1): **Group 1 will recite Psalm 9:1, 2.** Allow them to do that. **Today we are talking about one of the miracles God has done.**

Song (Group 2): **Group 2 will sing a song about Jesus.** After Group 2 has assembled at the front of the worship area, have the children in Group 2 put their blindfolds on. They will remove them during the second stanza of the song. If you prefer, have them put their blindfolds on first and have leaders and other children lead them to the front.

Lord's Supper: Jesus did wonderful things when He was on earth. The most important thing He did was to die and raise again so that we can be forgiven for the times when we do not obey Him. Let us ask Jesus to forgive us for the times we have not obeyed Him and promise to try harder to obey.

Offering (Group 6): **Group 6 will show us their pictures. These pictures are made with textures so that even the blind could learn about Jesus. At offering time we give the Lord our money and we promise to give Him our lives and talents to tell the good news about Jesus.**

Scripture (Group 4): **Group 4 has prepared a memory verse in action for our Scripture today.**

Devotional (Groups 3 and 5): **Group 5 will present a skit about what might have happened in our Bible story today.** Have Group 5 present their skit or paraphrase it yourself if this activity was not done.

What did the man miss out on? Healing. **Why?** He did not obey Jesus. **Do you think he would have told other people about Jesus?**

But the blind man in the Bible story obeyed Jesus and he was healed. Because he was healed, he told other people about Jesus.

Group 3 has prepared messages in Braille so that we can see one way that blind people today learn about Jesus. Please put your blindfolds on. Members of Group 3 will allow you to feel the messages. Allow time for this. **What are the messages?**

What? You don't know? Didn't Group 3 tell you anything? It is important to tell about Jesus, but maybe how we tell about Jesus is as important as what we tell. We must tell people in a way that they understand. You can tell your friends about Jesus because you understand them and they understand you. Group 3, please tell us the meanings of your messages. Allow time for the children to tell their messages. **Now you can understand, can't you? Let's tell the good news about Jesus to everyone we can in a way that he can understand.**

Closing Moments

(10-15 minutes)

Work on an addition to the worship focus banner. (Materials needed are butcher paper approximately four feet long, markers or crayons, and letter stencils if desired.) In previous sessions it has been suggested to have the children decorate and/or color in letters of a banner reading "We Worship Jesus Because. . . ." Additions to the banner have included "We have faith and trust in Him to take care of us," and "He can heal a deaf man." Today's addition is "He can make a blind man see."

Suggested Resources

Illinois Council of the Blind
P. O. Box 1336
Springfield, IL 62705
(217) 523-4967

Heart of Illinois Talking Books
845 Brenkman Drive
Pekin, IL 61554

National Library Service for Blind and Handicapped
Library of Congress
Washington, D. C. 20542

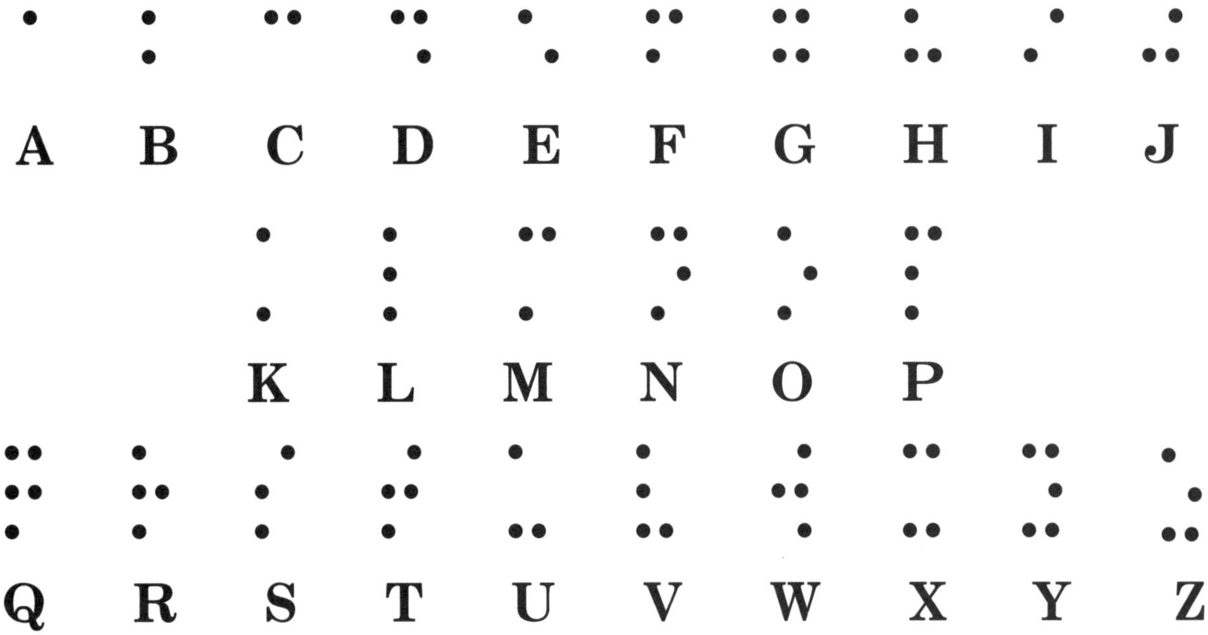
A B C D E F G H I J
K L M N O P
Q R S T U V W X Y Z

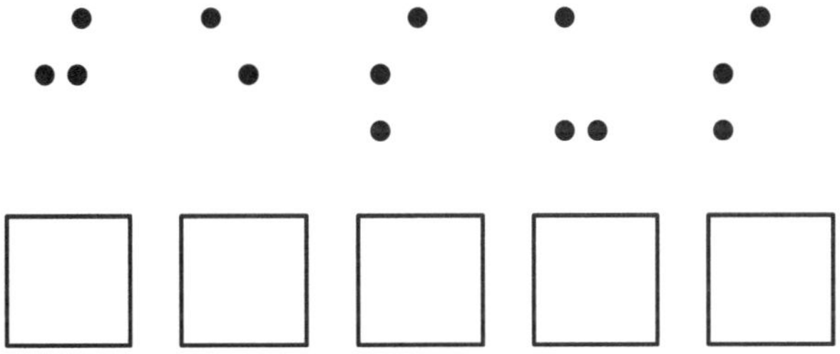

What If?

Characters: Jesus, blind man, crowd, disciples 1, 2, and 3

Disciple 1: Jesus, why is this man blind?

Jesus: He is blind so I can show people how God works. We must do the work God sent us to do. While I am in the world, I am the light of the world. *(Pretends to spit and make the mud. Jesus tries to put the "mud" on the blind man, who struggles and the crowd protests.)*

Blind man: What are you doing? Stop! That feels slimy! *(Begins to wipe off the "mud.")*

Crowd: Stop! Leave him alone! *(The disciples try to keep the blind man from wiping off the "mud.")*

Disciple 2: Jesus is trying to help you!

Disciple 3: Listen to what He is telling you!

Disciple 1: Do what He tells you to do!

Jesus: Go and wash in the Pool of Siloam.

Blind man: I know this won't do any good. I don't believe you can help me. You are a fake!

Crowd: Leave him alone! This man *(points at Jesus)* is fooling us all. Nobody can make people see with mud. We should chase him away.

(Part of the crowd gathers around the blind man, feeling sorry for him and wiping off the mud, while others chase Jesus and the disciples away.)

Disciple 2: Now he will be blind forever.

Disciple 3: That is what happens when people do not trust Jesus and obey Him.

Jesus Heals a Man's Hand

Worship Focus

We can worship Jesus because He can heal people.

Transition Time

(10-15 minutes)

Encourage the children to use the rest room and get drinks as they come to the room. Choose two student helpers and give each of them a badge.

(Prior to class, make badges for your helpers. Make two photocopies of the badge on page 26. Color, if desired, glue to poster board, cut out, and glue a safety pin on back. Cover with clear, adhesive-backed paper if desired.) Use these badges each week or make new ones to allow children to take them home. Alternate student helpers so every child takes a turn.

Shriveled Hand. Materials you will need are lace-up shoes, jars with screw-on lids, plastic containers with snap-on lids, wrapped candy, and bricks. You will also need cards with instructions: TIE ME; UNSCREW ME; TAKE MY LID OFF; UNWRAP ME; PICK ME UP. Arrange these at stations around the room.

You will also need tape. As the children return from their rest-room break, tape their thumbs securely against the palms of their hands. Have them try to follow the instruction at each station.

For a quieter activity, have the children decorate and/or color in letters of a banner reading "We Worship Jesus Because. . . ." Complete the sentence with the words "He can heal people." If you have used this activity throughout the unit, only add today's focus. (Materials needed are butcher paper approximately four feet long, markers or crayons, and letter stencils if desired.)

Use the song "It's Time to Praise the Lord!" to assemble the group.

Launching the Theme

(10 minutes)

We have discovered that hands are very important to us. Have a few children describe their experiences with "Shriveled Hands."

Listen as I read the Bible story for today. We know the man needs his hand hand healed, but there are some other people in the story who need another kind of healing. See whether you can figure out who they are. Read Mark 3:1-6 from your Bible. **Who else needed healing?** The Pharisees. **What kind of healing did they need?** Their attitudes toward other people needed healing. **There are two kinds of healing that Jesus can provide: for our bodies and for our minds and spirits. We will talk about both kinds of healing today.**

Describe the six activities for the children. If there are any left-handed children in your group, allow them to choose an activity first. Then allow the children with with the smallest handspan (check with a ruler) to choose next. Continue with bigger handspans until all children have chosen an activity. Try to have the groups be nearly the same size.

Building the Theme

(30 minutes)

1. Write a Chant. Not all music has to have musical instruments or singing. Many groups of people make songs with just their voice sounds and their hands and feet. Have the children write a simple chant. Add claps and foot stamps at appropriate times during the chant. An example is shown.

Jesus (stamp, stamp), help us see (clap, clap, clap)

You (stamp) died (stamp) to set (slap, clap) us (stamp) free (clap, clap, clap).

Experiment with combinations of stamps and claps. Allow the children to compose as many chants as they desire. You might also try using an echo effect. Point out to the children the difficulty they would have clapping with a withered hand.

The chant will be used as a special song during *Sharing in Worship.*

2. Pop-out Picture. We use our hands to do many things. Some of them are good things. Some of them are not so good. Let's make a poster to help us remember to do only good things with our hands.

Makes enough copies of activity 4A for the children in this group. (You may wish to have some extra copies in case the children have many ideas of good things their hands can do.) You will also need writing utensils, scissors, poster board, glue or tape, and extra paper.

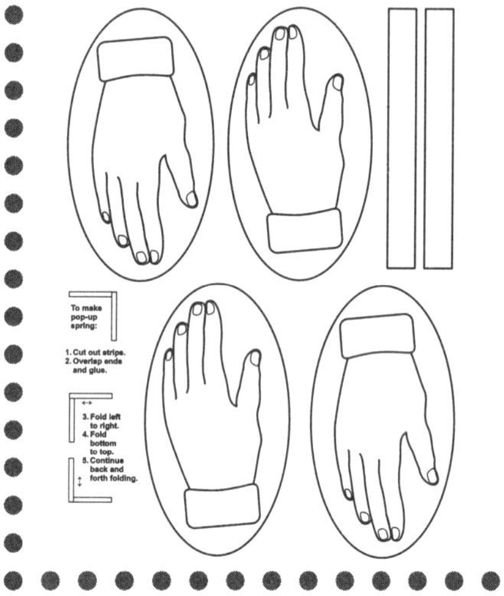

Write a good use of your hands on each of the hands on your paper. Some suggestions are to give hugs, write notes to sick people, clean room, do homework, wash dishes, applaud a good job. **After you have finished writing your ideas on the hands, cut out the hands. You may either cut out the oval around the hand or the outline of the hand itself. Then we will arrange them on the poster board here. After we are satisfied with the arrangement, we will glue the hands onto the poster board.**

The first four of you to finish will need an extra piece of paper. Please trace around your own hand. Then cut out the shape.

When the others of you finish, please follow the instructions on activity page 4A to make springs for the four large hands.

Each of the four hands should be labeled with a word: "Good," "Hands," "for," and "God." Attach them to the poster board with the "springs."

This group will present their poster during the Devotional.

3. Doctor Jesus. Materials you will need are an aspirin bottle, bandages, thermometer, crutch or sling, liquid medicine bottle, syringe, ice pack, and wooden cross.

Distribute the medical items and the cross to members of the group. **Some of you have objects that are used to make you well or feel better when you are sick. Let's talk about what each of these can do for a sick person.** Save the cross for last. **We have found out about many things that doctors use to heal us. What can a cross heal?** Our attitudes, thoughts, sinful actions. **In the Bible story, who needed healing as much as the man with the shriveled hand?** The Pharisees. **Why did they need healing?** Their hearts needed healing, their attitudes needed changing.

We will show each of these items and you will have a chance to tell the other children what these items can help heal. The cross will be the last item described. We will do this during the Lord's Supper portion of *Sharing in Worship.*

4. Finger Puppets. You will need enough copies of activity page 4B for this group. Also provide markers or crayons, scissors, glue, and construction paper. Before the session, cut the top portion of the activity page from the bottom portion. Also cut the construction paper to the same size as the top portion. That will make it easier for the children to make the puppets sturdier. After they color their puppets, they will glue the section with the puppets to the construction paper before they cut out the puppets. Then they will only have to cut the puppets out one time.

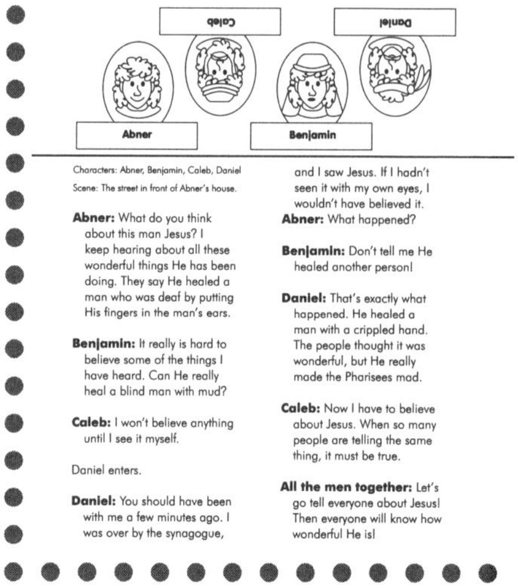

Color the finger puppets, glue that portion of the page to a piece of construction paper, and cut out the finger puppets. Help the children fit the puppets to their fingers. While the children are preparing their puppets, read the puppet skit aloud and then let children volunteer for the parts. If you have more than four children, assign some children just to be part of the group but not to speak. Each child will use one puppet for now but will be able to take the puppets and skit home to tell the story at home.

Let's practice our puppet skit. We will present this as part of the Devotional during *Sharing in Worship.* You can make a simple puppet stage by turning a table on its side and having the children crouch or sit behind it and hold their puppets above it.

5. Bible Health Care Book. You will need several blank sheets of paper for each student, construction paper for book covers, Bibles, glue, pencils, markers, crayons, and items to decorate the book covers (yarn, stickers, scraps of felt or paper). You will also need a list of Bible verses , such as Matthew 10:8; Mark 5:34; and Proverbs 15:13; Proverbs 17:22.

When you go to the doctor, quite often he gives you a prescription for medicine to make you feel better. The Bible gives us prescriptions also. Look up some of these verses, write them on your pages, then draw pictures to decorate the pages. Make a cover for your book. Put *Bible Health Care Book* for the title. Be ready to read one of your verses for the call to worship during *Sharing in Worship.*

6. Daily Prayer Folder. You will need white paper (full sheets and half sheets), construction paper, pencils, markers, scissors, and seven stickers for each child in this group.

Fold a whole piece of white paper in half crosswise. Then make an outline of your hands with your fingers together. This will make it look like praying hands. Make sure your wrist is on the fold. That way the hands will still be connected after you have cut them out.

As the children finish cutting the hands out, let them use glitter to decorate the hands. **Fold the sheet of construction paper in half crosswise. Place the praying hands with the wrist-fold on the construction paper fold, so the hands appear to be holding the folder. Glue them on.**

Get seven half sheets of paper. At the top of each one write a day of the week. Write a prayer for each day. Allow time for this.

Now place the prayer papers into the prayer folder. Here are seven stickers. Each day stick that day's prayer page to a door, mirror, bulletin board, or other place where you will see it several times during the day. Each time you see it, pray your prayer.

We will share our prayer ideas during the prayer time of *Sharing in Worship*. Choose which of your prayer ideas you would like to pray during that time. If any children are shy about praying audibly for the group, allow a time for silent prayer during which all of the children can pray.

Sharing in Worship

(20-25 minutes)

Omit any of the following sections if you did not offer the corresponding activity.

Summarize the points of Groups 2 and 3 during the Devotional and Lord's Supper if those activities were not offered. Read the skit or perform the finger puppet play yourself if you did not use the activity for Group 4.

Call to Worship (Group 5): Have several students read a verse from their *Bible Health Care Books* and show the pictures that correspond to the verses. **We can tell from these verses that the Bible tells us how to keep our bodies and our thoughts healthy.**

Song (Group 1): **Group 1 will show us another way to use our voices and hands to praise Jesus.** Perform the chant several times and allow the large group to participate.

Lord's Supper (Group 3): **Group 3 will share with us some thoughts about healing.** After they are done, add to their thoughts something they might have missed. **Jesus died on the cross to give us forgiveness for our sins. Let's think about that at this time.**

Offering: Paul tells the Hebrews to share what they have because it is pleasing to God. Let's please God now as we share what we have. Have the student helpers accept the offering.

Devotional (Groups 2 and 4): Use the finger puppets from Group 4 to set the mood.

Every day we hear about some wonderful new way that doctors can heal people. They have discovered machines and medicines that can make people well. (Name some diseases they know about.) **We swallow spoonsful of medicine or pills and we get well or at least feel better. The doctor gives us shots so we don't get some diseases at all. We are very healthy people on the outside. God gave us our bodies and people to help us take care of it.**

We also hear about people who are doing bad things. They kill and hurt each other. They steal, lie, and cheat. They sell drugs or take them. They have diseases inside them that no doctor can fix. These diseases have names like cruelty, selfishness, jealousy, and greed.

Sometimes we think, "I'm not that bad. I don't do any of those really bad things; and if I did, I would ask Jesus to help me." Think about the things you did last week that were just a "little bit" bad. Maybe you sassed your mom or said something mean to a friend or kept a pencil you found instead of looking for its owner. Or maybe on the way to the room today you ran down the hall or pushed at the water fountain or didn't wait your turn.

These may seem like small things, but if an apple or peach has a bruised spot or bread has a spot of mold, in a couple of days it will be spoiled. The spot grows from little to big and spoils the fruit or bread. In order to keep the little spot from spoiling the fruit or bread, we must cut the spot out of the fruit or bread.

In our lives, little bad things can get bigger and ruin us. But if we fill our lives with Bible verses, try to live like Jesus, and pray to God, we can stop the little bad things from getting bigger. In fact, we can replace

them with good things. Group 2 has some pop-out pictures that will show us good things that we can do with our hands.

Prayer (Group 6): **Group 6 has some prayer ideas to lead our closing prayer time.**

Closing Moments

(10-15 minutes)

Hands Necklace. Have enough copies of activity page 4A for all pupils; yarn, string, or dental floss; large-eye needles (threaded); scissors; and markers.

Write something you do with your hands on each hand on the page. Cut out the hands or the oval outlines and string them together to make a necklace.

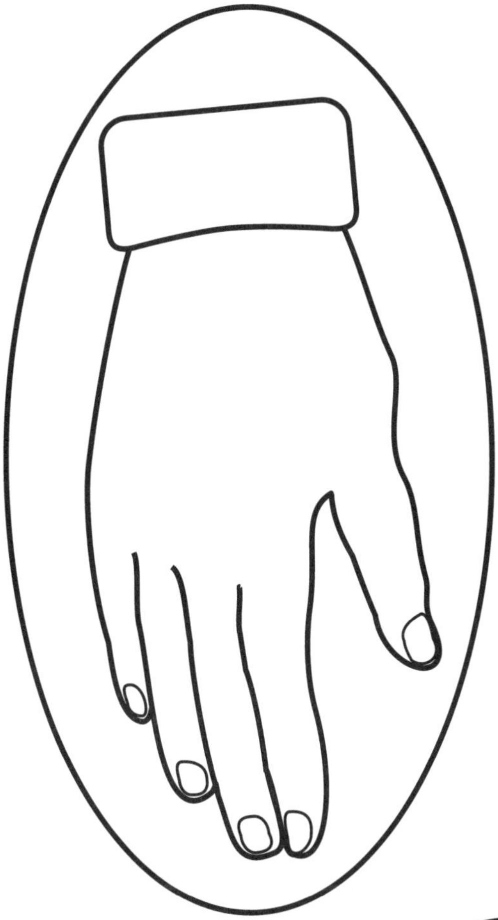

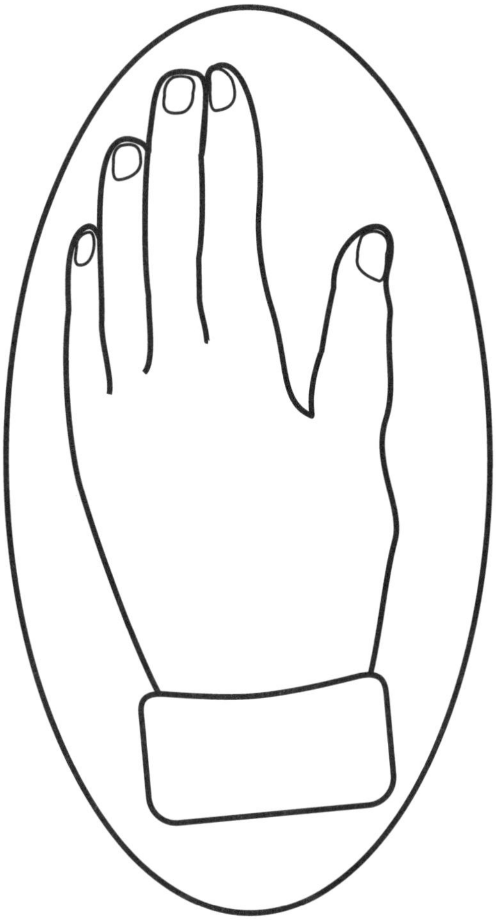

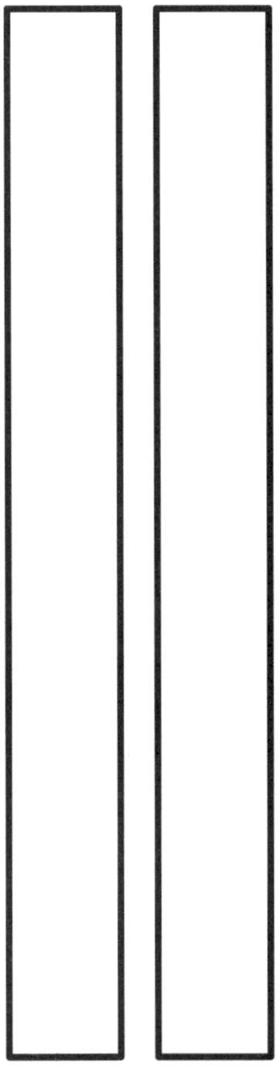

To make pop-up spring:

1. Cut out strips.
2. Overlap ends and glue.

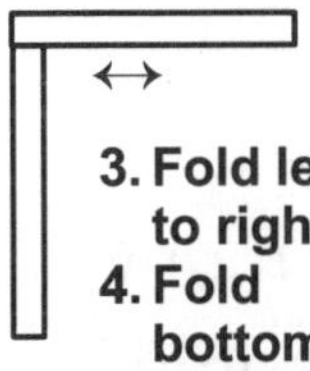

3. Fold left to right.
4. Fold bottom to top.
5. Continue back and forth folding.

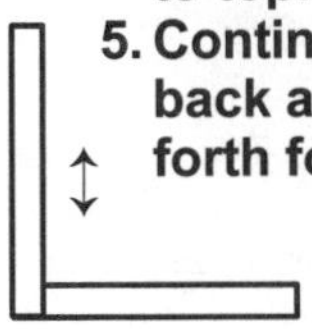

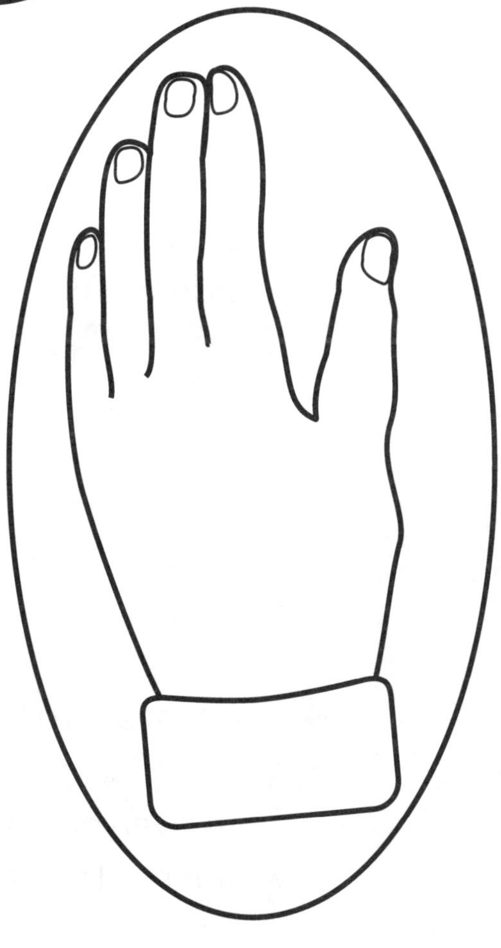

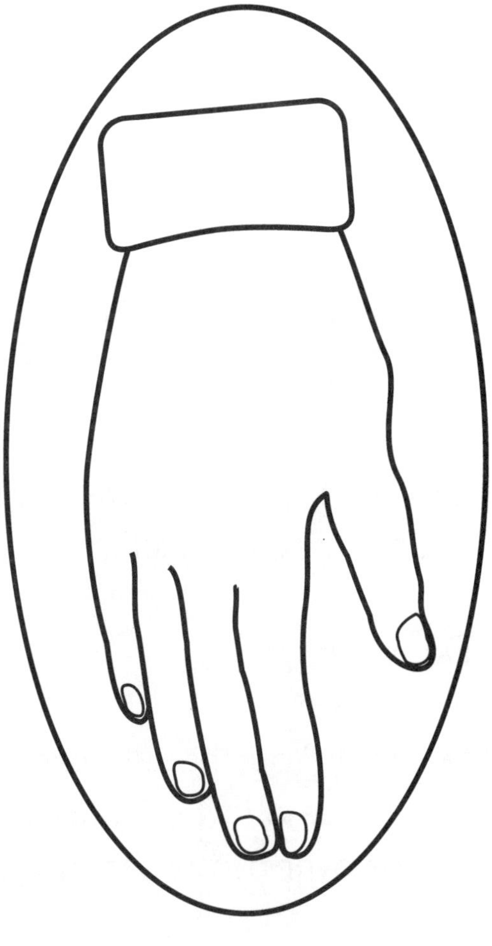

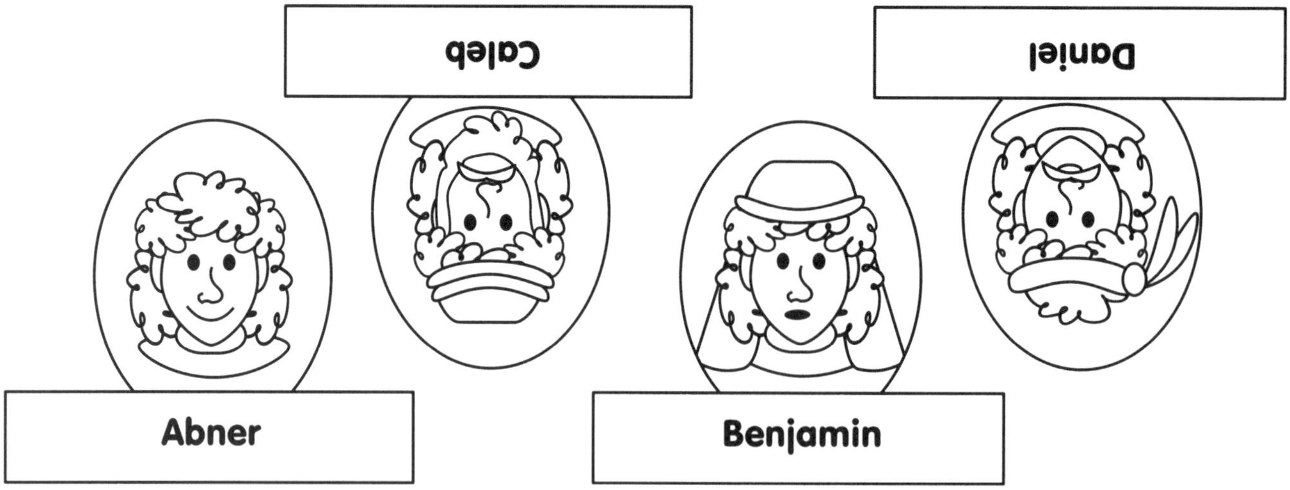

Characters: Abner, Benjamin, Caleb, Daniel

Scene: The street in front of Abner's house.

Abner: What do you think about this man Jesus? I keep hearing about all these wonderful things He has been doing. They say He healed a man who was deaf by putting His fingers in the man's ears.

Benjamin: It really is hard to believe some of the things I have heard. Can He really heal a blind man with mud?

Caleb: I won't believe anything until I see it myself.

Daniel enters.

Daniel: You should have been with me a few minutes ago. I was over by the synagogue, and I saw Jesus. If I hadn't seen it with my own eyes, I wouldn't have believed it.

Abner: What happened?

Benjamin: Don't tell me He healed another person!

Daniel: That's exactly what happened. He healed a man with a crippled hand. The people thought it was wonderful, but He really made the Pharisees mad.

Caleb: Now I have to believe about Jesus. When so many people are telling the same thing, it must be true.

All the men together: Let's go tell everyone about Jesus! Then everyone will know how wonderful He is!

Jesus Makes a Girl Live Again

Worship Focus

Worship Jesus because He can make people live again.

Transition Time

(10-15 minutes)

Encourage the children to use the rest room and get drinks as they come to the room. Choose two student helpers and give each of them a badge.

(Prior to class, make badges for your helpers. Make two photocopies of the badge on page 26. Color, if desired, glue to poster board, cut out, and glue a safety pin on back. Cover with clear, adhesive-backed paper if desired.) Use these badges each week or make new ones to allow children to take them home. Alternate student helpers so every child takes a turn.

Fix-it Display. Before the session, set up several displays where something needs to be fixed and the tools needed to fix it. (Examples: broken dish and glue; flat tire and tire pump; torn cloth and needle and thread; wilted plant and water; picture of Jairus' dead daughter from Sunday-school materials or picture of a tombstone.) By each display place a sign reading, "Can you fix me?" or "Can you make me like new?" By the daughter or tombstone, write, "Can you bring me back to life?"

Death to Life! Relay. Before the session, make two sets of index cards. Each set should have the words "Death" and "Life!" spelled out with one letter per index card. (Be sure to put the exclamation point on an index card too.) Prepare an area for your relay. For each team you will need a chair by the starting point where you will place the cards for the word "Death." At the far end of the course, have a chair for each team on which you will place the cards for the word "Life!"

Divide the group into teams of no more than five children each. (If you have a large group, you may need more than two teams. You will need a set of letters for each team.) Line the children up by the first chair. The first child on each team will take the first letter of the word "Death" and run (or walk quickly) to the other chair at the far end of the course. There he will leave that letter and pick up the first letter of the word "Life!" He will return to the first chair and put the letter down. The second child picks up the second letter, goes down, exchanges it, and returns. Play continues until the word "Life!" is completed on the first chair. The first team to exchange the letters completely calls out, "Jesus changes death to life!"

If you have fewer than five children per team, have as many of the team members as is necessary run again. If you have more than five members per team or a large class, the first child may take the letter "D" to the far end of the course where another child runs the return course with the letter "L." Play continues until the word "Life!" is spelled out at the beginning of the course.

Launching the Theme

(10 minutes)

Use "It's Time to Praise the Lord!" to assemble the group.

For several days, Jesus had been traveling around the countryside telling about God's love and healing. In those days there were no newspapers or radios and televisions to spread news, so people learned about things by talking to each other.

Someone recognized Jesus and the news spread quickly through the town. A crowd gathered around Jesus.

Jairus was an important man in the town, but even he probably had to push his way through the crowd. Jairus was one of the leaders of the men who were enemies of Jesus. Probably his friends would not like it that he was asking Jesus for help.

But someone even more important than his friends needed help. Jairus' daughter was dying! Jairus didn't care what everyone was going to think about him. He had heard about the other people Jesus had healed and believed what he had

heard. Now he was begging Jesus' help for her.

I am sure Jesus knew that Jairus was His enemy, but He still went with Jairus. You can imagine how Jairus must have felt when Jesus stopped along the way to heal a sick woman. How terrible Jairus must have felt when some of his friends came and told them that it was too late because the little girl had died.

Jesus told Jairus not to give up and to keep believing. Sure enough, when they got to the house, Jesus went in, touched the little girl, and brought her back to life.

Describe the six activities available. Choose three boys representing Jairus, the men in the crowd, and Jesus. Choose three girls representing the little girl, the woman who was healed, and the women in the crowd. Let these six children take turns choosing students to fill out the groups.

Building the Theme

(30 minutes)

1. Song. You will need poster board, the words to the song "I Love to Tell About Jesus," butcher paper approximately four feet long, markers or crayons, and letter stencils if desired.

Let the children prepare a song chart to learn the song and to use to teach the large group the song. Discuss the words to the song and what they can tell about Jesus. Also discuss whom they can tell about Jesus.

Have the children decorate and/or color in letters of a banner. (This is a unit activity introduced during *Transition Time* of session one.) Add today's worship focus, "He can make people live again," if you have used this activity previously. If this is the first time you have used a banner during this unit, have the banner say, "We Worship Jesus Because He can make people live again."

The song and banner will be used as the Call to Worship during *Sharing in Worship.*

2. Bible Research. Let the children take turns reading John 11:1-44 aloud from their Bibles. (If you have younger children, allow a few good readers to read aloud or read the passage aloud yourself while the children listen.)

This is another story about a time when Jesus made someone who was dead live again. Lazarus was sick, so Mary and Martha sent a message to Jesus. What do you think they wanted Jesus to do? They wanted Jesus to come heal Lazarus. They knew that Jesus could do special things like that. But Jesus didn't come and Lazarus died? How do you think Mary and Martha felt then? How do you think they felt after Jesus came and made Lazarus alive again?

Discuss the story with the children. Then help them to choose an aspect of the story to pantomime as you tell that part of the story. They might choose to travel with Jesus as His disciples and then be there when Jesus makes Lazarus live again. They might choose instead to be Mary and Martha waiting for Jesus, knowing their brother is sick and then has died, and then getting their brother back alive again. Tell the story from the perspective they have chosen. Emphasize how much the people must have praised and worshiped God after Jesus made Lazarus live again.

This group will present its pantomime during the devotional part of *Sharing in Worship.*

3. Thank-you letter. You will need enough copies of activity page 5A and pencils for the students in this group. **When someone gives us a gift or does something nice for us, we sometimes write a thank-you letter. Pretend you are Jairus or the little girl and write a thank-you letter to Jesus.**

Volunteers from this group will read their thank-you letters before the offering during *Sharing in Worship.*

4. Choral Reading. Provide Bibles and enough copies of activity page 5B for the pupils in this group. Have the children look up Luke 7:18-22 in their Bibles or read from the activity page.

Luke 7:18-22, *ICB*

18 John's followers told him about all these things. He called for two of his followers. **19** He sent them to the Lord to ask, "Are you the One who is coming, or should we wait for another?"
20 So the men came to Jesus. They said, "John the Baptist sent us to you with this question: 'Are you the One who is coming, or should we wait for another?'"
21 At that time, Jesus healed many people of their sicknesses, diseases, and evil spirits. He healed many blind people so that they could see again. **22** Then Jesus said to John's followers, "Go tell John the things that you saw and heard here. The blind can see. The crippled can walk. People with a harmful skin disease are healed. The deaf can hear, and the dead are given life. And the Good News is told to the poor."

Speaker 1: Then Jesus said to John's followers,

All: "Go tell John the things that you saw and heard here.

Speaker 2: "The blind can see.

Speaker 3: "The crippled can walk.

Speaker 4: "People with a harmful skin disease are healed.

Speaker 5: "The deaf can hear,

Speaker 6: "And the dead are given life.

All: "And the Good News is told to the poor."

Jesus did many wonderful things while He was on the earth. John the Baptist sent some of his followers to make sure who Jesus was. Today we will tell the large group what Jesus told

John's followers to tell John. We will do this as a choral reading for the Scripture. A choral reading means that we will read parts of Luke 7:22 together and some of it will be read by one or two of you. This is like a choir but without the music. Look at your activity page and we will practice the reading.

Assign your better readers to the solos or ask for volunteers. The solos could be read by two children at the same time also. Practice so that the reading goes smoothly. The children should feel (and show) more excitement with the mention of each successive miracle. This will be the Scripture reading for *Sharing in Worship*.

5. **Role Play.** You will need poster board and marker or chalkboard and chalk. Let the children create a role play, pretending they are a child and his family at supper with the child's telling about what he saw that day—Jesus' making Jairus' daughter alive again.

Let's imagine what it might have been like to be nearby when Jesus made the little girl alive after she had been dead. We will act this out later for the other children.

Write down the children's ideas about what they might say and how they might react as family members hearing about Jesus' making Jairus' daughter alive again.

Help the children choose parts and what they might say. They should not read the parts but have a general idea of what their characters might say and how they might act. The children will role play during the devotional portion of *Sharing in Worship*.

6. **Montage.** Provide poster board; construction paper; scissors; glue; letter stencils; magazines; and Sunday-school visuals, teaching pictures, activity book pages with pictures, and take-home papers with pictures.

Today we will make a montage, a collection of pictures arranged on poster board and then glued to it. The theme of our montage will be "Jesus does wonderful things." Cut out pictures that remind you of wonderful things that Jesus has done. Some of you will need to use the letter stencils to make construction paper letters for our title. In the center of our montage, we want to have pictures about how Jesus can make dead people live again.

We will tell the other children about our montage before the closing prayer time.

Sharing in Worship

(20-25 minutes)

Omit any of the following sections if you did not offer the corresponding activity.

The offering thoughts and devotional can be completed without the contributions of Groups 2 and 3. Summarize what Jairus or his daughter might have said in thanks to Jesus for the offering. Tell the story of the raising of Lazarus from the dead during the devotional.

Use "It's Time to Praise the Lord!" to assemble the groups.

Call to Worship (Group 1): Allow Group 1 to sing their song and present their banner.

Songs: Sing songs that worship Jesus for the wonderful things He has done.

Lord's Supper: During the Lord's Supper, we take time to think about Jesus and the most wonderful thing He did. He died on the cross for us. Because He died on the cross, we can be forgiven for our sins, the wrong things we do. Let's pray silently to God, thanking Him for sending Jesus to earth for us.

Offering (Group 3): Have volunteers from Group 3 read their thank-you letters.

Another way to show that you are thankful is to give something to the person who has given you something or has done something nice for you. We can thank Jesus by giving our offerings to Him.

Scripture (Group 4)**: Group 4 has a choral reading about the wonderful things Jesus did. The reading is from Luke 7:22.** Let Group 4 read the Scripture now. **One very special thing Jesus did was to make people who were dead become alive again.**

Devotional (Groups 2 and 5): **Jesus did many wonderful things! He made people who couldn't walk able to walk. He made people who couldn't hear able to hear. He healed people and He fed many people with only a little bit of food.**

The people who were around Jesus were amazed and praised God for the wonderful things and miracles Jesus did. One thing that was especially wonderful was when Jesus made someone who was dead live again. Group 5 will show us what it might have been like to be in a family who lived in the same town that Jairus lived in. Let Group 5 role play the family.

The Bible also tells us about another person whom Jesus made alive after he was dead. Group 2 will pantomime what happened when Jesus made Lazarus live again after he was dead. While Group 2 pantomimes the story, tell the story in your own words based on the aspect of the story that the children decided to portray.

Prayer (Group 6): **Today we want to thank God for the special things that Jesus did. Group 6 will remind us of some of the wonderful things that Jesus did.** After Group 6 has shown and explained its montage, allow a time for all the children to offer prayers of praise and thanksgiving for the wonderful things Jesus did. Close the prayer time with a prayer praising God for Jesus and His making dead people live again.

Closing Moments

(10-15 minutes)

Write the words "WORSHIP JESUS" vertically on the chalkboard. Make an acrostic with these letters, concentrating on reasons to worship Jesus. Especially encourage words or phrases that have to do with today's focus, "Worship Jesus because He can make people live again." If time allows, make more than one acrostic. Use the words "JESUS DOES WONDERFUL THINGS" for another acrostic.

Luke 7:18-22, *ICB*

18 John's followers told him
about all these things. He
called for two of his followers.
19 He sent them to the Lord
to ask, "Are you the One who
is coming, or should we wait
for another?"
20 So the men came to
Jesus. They said, "John the
Baptist sent us to you with this
question: 'Are you the One
who is coming, or should we
wait for another?'"
21 At that time, Jesus healed
many people of their
sicknesses, diseases, and evil
spirits. He healed many blind
people so that they could see
again. **22** Then Jesus said to
John's followers, "Go tell
John the things that you saw
and heard here. The blind
can see. The crippled can
walk. People with a harmful
skin disease are healed. The
deaf can hear, and the dead
are given life. And the Good
News is told to the poor."

Speaker 1: Then Jesus said to John's followers,

All: "Go tell John the things that you saw and heard here.

Speaker 2: "The blind can see.

Speaker 3: "The crippled can walk.

Speaker 4: "People with a harmful skin disease are healed.

Speaker 5: "The deaf can hear,

Speaker 6: "And the dead are given life.

All: "And the Good News is told to the poor."

Jesus Eats Supper With His Friends

Worship Focus

We worship Jesus when we remember Him.

Transition Time

(10-15 minutes)

Encourage the children to use the rest room and get drinks as they come to the room. Choose two student helpers and give each of them a badge.

(Prior to class, make badges for your helpers. Make two photocopies of the badge on page 26. Color, if desired, glue to poster board, cut out, and glue a safety pin on back. Cover with clear, adhesive-backed paper if desired.) Use these badges each week or make new ones to allow children to take them home. Alternate student helpers so every child takes a turn.

Remembrance Chain. Materials you will need are six-inch by one-inch strips of paper, glue, clothespins, and markers. Hang a rope across part of your assembly area. It should be low enough for the children to reach but not low enough for the children to get caught in it. A corner area or along a wall would be a good location for this rope (or string).

Make a poster with these instructions: "On each strip, write words that remind you of something Jesus did or that tell about what Jesus is like. For example: 'Jesus healed the sick'; 'Jesus was gentle.' Then make a chain of your 'Reminder Strips.' When you are finished, hang your chain from the rope.

During the session, have the student helpers give each arriving child several strips of paper and help the child read the instruction poster. If the children need assistance or have questions, allow the student helpers to help as much as they are able.

Launching the Theme

(10 minutes)

Before the session, you will need to prepare your classroom/ worship area for this special time. Set up low tables so the children can sit on the floor to participate. Provide a large loaf of unleavened bread and a pitcher of grape juice and small cups for each table or small group. (If this is not possible, have the children sit in a circle on the floor. Have the bread and grape juice available to be passed at the appropriate time.) It is preferable to have the children seated in small groups with an adult or teenager in each group. That will help the children to remain quiet and reverent and will make it easier to pass the grape juice and bread later.

To assemble the children, go to each one or to small groups of them and whisper excitedly, **Come, our special meal is about to begin. Let us remember what the Lord has done for us. Follow me quietly and with respect for our God.** Lead them to the worship area and encourage them to sit quietly and reverently.

Why do we have birthday parties or Fourth of July picnics? Allow for answers. **We remember what happened on those days—our births and the day the United States declared independence from England. We celebrate these occasions.**

On the night before Jesus died, He and His disciples celebrated the Passover Feast. This was a special time when God had commanded the people of Israel to remember what had happened one night in Egypt. It was an exciting time, but it was a serious and reverent time. We will learn about the Passover and especially about what happened when Jesus and His disciples were together the night before Jesus died.

The Jews observed the Passover as a reminder of the time when they were freed from being slaves in Egypt. Turn to Exodus 12 in your Bible. **In Exodus in the Bible it tells about**

the things to fix for the Passover feast. It also tells how to fix the food and how to eat it. Read Exodus 12:3-14. **Did you notice that the last part I read talked about how they must remember this feast and celebrate it always, even their children and their grandchildren, and their great-grandchildren, and so on?**

Listen to some more verses that explain how and why they were to celebrate the Passover feast. Read Exodus 12:24-28. **Notice that this is called a command, a law. The Jews were to do this because God commanded them to. What did they tell their children when the children asked why they did those things?** The parents told the children they did those things because the the Lord passed over the houses of Israel.

Why did Jesus celebrate the Passover? Because Jesus always obeyed God's laws.

In the book of Luke in the Bible we read about the last Passover Jesus took part in. Listen. Read Luke 22:14-18. **Today, we will have a part of the Passover as we find it in Luke 22. As I read, we will also do what the Scripture is describing.**

If you are not seated with the children, sit with them at this time. Read Luke 22:19. Then thank God for the bread, tear off a small part and pass it to the children, who will tear off small pieces as they pass the loaf on. Then eat the bread. Each leader will tear and pass the loaf to his group of children.

Read Luke 22:20. Then thank God for the grape juice, pour enough for your group. Then pass the cups to the children and all of you drink your grape juice. Each adult or teenager will pour and pass the grape juice.

This Passover meal was different from every other Passover that Jesus and His friends had ever had. This time Jesus explained how the Passover could be seen as a symbol for Jesus' death. We call this special Passover the Last Supper or the Lord's Supper. After Jesus died and became alive again, this became a special time in prayer with God for remembering Jesus' death. Jesus died so that our sins can be forgiven. The Lord's Supper, or Communion, as we call it, is an important reminder for Christians of the fact that Jesus came to earth to die so we could be forgiven.

Today in our worship time we will learn more about the Lord's Supper and how we remember Jesus because of and through it, even if we are not Christians yet. Explain the activities that are available. Encourage the children to move quietly and reverently to the activity of their choice.

Building the Theme

(30 minutes)

1. Communion Hymn. Teach new words to the hymn "Communion Hymn." You will need poster board and markers so the children can make a song chart.

This is a very special song about the Lord's Supper. It is called "Communion Hymn." Communion is a word used to mean the Lord's Supper. It means a time for remembering what Jesus did for us, talking to Him in prayer.

Read the original words to the hymn. Then read the following words to the hymn to the children. Let the children copy the new words onto a song chart. Then have the children read the new words with you.

Sing the song for the children. Practice the song with the children until they know it well enough to sing it as special music during *Sharing in Worship.*

On this holy Lord's day
  morning,
We want to remember You;
How You helped so many
  people,
How You cared and loved
  them, too.

May this bread and juice
  remind us
Of Your life You gave for us;
Dying for us on a cross and
Coming back to life again.

If you have extra time, encourage the children to tell things they remember about Jesus. Explain to them that we remember Jesus at the Lord's Supper, especially how He died to forgive our sins.

2. Bible Verses About Remembering. Help the children in your group find and read 1 Corinthians 11:23-26. Discuss the verses. From a collection of pictures about Jesus (birth, miracles, teaching), ask each child to select one that is a picture of something to remember about Jesus. The children may mount their pictures on construction paper. Ask two or three children who are good readers to read the verses for the Scripture reading during *Sharing in Worship* as the other children hold up their pictures.

3. Scripture Study. Provide enough copies of activity page 6A and pencils for each child in this group to have one. Also have Bibles available in case some children do not have their Bibles with them.

Today we will do a Bible study that will help us to understand the purpose of the Lord's Supper and the attitudes that we should have during that portion of a worship time. Then we will share our new

understanding with the rest of the group.

Each of you will have a Scripture to look up. Then you can fill in the blanks in your verse on your activity page. After you have completed your verse, read the explanation about the verse. During our worship time, each of you will take a turn reading a Scripture and its explanation. After all of you have read, we will recite John 3:16 together as a group.

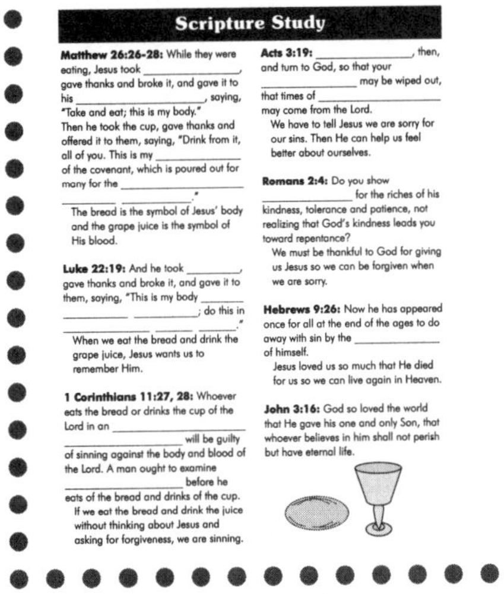

Scripture Study

Matthew 26:26-28: While they were eating, Jesus took ______________, gave thanks and broke it, and gave it to his ______________, saying, "Take and eat; this is my body." Then he took the cup, gave thanks and offered it to them, saying, "Drink from it, all of you. This is my ______________ of the covenant, which is poured out for many for the ______________ ______________ ______________."

The bread is the symbol of Jesus' body and the grape juice is the symbol of His blood.

Luke 22:19: And he took ______________, gave thanks and broke it, and gave it to them, saying, "This is my body ______________ ______________ ______________; do this in ______________ ______________ ______________."

When we eat the bread and drink the grape juice, Jesus wants us to remember Him.

1 Corinthians 11:27, 28: Whoever eats the bread or drinks the cup of the Lord in an ______________ ______________ will be guilty of sinning against the body and blood of the Lord. A man ought to examine ______________ before he eats of the bread and drinks of the cup.

If we eat the bread and drink the juice without thinking about Jesus and asking for forgiveness, we are sinning.

Acts 3:19: ______________, then, and turn to God, so that your ______________ may be wiped out, that times of ______________ may come from the Lord.

We have to tell Jesus we are sorry for our sins. Then He can help us feel better about ourselves.

Romans 2:4: Do you show ______________ for the riches of his kindness, tolerance and patience, not realizing that God's kindness leads you toward repentance?

We must be thankful to God for giving us Jesus so we can be forgiven when we are sorry.

Hebrews 9:26: Now he has appeared once for all at the end of the ages to do away with sin by the ______________ of himself.

Jesus loved us so much that He died for us so we can live again in Heaven.

John 3:16: God so loved the world that He gave his one and only Son, that whoever believes in him shall not perish but have eternal life.

Assign each child a Scripture to look up. Help those who need it to find their Scriptures. Then go over the verses one at a time with each child reading his assigned Scripture and all children filling in the blanks. Help the children practice reading their verses and explanations. Expand the explanations if the children have questions about the Scriptures or explanations they are to read.

During *Sharing in Worship* the children will read their verses and explanations in order for the devotional. If you expanded the explanations, add those comments after the appropriate explanations.

4. Call to Worship. This group will read Psalm 77:11-15a as a call to worship during *Sharing in Worship.* You will need a copy of activity page 6B for each child and crayons or colored pencils. You will also need scissors, construction paper, and glue.

Distribute the activity page and crayons or colored pencils. **Today we will prepare a Scripture which will begin our worship time in the large group. May I have a volunteer to read the verse?** Pause. **You can't read the verse until you have put it right, can you? While you color the pieces of the puzzle, listen. I will help you understand how important it is to have things right when you worship.**

When we worship, we must have our actions right. We must sit still at the appropriate times. When we are to move about, we should do it in a polite way, without pushing or rushing. We should listen at the right times and speak when we should.

In addition to our actions, our attitudes should be right. We should be respectful toward our leaders and especially toward God. We should be loving. We should be joyful.

When we have our attitudes and actions right, then we are able to worship God in the best way possible. One important way to worship is to remember Jesus and the wonderful things He has done.

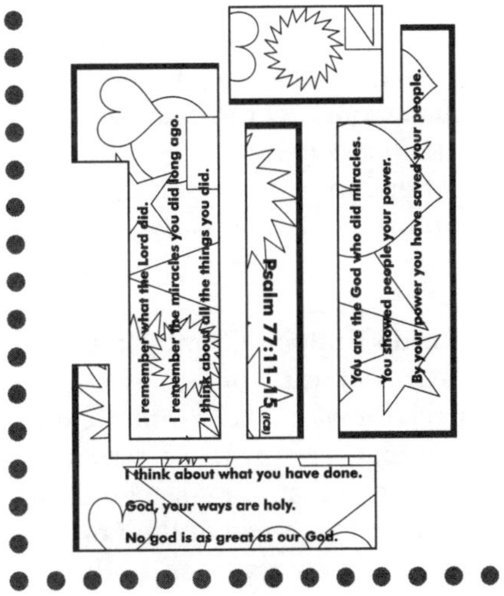

Allow the children to cut their puzzles apart and work them. After all the children have completed their puzzles, they should glue the puzzle to a piece of construction paper in the correct form. While they do this, read the verses aloud. Then lead the children in reading the verses together.

Practice reading the verses together until the children feel comfortable with it. If necessary, divide your group into smaller groups and assign a portion of the Scripture for each group.

5. Hymn Search. This is a challenge activity for older or advanced children. Provide hymnals for the children in this group. Also provide markers and several pieces of chart paper or poster board. The children in the group will read through several Communion hymns and choose a few which will be used for a song time. They will write the words to these songs on song charts. Show the children how to use the topical index of the hymnal to find hymns which concern Communion or the Lord's Supper. If these hymns are grouped together in the book, you may wish to put a bookmark in that section.

There are many hymns which talk about the Lord's Supper. They can help us understand more about the what the Lord's Supper should mean to us. Today we will read several hymns about the Lord's Supper. Then we will choose a few that we will lead the large group in singing. We will write the words to these songs on charts.

Read several songs with the children. Help them to choose which songs they will lead. Let them make the song charts. Then help them practice the songs. Select one song to be used at the Lord's Supper time. The others will be used during the song time.

6. Prayer. This group will lead in the closing prayer time of *Sharing in Worship.* Have Bibles ready for the children and papers and pencils.

Find Acts 2:42 in your Bibles. Help the children who need help. Let a volunteer read the verse. Discuss what it means to be devoted to prayer.

Prayer is a very important part of the lives of those who love the Lord. There are many Bible verses where we can read the prayers of people from the Old Testament. We read of many times when Jesus prayed. We also can find verses that tell about the prayers of Jesus' followers.

Today we will write prayers that will be used to close our worship time. In our prayers today we want to concentrate on thanking God for Jesus and remembering the things that Jesus has done. Help the children as needed when they write their prayers.

Sharing in Worship

(20-25 minutes)

Omit any of the following sections if you did not offer the corresponding activity. You can present the Scriptures and explanations during the devotional if activity 3 was not offered.

Note: Because this session highlights the Lord's Supper, the order of service has been changed to have Communion just before the closing prayer time. The entire service will focus the children's thoughts on the reason for the Lord's Supper.

Call to Worship (Group 4): Allow Group 4 to read Psalm 77:11-15a. **An important part of worship is remembering what the Lord has done for us. This is especially true when we remember that Jesus died on the cross so that our sins could be forgiven.**

Songs (Group 5): Group 5 will lead the large group in two or three songs. **Our songs that we sang have reminders in them. They help us remember what the Lord has done, what our attitude and actions should be, and also what the Lord's Supper means.**

Offering: Because we remember God's love for us and what the Lord has done, we are grateful. We give back to the Lord what He has given us. When we offer our gifts to Him, we remember Him.

Scripture (Group 2): Allow Group 2 to read the Scripture and show their pictures.

Special Music (Group 1): **Group 1 will sing a special song about the Lord's Supper.**

Devotional (Group 3): **Group 3 will read and explain some Scriptures that will help us understand more about the Lord's Supper, what it means, and what our attitudes should be.**

The Scriptures that will be read and discussed are Matthew 26:26-28; Luke 22:19;1 Corinthians 11:27, 28; Acts 3:19; Romans 2:4; and Hebrews 9:26. John 3:16 is to be recited by Group 3. If you are reading the Scriptures and making the comments instead of the group's doing it, use activity page 6A for ideas about the explanations. Let the large group recite John 3:16.

After Group 3 has read the Scriptures and made the explanations, lead right into the Lord's Supper.

Lord's Supper (Group 5)**: At this time of our worship, we especially want to concentrate on remembering how Jesus died on the cross so that our sins could be forgiven. The bread of the Lord's Supper represents Jesus' body and the juice represents Jesus' blood. When He died on the cross, He was giving His body and His blood as a sacrifice so that we might be forgiven. Group 5 will sing a song that will guide our thoughts during this time.**

Prayer (Group 6): **Group 6 has written some prayers to direct our prayer time today.**

Closing Moments

(10-15 minutes)

Involve the children in a discussion about remembering Jesus. Begin the discussion using these thoughts: **When I remember Jesus, I remember the story of Jesus' feeding five thousand people with a boy's lunch of two fish and five small loaves of bread. I think about what the crowd must have thought and what Jesus' followers must have though—Jesus is so special. Only Jesus could feed so many people with a little bit of food.**

When you remember Jesus, what do you think about? Ask the children to fill in the sentence, "When I remember Jesus, I. . . ." Encourage each child to participate as well as other adult leaders. You may wish to provide old visuals or teaching pictures or take home papers of miracles Jesus did to help the children remember different stories.

Scripture Study

Matthew 26:26-28: While they were eating, Jesus took ________________, gave thanks and broke it, and gave it to his ______________________, saying, "Take and eat; this is my body." Then he took the cup, gave thanks and offered it to them, saying, "Drink from it, all of you. This is my ______________ of the covenant, which is poured out for many for the ____________________ ________ ____________."

The bread is the symbol of Jesus' body and the grape juice is the symbol of His blood.

Luke 22:19: And he took _________, gave thanks and broke it, and gave it to them, saying, "This is my body ________ __________ ___________; do this in _____________ ______ _______."

When we eat the bread and drink the grape juice, Jesus wants us to remember Him.

1 Corinthians 11:27, 28: Whoever eats the bread or drinks the cup of the Lord in an ______________________ ___________________ will be guilty of sinning against the body and blood of the Lord. A man ought to examine ___________________ before he eats of the bread and drinks of the cup.

If we eat the bread and drink the juice without thinking about Jesus and asking for forgiveness, we are sinning.

Acts 3:19: _______________, then, and turn to God, so that your _______________ may be wiped out, that times of ____________________ may come from the Lord.

We have to tell Jesus we are sorry for our sins. Then He can help us feel better about ourselves.

Romans 2:4: Do you show ______________ for the riches of his kindness, tolerance and patience, not realizing that God's kindness leads you toward repentance?

We must be thankful to God for giving us Jesus so we can be forgiven when we are sorry.

Hebrews 9:26: Now he has appeared once for all at the end of the ages to do away with sin by the ______________ of himself.

Jesus loved us so much that He died for us so we can live again in Heaven.

John 3:16: God so loved the world that He gave his one and only Son, that whoever believes in him shall not perish but have eternal life.

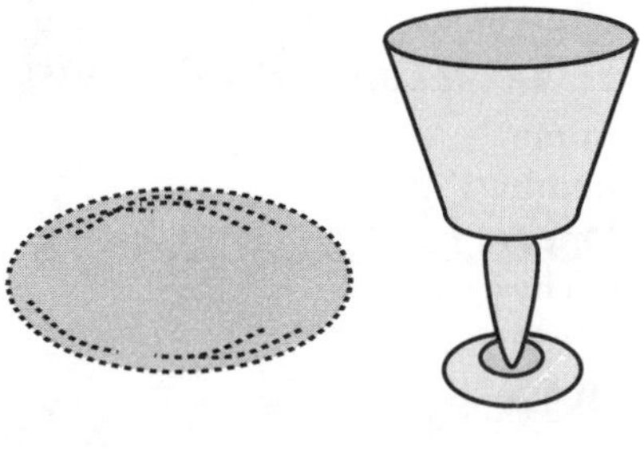

Scriptures are taken from the *New International Version.*

I remember what the Lord did.
I remember the miracles you did long ago.
I think about all the things you did.
I think about what you have done.
God, your ways are holy.
No god is as great as our God.
You are the God who did miracles.
You showed people your power.
By your power you have saved your people.
Psalm 77:11-15 (ICB)

Jesus Is Alive

Worship Focus

Worship Jesus because He arose from the dead.

Transition Time

(10-15 minutes)

Encourage the children to use the rest room and get drinks as they come to the room. Choose two student helpers and give each of them a badge.

(Prior to class, make badges for your helpers. Make two photocopies of the badge on page 26. Color, if desired, glue to poster board, cut out, and glue a safety pin on back. Cover with clear, adhesive-backed paper if desired.) Use these badges each week or make new ones to allow children to take them home. Alternate student helpers so every child takes a turn.

Good News Telephone. Have the children sit in a circle. If your group is larger than ten or fifteen children, have two circles. Whisper a message into the ear of one child in each circle. Proceeding clockwise around the circle, that child whispers in the ear of his neighbor, who whispers in the ear of his neighbor, and so on until the message gets back to the child sitting next to the first child. That last child will tell the message aloud. Then you tell the original message and check the accuracy of the passed message. (If you have two or more circles, have the child stand silently until all circles have completed sending the message. Then see which circle has relayed the message most accurately.)

Some suggested messages for you to whisper follow: "Jesus died for you and me." "Jesus was buried in a tomb." "Jesus is alive!" The smaller the group, the more complicated you might make your message. It is fun to hear how the message changes from beginning to end. Always make sure the correct message is announced at the end, so that the good news is told accurately. Use several phrases if time allows. Start with different children each time.

Launching the Theme

(10 minutes)

Recruit an adult or teenager who will portray Mary Magdalene for an interview. If possible, have her dress in costume. The interview can be conducted in either of two ways: interview Mary yourself, either as a print or broadcast journalist; or have Mary hold a news conference in which the children ask the questions. Distribute the questions from the interview printed below to volunteers among the children. Either way, introduce Mary and the occasion for the interview before beginning the actual interview/press conference.

Today we are pleased to have with us Mary, a friend of this unusual religious leader called Jesus. Perhaps Mary can shed some light on what has been going on in Jerusalem this past weekend. Mary, thank you for joining us today.

Mary: It's my pleasure. I'm always glad to talk about Jesus.

Interviewer: Why don't you tell us a little about what happened last Friday?

Mary: It was so awful. They crucified Him! They nailed Him to a cross to die. He was perfect, but they sentenced Him to a horrible death on a cross. Then they divided His clothes among themselves by casting lots. They placed a sign over His head. It said, "This is Jesus, the king of the Jews." (Begins to laugh ironically.)

Interviewer: What's so funny about that?

Mary: If only they knew! He *is* the king of the Jews; and more than that, He's the Son of God! But they put Him on a cross in between two thieves who were also crucified. They might have deserved their punishment, but Jesus didn't. He healed people; He helped people; He fed people; He made people live again. He wasn't a criminal. He loved people, but the people who went by Him when He was on the cross shouted awful insults to Him.

Interviewer: Insults? What kind of insults?

Mary: They told Him to get off the cross if He were really the Son of God. They also said, "He saved others, but He can't save himself!" They said God could rescue Him if God really wanted to! Even those awful robbers insulted Him! But then the worst thing happened. (Begins to sob.) Jesus died. (Continues sobbing.)

Interviewer: I'm sorry. I know this is hard for you. What a horrible death Jesus died. Please tell us what happened next.

Mary (calmer): What happened next was amazing and frightening! The earth shook. Rocks split. The curtain in the temple was torn in two—from the top to the bottom! Tombs were open and holy people who were dead came to life again. Then one of the soldiers who was guarding Jesus finally realized that Jesus was the Son of God. But that didn't change the fact that Jesus was dead.

Interviewer: What happened to Jesus' body?

Mary: Joseph of Arimathea asked for Jesus' body. He took it, wrapped it in cloth, and placed it in his own tomb. Then he rolled a big stone across the entrance and went away. How sad I was as I watched Joseph bury Jesus and seal His body in the tomb. (Sobs again.)

Interviewer: Thank you, Mary. That concludes our interview.

Mary: Wait! That's not the whole story. Early in the morning on Sunday, after the Sabbath was over, Mary and I went to look at the tomb again. Once again there was a terrible earthquake! What happened was that an angel came from Heaven, rolled back the stone in front of the tomb, and sat on that huge stone. He was so bright! His appearance was like lightning. His clothes were as white as snow. The guards at the tomb were so frightened that they fainted. Then the angel told us something incredible! He told us not to be afraid. He knew we had come to see Jesus. But he told us that Jesus had risen from the dead! The angel even showed us where Jesus' body had been! Then he told us to go tell the disciples the good news.

Interviewer: That's exciting! But I'm not sure I would believe some guy dressed in white. How can you be sure he was telling the truth?

Mary: As we ran to tell the disciples, the best thing of all happened! JESUS came to us! Jesus is alive! I've seen Him! I've talked to Him! He is alive! He is alive!

Thank you, Mary. That's an amazing story. I don't know quite what to say. I think I'd better make my report to my newspaper (radio or television station).

As Mary leaves, explain the activity choices to the children. Let them choose which activity to participate in, but try to keep the groups approximately the same size.

Building the Theme

(30 minutes)

1. Call to Worship. This group will lead the larger group in a responsive reading. You will need paper, pencils, and poster board and markers or chalkboard and chalk.

What is special about Jesus? Let the children write their ideas on the paper you have provided. You will use these ideas for the responsive reading. Be sure they include several of His miracles, the fact that He is God's Son, that He died so that our sins could be forgiven, and that He arose from the dead. **Today is a special day! Tell me, what is the most important thing about today?** Steer conversation away from the Easter bunny, new clothes, spring time, and other ways of celebrating the day. Be excited about Jesus' becoming alive again and respond with excitement to any mention of Jesus' resurrection.

We want to help the other children praise God for His special Son and for this special day. Let's write some praise sentences to tell at the beginning of our worship time. First let's choose a sentence that can be repeated several times. Then we will write several other sentences.

Your responsive reading might be something like this:

All: Let's praise the Lord together!
Individual (or small group): Jesus is God's Son.
All: Let's praise the Lord together!
Individual (or small group): Jesus does wonderful things.
All: Let's praise the Lord together!
Individual (or small group): Jesus heals sick people.
All: Let's praise the Lord together!

Continue in this way, including some of Jesus' miracles and His death, burial, and resurrection. End with all children saying, "Let's praise the Lord together!" Use the poster board or chalkboard to write the responsive reading so that all children will be able to see it.

This small group will lead the reading for the call to worship during *Sharing in Worship.*

2. Special Music. This group will sing a the song "One Day!" You will need to provide hymnals for the children to use. If possible, have an instrumentalist in the session who can help the children learn the song as well as accompany them during *Sharing in Worship.* If no instrumentalist is available, record either an instrumental or vocal version of the song for the children to listen to as they follow along in the hymnal.

This song describes the life of Jesus, especially His death, when He was buried, and His coming back to life again. Today we will sing this song to tell the other children about Jesus' life.

Explain any parts of the song the children don't understand. Practice the song until the children feel comfortable with it.

If you feel the children will have trouble mastering the tune and the words, have the children present this as a choral reading. Assign phrases to different children or allow two or three children to read a stanza in unison and then two or three others to read another and so on.

Whether the group presents a song or a choral reading, the children's voices should be filled with the feelings that are appropriate for the words that are being sung or said.

3. Scripture. This group will draw a mural which will illustrate the Scripture to be read during *Sharing in Worship.* You will need a long section of butcher or shelf paper and markers or crayons. Also provide Bibles.

Have a good reader find 1 Corinthians 15:3, 4 and read the verses to the group. **In these verses, Paul is reminding the Christians in the city of Corinth that he told them how important it is that Jesus died, was buried, and became alive again. That is the most important thing Paul told the people in Corinth.**

We will draw a mural showing three scenes: Jesus on the cross, the tomb where Jesus' body was buried, and Jesus after He was raised from the dead. In each of these scenes, we should also include people who were there. Be sure to draw expressions on their faces showing how they might have felt.

Allow time for the children to draw the mural. If they have questions, refer to Matthew 27:35-54, 57-60; 28:1-10. During *Sharing in Worship,* one child should read 1 Corinthians 15:3, 4 while the other children present the mural at the Scripture time.

4. Praise Poems. This group will write poems of praise to be read during *Sharing in Worship.* You will need copies of activity page 7A and pencils for the children.

This is a very exciting day. We celebrate the resurrection of Jesus—that He became alive again. Today we will write poems of praise to God for bringing Jesus to life again.

Let the children brainstorm a few ideas for poems. Write these ideas on the chalkboard. Then let the children write and title their own poems. Let the children read their poems to each other. Then ask for volunteers who will read their poems during *Sharing in Worship.*

5. Devotional. This group will create a newspaper writing articles about Jesus' death, burial, and resurrection from different peoples' perspectives. You will need copies of activity page 7B, pencils, Bibles, and scrap paper for rough drafts of the articles. This activity is a challenge activity, better for older students.

On the weekend when Jesus was crucified and buried and then raised from the dead, many unusual things happened. We are going to write newspaper articles about that weekend. We will try to have articles written about the events from different people's perspectives.

Here are two suggestions for your newspaper: have each child write about a different part of that weekend or have more than one child write about a particular part but from the perspectives of various followers of Jesus as well as people who were against Jesus. Help the children as needed. Let their imaginations run, but keep them true to the Scriptural account and be sure they include Jesus' death, burial, and resurrection.

The children will read their newspaper articles as part of the devotional portion of *Sharing in Worship.* If possible, after the children have copied their articles onto the copies of activity page 7B, make copies of the "newspaper" pages for each of the children.

6. Prayer Acrostic. This group will prepare a prayer acrostic to lead the closing prayer of *Sharing in Worship.* You will need poster board and markers.

Before the session, write the words "Jesus Lives" vertically in the middle of the poster board.

Today we remember how wonderful Jesus is. He died a horrible death, was buried, and then was raised to life again. He did all that so we could live in Heaven with Him someday. We want to have a praising prayer time today, praising God for Jesus. We will use these words, "Jesus Lives," as a basis for our prayers. Think of words that have these letters in them that are about Jesus or show how we should feel today. The words can begin with one of these letters or have one of these letters in them.

At the closing prayer time during *Sharing in Worship,* the children will present their acrostic. Let each child who is willing choose a part of the acrostic as a basis for an oral prayer. Close the prayer time including other ideas from the acrostic that might not have been used by the children.

Sharing in Worship

(20-25 minutes)

Omit any of the following sections if you did not offer the corresponding activity.

Call to Worship (Group 1): Group 1 will lead the larger group in the responsive reading.

Special Music (Group 2): Group 2 will sing or read "One Day!" at this time.

Lord's Supper: Each week at this time of our worship, we remember Jesus' death. The Communion bread reminds us of His body, and the juice reminds us of Jesus' blood. Every Sunday we think about how Jesus died to save us from our sins. We also celebrate Jesus' resurrection, His coming to life again. Let's prayerfully remember Jesus during this special time.

Offering: One way that we can celebrate the wonderful things Jesus has done for us it to give our offerings so that other children can learn about Jesus too. Then they can know that Jesus, God's Son, died, was buried, and became alive again.

Scripture (Group 3): Group 3 will present a mural while one of the students reads 1 Corinthians 15:3, 4.

Praise Poems (Group 4): Children from Group 4 will read their praise poems at this time.

Devotional (Group 5): **Extra! Extra! Group 5 is going to read all about it!** Allow the children from Group 5 to read the newspaper articles they have written and, if possible, distribute copies of the newspapers. After they have finished, fill in any important facts they might have omitted.

Jesus is God's Son. He had everything—God's power, Heaven, glory, praise. Yet He came to earth and was born in a stable. He lived as an ordinary child. He grew to be a man, a very special man. Jesus loved people; He healed them; He fed thousands of them; He made some of them live again after they were dead. Then He was crucified, He was buried, and on the third day He rose from the dead.

Jesus did all of that because He loves us so much. He knows that we do wrong, that we sin. But Jesus made a way for God to forgive us. Let's praise God for letting Jesus die for us and for making Him live again!

Prayer (Group 6): Let the children from Group 6 present their prayer acrostic and lead in the closing prayer.

Closing Moments

(10-15 minutes)

Worship Poster. Provide materials for the children to make worship posters to take home with them. Encourage them to use the theme "Jesus Is Risen" or "Jesus Lives." You will need poster board or construction paper, glue, markers, scissors, yarn, glitter, rickrack, sequins, and whatever other materials you have available.

Praise Poem!

Use the lines below to write a poem praising God for bringing Jesus to life again.

The Jerusalem News

Paul Begins to Tell About Jesus

Worship Focus

Worship Jesus because He changes enemies into friends.

Transition Time

(10-15 minutes)

Encourage the children to use the rest room and get drinks as they come to the room. Choose two student helpers and give each of them a badge.

(Prior to class, make badges for your helpers. Make two photocopies of the badge on page 26. Color, if desired, glue to poster board, cut out, and glue a safety pin on back. Cover with clear, adhesive-backed paper if desired.) Use these badges each week or make new ones to allow children to take them home. Alternate student helpers so every child takes a turn.

Trust walk. After all the children are in the room, have them participate in a trust walk. You will need to group the children into pairs. Using a simple cloth blindfold, cover the eyes of one of the children in each pair. The child whose eyes are not blindfolded should then lead the other child around the room. Make sure the children walk carefully to avoid possible injury. After one or two minutes, have the children trade roles and continue the "walk." After you are finished, collect the blindfolds and have the children sit in a circle.

Launching the Theme

(10 minutes)

After the children are settled, have them tell how it felt to be blindfolded and led around the room. Then continue the discussion. **It can be very scary to be blind, especially if you suddenly become blind. You would not be able to tell where you were going or what might be in your way. You couldn't be sure who was near you or whether you were in danger. You would have to depend on others around you for your safety and guidance.**

What if you were blind and you suddenly received your sight? Allow discussion. **You would feel great, wouldn't you? You'd be so happy! You would tell everyone about the change.**

What if there could be an even better change? Saul had both. He was an enemy of God's people. God made him blind for three days. Then God gave Saul his sight back. But the better change was that Saul became a friend to God and His people. He told everyone he could how God could change them from enemies into friends.

At this time, explain to the children what activities will be offered during *Building the Theme.* Allow the children to choose which group interests them, but try to have the groups be approximately the same size.

Building the Theme

(30 minutes)

1. Memorization. Provide a set of Scripture cards for each child in this group. A "set" consists of twenty cards cut from activity page 8A, nineteen with one word from 2 Corinthians 5:17 (ICB) written on each one and the twentieth with the Scripture reference. If your children are able and are quick workers, they can cut the cards on activity page 8A apart themselves. Otherwise, do it before class. Put each set of twenty cards in a separate envelope (or provide envelopes for the children to put their cards in to take them home).

Arrange the cards in order, and they will spell out a verse that tells how God changes enemies into friends. Try to arrange them without looking up the verse. After a few minutes, you can look it up for help. Give a few minutes to arrange; make sure everyone has the verse correct.

Now let's read the verse together. Do so. **Now take out one card—it doesn't matter which. Then we'll read it again, but pretend the missing card is there.** Read. **Take out another**

card. Continue until students can "read" the verse with no cards.

The children will recite this verse as the Call to Worship during *Sharing in Worship.*

2. Song. This group will present a song during *Sharing in Worship.* Make a song chart using the words below. The tune of the song is "Have You Ever Seen a Lassie?"

Have you ever had an enemy,
  an enemy, an enemy?
Have you ever had an enemy?
God wants you to be friends.
God loves you.
He cares for you.
He wants what is best for you.
Have you ever had an enemy?
God wants you to be friends.

Now Saul was once an enemy,
  an enemy, an enemy.
Now Saul was once an enemy.
God made him a friend.
God loved him.
He cared for him.
He wanted what was best for
  him.
Now Saul was once an enemy.
God made him a friend.

Today we will worship God because He can make enemies into friends. We will sing this song to remind us of that.

Sing the song for the children. Then have them sing along. Practice the song until the children are comfortable with it.

3. Scripture play. This group will review the Scripture lesson (Acts 9:1-30) during the devotional portion of *Sharing in Worship.* You will need copies of the script from page activity page 8B. If possible, provide simple costumes and props for the children. This play has three scenes: the road to Damascus, Damascus, and Jerusalem. You will need the following cast: Narrator, Voice of the Lord, Saul, at least one man traveling with him to Damascus, Ananias, at least one Christian in Damascus, Barnabas, and at least one Christian in Jerusalem. (Some of the children can overlap in the parts of the "anonymous" people.) Group 4 will prepare scenery for this play.

Saul Becomes a Friend

Cast: Narrator, voice of the Lord, Saul, man traveling with him, Ananias, Christian in Damascus, Barnabas, Christian in Jerusalem

Scene 1: The road from Jerusalem to Damascus

Narrator: Saul was traveling from Jerusalem to Damascus one day, planning to cause trouble for the Christians in Damascus. Suddenly there was a light from Heaven. As Saul fell to his knees, he heard a voice.

Voice of the Lord: Saul! I am Jesus. Why are you persecuting me? Go to Damascus. You will be told what to do.

Saul: I can't see! Please help me. Lead me to Damascus.

Man: I don't know what happened, but I'll help you. (Leads Saul to Damascus.)

Scene 2: Damascus

Narrator: Saul was blind for three days. During that time he did not eat or drink. The Lord sent Ananias to see Saul.

Ananias (putting hands on Saul's shoulders): Saul, Jesus sent me to you so that you may see again and receive the Holy Spirit.

Saul: I can see! Thank you, Lord.

Narrator: Then Ananias baptized Saul. Immediately Saul began telling about Jesus. But then the enemies of God's people learned about Saul's change.

Christian in Damascus: Saul, you must leave! Those people will kill you if you don't. I have a plan, we'll let you over the city walls tonight in a basket. Then you can escape.

Scene 3: Jerusalem

Narrator: Saul went back to Jerusalem and tried to be with other Christians. But the Christians were afraid Saul was still their enemy and was trying to trick them. Barnabas believed Saul and took him to the other Christians.

Barnabas: The Lord himself talked to Saul when Saul was on the way to Damascus. Now Saul is a Christian too. In fact, he was talking about Jesus so much that he had to leave Damascus at night by being lowered over the wall in a basket.

Christian in Jerusalem: Saul, I'm glad you are one of us! I'm sure you will tell many people about Jesus.

Saul: I will tell everyone I can the good news about Jesus. I'm glad God made us friends.

We will be preparing a play showing how Saul, who had been an enemy of God and God's people, became a friend to God and God's people. Who knows who Saul was? Allow the children to respond. **That's right. Saul is the one who later became known as Paul, and he traveled all over the world telling people about Jesus. He also wrote many of the books of the New Testament. Can you name some of them?** Again, allow student response. (Paul wrote all the books from Romans through Philemon, and he may also have written Hebrews.)

During the last five minutes of *Building the Theme,* rehearse with Group 4 so that scene and scenery changes go smoothly during *Sharing in Worship.*

4. Scenery. This group will prepare the scenery for the Scripture play that Group 3 will present during the devotional portion of *Sharing in Worship.* You will need copies of activity page 8B, poster board, markers or paints, letter stencils, Bibles, and Bible reference books that would show Bible-times buildings.

The play will have three scenes: the road to Damascus, Damascus, and Jerusalem. This group will prepare a sign telling the location of each scene and also a basic, not detailed, background for each scene.

Scene one background should be a simple road with a few small plants and rocks around it. Scene two background should show a city wall on one side, a few buildings in the middle, and a river on the other side. Scene three scenery should be another city with a few buildings.

Group 3 will be doing a play about how Saul, who was later called Paul, changed from being an enemy of God and God's people to being a friend to God and God's people. We will make the signs that tell which scene it is and also background for each scene to make it easier to understand.

Read the play with the children and help them make the signs and simple background sketches. If you need more information about what happened, read Acts 9:1-30 and refer to the Bible references.

During *Sharing in Worship,* the children will hold the appropriate scene signs and backgrounds during the play. Rehearse with Group 3 during the last five minutes of *Building the Theme.*

5. Lord's Supper. This group will present a Lord's Supper meditation. You will need construction paper, markers, and (if desired) letter stencils. The children will make signs with one letter of the word "Enemies" on one side and one letter of the word "Friends" on the other side. You will need to assign the letters so that the children will be able to stand in order showing the word "Enemies" and at the appropriate time turn the letters over to show the word "Friends." If you do not have seven children in this group, let at least one child hold two letters. You may want to tape these letters together to make it easier for the child holding them. In this case, you will either switch the order of the letters on the back or put them upside down and have the child flip the papers end over end. As the children work making and drawing the letters, use the following explanation.

God loves us very much and wants us to be His friends. But because we sin, we are His enemies. Although God loves us, He cannot stand the wrong things that we do. But God made a plan so that we could be friends. He let His Son Jesus come to earth as a baby. Jesus lived on the earth but did no wrong. Then one day Jesus was crucified—He was killed on a cross. He was buried in a tomb, and then He rose to life again. Because Jesus did that, He made it so that we could be God's friends.

Today during the Lord's Supper time, we want to remember that Jesus turns enemies into friends.

Use the above talk for the Communion meditation. The children should stand at the front of the room showing the word "Enemies." Then at the end of your talk, they should turn the letters to show the word "Friends." Practice with the children until everything goes smoothly. It is important to keep all the children's thoughts on what God has done through Jesus rather than on a mistake in turning the letters.

6. Prayer Montage. This group will make a montage showing how God can make enemies friends. You will need poster board, markers, old magazines and catalogs, scissors, and glue. Before the session, make a large construction paper cross and glue it to the middle of the poster board. On the cross write the words "God's love." Label the section of the poster to the left of the cross "Enemies" and the section to the right of the cross "Friends."

Today we are worshiping God because He can make enemies into friends. We will be leading the closing prayer time. So we will make a montage showing enemies on one side of the cross which stands for God's love and showing friends on the other side of God's love. God's love, especially how He let Jesus die so our sins could be forgiven, is the main difference between enemies and friends. Look through the magazines and catalogs here. Find and cut out pictures of people who are angry or maybe fighting or are unhappy. We will put them on the left side of the cross on this poster. Also find and cut out pictures of people who are friends, people who look happy, people who are helping others. We will put these on the right side of the cross.

During our prayer time, we will show this poster to the other children and explain it. Then I will have a prayer thanking God for making enemies into friends.

Sharing in Worship

(20-25 minutes)

Omit any of the following sections if you did not offer the corresponding activity.

Call to Worship (Group 1): **Group 1 will recite 2 Corinthians 5:17 (ICB).**

Song (Group 2): **Group 2 will sing a song for us.** If time allows, have the group teach the large group the song also.

Lord's Supper (Group 5): The children from Group 5 should stand at the front showing the word "Enemies." A leader will giving the following Communion meditation.

God loves us very much and wants us to be His friends. But because we sin, we are His enemies. Although God loves us, He cannot stand the wrong things that we do. But God made a plan so that we could be friends. He let His Son Jesus come to earth as a baby. Jesus lived on the earth but did no wrong. Then one day Jesus was crucified—He was killed on a cross. He was buried in a tomb, and then He rose to life again. Because Jesus did that, He made it so that we could be God's friends. Today during the Lord's Supper time, we want to remember that Jesus turns enemies into friends. The children will turn the letters to show the word "Friends."

Offering: When we are friends with someone, we often give him things. God is our friend in a very special way. He has given us everything we have. He has even given us a special way to become His friends. Since we can be friends with God, we want to give Him things. Our offering time is one time we can give to God to show Him that we are His friends.

Devotional (Groups 3 and 4): **Groups 3 and 4 have a play to show us how God made Saul into a friend.** Allow the children to perform their play with scenery.

Saul had been an enemy of God and God's people. He wanted to put the people who believed in Jesus in jail and he wanted to frighten God's people by saying he would kill them. That certainly sounds like an enemy!

But anyone who does something against God is like an enemy to God. That means that anyone who does wrong, anyone who sins is an enemy of God. The Bible tells us in Romans 3:23 (ICB), "All people have sinned and are not good enough for

God's glory." That means that all of us are like God's enemies because God cannot stand sin.

But God loves us anyway. In fact, He had a plan to make us His friends. Romans 5:8 (ICB) tells us, "Christ died for us while we were still sinners. In this way God shows his great love for us." That's wonderful! God loves us so much that He sent His own Son Jesus to die on the cross for our sins. That way we could be forgiven and be friends with God.

When Peter told the Jews that they had crucified God's only Son Jesus, they felt awful! They asked Peter what they could do about that to make things better. Listen to what he said, "Change your hearts and lives and be baptized, each one of you, in the name of Jesus Christ for the forgiveness of your sins. And you will receive the gift of the Holy Spirit" (Acts 2:38, ICB).

Did you notice that Saul did that? He changed his heart and life and was baptized. After that he was forgiven. He was now one of God's friends. He was so happy that he told everyone he knew about Jesus. He tried to please and obey God the rest of his life.

We can please and obey God, too, and be His friends.

Prayer (Group 6): **Group 6 has prepared a montage showing how God changes enemies into friends.** Group 6 will show and explain the prayer montage at this time. Then a leader will close with prayer.

Closing Moments

(10-15 minutes)

Enemy-to-friend Puppet. Help the children make enemy-to-friend puppets to tell the story of Saul. Before the session prepare a few more construction paper circles (approximately four inches in diameter) than you expect children. Also provide large craft sticks or dowels at least eight inches long. You will need markers or crayons, glue, yarn for hair, and felt for clothing.

Allow the children to draw a happy Saul face on one side of the circle and a sad Saul face on the other side. Have them glue a craft stick or dowel to the bottom of the circle. Allow the children to add hair and clothing. Be sure they decorate both sides of the puppet.

When the children have completed their puppets, have them tell the story of how Saul changed from an enemy to a friend. Use the sad face for the enemy Saul and the happy face for the friend Saul.

Send the puppets home with the children as they leave.

things	old
everything	then
new.	made
Christ,	gone;
is	2 Corinthians 5:17 *(ICB)*
anyone	The
belongs	have
to	new!
he	If
is	made

Saul Becomes a Friend

Cast: Narrator, voice of the Lord, Saul, man traveling with him, Ananias, Christian in Damascus, Barnabas, Christian in Jerusalem

Scene 1: The road from Jerusalem to Damascus

Narrator: Saul was traveling from Jerusalem to Damascus one day, planning to cause trouble for the Christians in Damascus. Suddenly there was a light from Heaven. As Saul fell to his knees, he heard a voice.

Voice of the Lord: Saul! I am Jesus. Why are you persecuting me? Go to Damascus. You will be told what to do.

Saul: I can't see! Please help me. Lead me to Damascus.

Man: I don't know what happened, but I'll help you. (Leads Saul to Damascus.)

Scene 2: Damascus

Narrator: Saul was blind for three days. During that time he did not eat or drink. The Lord sent Ananias to see Saul.

Ananias (putting hands on Saul's shoulders): Saul, Jesus sent me to you so that you may see again and receive the Holy Spirit.

Saul: I can see! Thank you, Lord.

Narrator: Then Ananias baptized Saul. Immediately Saul began telling about Jesus. But then the enemies of God's people learned about Saul's change.

Christian in Damascus: Saul, you must leave! Those people will kill you if you don't. I have a plan, we'll let you over the city walls tonight in a basket. Then you can escape.

Scene 3: Jerusalem

Narrator: Saul went back to Jerusalem and tried to be with other Christians. But the Christians were afraid Saul was still their enemy and was trying to trick them. Barnabas believed Saul and took him to the other Christians.

Barnabas: The Lord himself talked to Saul when Saul was on the way to Damascus. Now Saul is a Christian too. In fact, he was talking about Jesus so much that he had to leave Damascus at night by being lowered over the wall in a basket.

Christian in Jerusalem: Saul, I'm glad you are one of us! I'm sure you will tell many people about Jesus.

Saul: I will tell everyone I can the good news about Jesus. I'm glad God made us friends.

Paul Tells About Jesus in Lystra

Worship Focus

Worship Jesus when you tell others about Him.

Transition Time

(10-15 minutes)

Encourage the children to use the rest room and get drinks as they come to the room. Choose two student helpers and give each of them a badge.

(Prior to class, make badges for your helpers. Make two photocopies of the badge on page 26. Color, if desired, glue to poster board, cut out, and glue a safety pin on back. Cover with clear, adhesive-backed paper if desired.) Use these badges each week or make new ones to allow children to take them home. Alternate student helpers so every child takes a turn.

Jesus Chant. Help the children learn a chant about the previous sessions in units one and two. Make a poster of the sentences about Jesus that follow. Read the sentences with the children. To make this more challenging, have the children pair off to add patting and clapping to the chant. Each child will do the same motion as his partner. The partners should sit facing each other, with knees almost touching.

Use this pattern of pats and claps—one pat or clap for each syllable. Pat your knees. Clap your hands. Use your right hand to pat your partner's right hand. Clap your hands. Use your left hand to pat your partner's left hand. Clap your hands. Pat both hands of your partner. Clap your hands. Repeat the sequence for each sentence below. Practice slowly at first and then speed up as you are able.

Jesus can do wonderful things.
Jesus can calm the wind and sea.
Jesus can make a deaf man hear.
Jesus can make a blind man see.
Jesus can make a man's hand well.
Jesus can make a dead girl live.
Jesus wants to be remembered.
Jesus died but He lives again.
Jesus can make enemies friends!

Launching the Theme

(10 minutes)

Before the session, prepare small slips of paper on which you have written the names of the characters in today's Scripture. Include Paul, Barnabas, man who couldn't walk, and at least three members of the crowd. Distribute the slips of paper to volunteers who will act out the Scripture while you are reading it. Briefly give these volunteers an overview of the story, so they will be prepared to act in appropriate ways during the Scripture reading.

Read Acts 14:8-18 directly from the Bible with the children following the story action in their movements.

After the pantomime is finished, be sure to thank each participant for his help.

Paul and Barnabas told about Jesus. Everyone who heard them did a different thing. When the man who couldn't walk heard Paul speak about Jesus, he believed what Paul was saying. And because he believed what Paul was saying, he was healed. When the people of Lystra heard Paul speak and saw what he did for the man who couldn't walk, they thought that Paul and Barnabas were gods. Paul and Barnabas had to teach the people that they were messengers from the only God, not gods.

It is important that we tell everyone about Jesus, and that we keep telling them until they understand that Jesus is God's Son, that He loves us, and that He died for each of us.

Building the Theme

(30 minutes)

1. Call to Worship. This group will make posters to help the large group learn Matthew 28:19, 20 during the call to worship portion of *Sharing in Worship.* You will need Bibles (the same version, preferably NIV or ICB), poster board or drawing paper, and markers.

Find Matthew 28:16-20 in your Bibles. One of the things Jesus told His disciples was to teach everyone. Listen to what Jesus told them. Read it aloud. **We will make posters of the last two verses to help us learn the verses and also to help us teach the verses to the other children.**

Divide Matthew 28:19, 20 into phrases. Let the children illustrate each phrase. During *Sharing in Worship* one child will explain the background from verses 16-18. Then the children will recite verses 19, 20 while displaying the posters. Practice this with the children after they have finished drawing the posters.

2. Song. This group will sing "If You Got Good News, Tell It Brother" during *Sharing in Worship.* Provide poster board and markers. The children will make and decorate a song chart with the words to the song on it. They will learn the song well enough to teach it to the other children.

One way we can worship Jesus is to tell other people the good news about Him. That can mean we sing about Him in a group as we are doing today. That can mean we tell our best friends about Him. That can mean we write a letter to someone to tell about Jesus. Maybe it means that our family will go to another country to teach other people about Jesus. Let's draw some of these ways to tell about Jesus in the borders around the words of the song.

Practice the song until the children are comfortable with it.

3. Scripture Search. This activity would be good for older or gifted students. Provide copies of activity page 9A, pencils, and Bibles for these children. The children will study Scriptures to find the answer to missionary-related questions.

Paul and Barnabas told people about Jesus every chance they got. We call people who tell others about Jesus missionaries. Today we will look at some questions about being a missionary. Then we will look up Scriptures to answer these questions. Later we will tell the other children what we found out about missionaries.

Depending on the ability and initiative of the children in this group, you may work together on all the Scriptures or you may assign individual questions and Scriptures to particular children. If you choose the second option, let the children report their findings after all have completed their research. Let each child read one Scripture aloud and answer the corresponding question during the Scripture portion of *Sharing in Worship.*

Here are the questions and Scriptures that are on activity page 9A.

Who should be a missionary? Isaiah 6:8

Whom should the missionaries tell? 1 Chronicles 16:23, 24

Why should missionaries tell everybody about Jesus? Mark 16:15, 16

Should we stop telling about Jesus if someone makes fun of us? 2 Timothy 1:8

Why is it important to send many missionaries? Romans 10:14, 15

Can you be a missionary? James 5:20

4. Bible Story Review. This group will review Acts 14:8-18 as a part of the devotional during *Sharing in Worship.* Provide Bibles, pencils, and paper.

It must have been very exciting to have lived in Bible days. Let's read about what happened in Acts 14:8-18. Read the account from the Bible or have several volunteers read it. **I wonder what Paul or Barnabas might have written in a letter to a friend about that day. Wouldn't you like to read what the lame man wrote to his parents about what happened? I imagine it was very exciting to have seen all of this happening.**

Today we will write letters to someone telling about this event. Think about what it would be like to have been Paul, Barnabas, the man who couldn't walk but was healed, or someone in the crowd. Choose one person and write a letter to your parents or a friend telling about what happened on that special day in Lystra.

Allow time for the children to write their letters. Provide help and encouragement as needed, but make sure the letters really are from the children. When the children are done writing their letters, let them practice reading them to one another. They will read their letters as part of the devotional during *Sharing in Worship.*

5. Cartoon Story. This group will write and draw a cartoon application story showing children telling others about Jesus. Provide copies of activity page 9B, pencils, and markers or crayons. Encourage the children to brainstorm ideas before you distribute the supplies.

Throughout the New Testament, we find that many people told other people the good news about Jesus. They told as many people as they could. It is just as important today to tell about Jesus, but sometimes it's hard to know when or how to do it. Today we will write and draw a cartoon story showing children telling others about Jesus. Let's talk about some places we might tell others about Jesus. Discuss, including school, in the neighborhood, and on the playground. **What things might you tell someone else about Jesus?** Discuss, including that He is God's Son, that He does wonderful things, and that He died and rose again so that we might go to Heaven. **Now choose an idea of where and what you want to tell about Jesus. You may be one of your cartoon characters telling a real friend or you might have two real or imaginary people talking.**

Encourage the children to draw two simple scenes (part of one story or two separate incidents) and include simple dialog. The dialogue could be written in "balloons" in the scene or written on the lines below each scene.

The children will show and read their cartoons as part of the devotional during *Sharing in Worship.* Allow the children time to practice their reading cartoons aloud.

6. Prayer. This group will lead the large group in a time of prayer for people who tell about Jesus and also for asking the Lord to help them tell other people about Jesus. You will need markers and poster board to make the prayer list. You may wish to divide the list into categories, such as "In our neighborhood," "In our city (town)," "In our country," "In the whole world."

Paul told other people about Jesus whenever he could. We need to tell others about Jesus too. Today we will make a prayer list so that we can ask God to help people who tell others about Jesus. Let's name some people or groups of people who need to tell about Jesus.

Guide the children in their listing. Point out specific ways in which the people on the list might need prayers, such as through whatever difficulties might fit the specific situations. Help the children learn how they can pray for individuals or groups in a particular way. This will make their prayer time more meaningful. They will also begin to see missionaries, preachers, and teachers in a more personal way. Be sure the children include themselves on the list as people who tell about Jesus.

During *Sharing in Worship,* the children will present their prayer list. The prayer time can be led by an adult or the children can present individual prayers for the people on the list.

Sharing in Worship

(20-25 minutes)

Omit any of the following sections if you did not offer the corresponding activity.

Use soft music to call the groups together for the worship time.

Call to Worship (Group 1): **Group 1 will lead us in a Scripture as we worship together.** Allow Group 1 to show their pictures and recite the Scripture, Matthew 28:19, 20, and explain the background. **What do these verses tell us to do?** Go everywhere and make disciples. **Whom should we tell?** Everybody. **What should we do next?** Baptize them. **Then after that what should we teach them?** To obey everything Jesus commanded.

Song (Group 2): **Group 2 is going to sing a song that tells us about the things a missionary should do. What is a missionary? That's right. Anyone who tells about Jesus—including us! Listen to the song to learn what we should do.**

Let Group 2 sing the song and then teach it to the large group. Discuss the message of the song.

Lord's Supper: Jesus has told us to remember Him. One special way we remember Him is with the Lord's Supper. This special time of our worship reminds us that Jesus died on the cross so that our sins could be forgiven. In fact, not only is this time a reminder for us, Paul says it tells about Jesus' death. Listen while I read 1 Corinthians 11:26. Do so, preferably from the ICB.

Offering: When we worship God by giving Him our offerings, we are also helping to tell others about Jesus. Our offerings can be used in many ways: to provide Bible-school materials that tell about Jesus, to help pay our minister to talk about Jesus, to help missionaries be able to tell about Jesus. In addition, giving our offering tells the people around us that we love Jesus.

Scripture (Group 3): **Group 3 did some research on missionaries and telling about Jesus. They will share that with us now.** Allow time for the children to read their Scriptures and answer the questions they have.

Devotional (Groups 4 and 5): **Group 4 reviewed our Bible story from Acts 14:8-18. The children have some interesting letters to share with us now.** Allow the children to read their letters.

Although these letters the children have written were imaginary, they have an important message for us. It is important for us to tell people about Jesus—in any way that we can. We can write letters, sing songs, tell stories, read the Bible, learn another language to tell in, use sign language. The important thing is that we do tell.

The children from Group 5 will share with us their ideas of some places and ways to tell about Jesus. Let the children show and read their cartoons of children telling about Jesus.

What are some other times, places, and ways to tell about Jesus? Who should tell about Jesus? Whom should we tell?

Why is it so important? Listen again to Matthew 28:19, 20. Read the verses yourself or allow Group 1 to recite it again. **Who spoke these words? That's right. Jesus told us to teach others about Him. We must obey Him and tell the good news about Him to everyone we can.**

Prayer (Group 6): **The members of Group 6 have prepared a prayer list to help us remember some people and things for which to pray.** Allow the group to show the prayer list. Have a time of silent prayer encouraging the children to pray for people on the list in a specific way. Then have a leader close, being as specific about the requests on the list as possible. This is an important aspect of prayer which the children should learn early.

Closing Moments

(10-15 minutes)

Missionary Billboard. Use this time to develop a slogan and design a billboard that a missionary could use to advertise Jesus. You could have the children work together using a bulletin board for the billboard or you could provide poster board or drawing paper for the children to make individual billboards. Provide materials needed for whichever method you use. These supplies might include: poster board, construction paper, markers, thumb tacks, letter stencils, and paints.

Who should be a missionary?
Isaiah 6:8

Whom should the missionaries tell?
1 Chronicles 16:23, 24

Why should missionaries tell everybody about Jesus?
Mark 16:15, 16

Should we stop telling about Jesus if someone makes fun of us?
2 Timothy 1:8

Why is it important to send many missionaries?
Romans 10:14, 15

Can you be a missionary?
James 5:20

Paul Tells a Jailer About Jesus

Worship Focus

Worship God because He sets us free from problems.

Transition Time

(10-15 minutes)

Allow time for the pupils to use the rest room and get drinks of water.

Pupils may help arrange the chairs around tables supplied with magazines, scissors, and tacks, Plasti-tak, glue, or tape.

Problems pictures. Before class prepare an empty bulletin board or a large sheet of paper mounted on the wall. **Children, people have many kinds of problems: sickness, injuries, accidents, not enough money, no home, being lonely or angry. Please see how many pictures you can find of people with problems. Cut them out and put them on this background. We are going to talk about what Jesus will do about these problems.**

Commend each child who finds a picture or who helps another child find a picture. Talk with the children about the problems represented and others not pictured and how Jesus can solve them. Stress that all people need to be told about God's love and power so that they can call on Him for help. **No problem is too difficult for God. Just as God made an evil spirit leave a servant girl and freed Paul and Silas from prison, and just as He kept the jailer from killing himself and then saved the jailer and his family, God can help with all the problems people have today.** Encourage the children to share that good news with everyone they know.

Have the children set up the chairs facing a puppet stage. (Use a short screen or a table with a cloth or paper over it if no puppet stage is available.)

Launching the Theme

(10 minutes)

Puppet show. Use six or more puppets, preferably hand puppets. (These could be socks with features drawn on them with markers.) You will need these puppets:
Servant girl—with yarn hair;
Paul and Silas—cloth robes draped over them;
Jailer—needs a block of wood;
Men—two or more, with a craft stick for each.

Teachers may want to be Paul and Jailer and let children be the other characters. A teacher (or two) should read the speaking parts, using a different tone of voice for each different person. Prompt the children on what the puppets should do as you go along.

Scene 1

Paul and Silas are walking along. Servant girl is following, hollering repeatedly: "These men are servants of the Most High God! They are telling you how you can be saved!"

Paul turns and says to girl, "By the power of Jesus Christ, I command you to come out of her!" Servant girl is quiet.

The men grab Paul and Silas and shout, "These men are making trouble!" The men tear the robes of Paul and Silas and beat them with sticks (craft sticks).

Scene 2

Jailer says, "We know how to take care of troublemakers. You won't get out of my jail!" as he puts a block of wood in front of Paul and Silas (to represent stocks).

Jailer and men are listening while Paul and Silas sing:

God is so good.
God is so good.
God is so good.
He's so good to me.

He sets me free.
He sets me free.
He sets me free.
He's so good to me.

Then Paul and Silas pray: "Thank You, Lord Jesus, for setting us free from the bondage of sin."

There is an earthquake—puppets shake, block of wood falls to the floor, puppets jump up.

Jailer yells, "Oh, no! The prisoners are loose! They'll get

away! I'm in *bad* trouble! I'm going to kill myself!"

Paul calls out: "Don't hurt yourself! We are all here!"

Jailer ask, "What must I do to be saved?"

Paul and Silas tell him, "Believe in the Lord Jesus, and you will be saved, you and all the people in your house."

Scene 3

Jailer, girl, and men (family) say, "Thank you for telling us about Jesus who came to save us!"

Jailer washes the backs of Paul and Silas. Paul and Silas tell him, "Thank you for washing our sore backs. We feel much better now."

Jailer asks, "Will you baptize us now?"

Paul and Silas baptize Jailer and family. Paul says, "Since you have accepted Jesus as God's sacrifice for your sins, I baptize you into His death and resurrection. Rise to walk in a new life in Christ!"

Jailer gives Paul and Silas food. Paul and Silas tell him, "Thank you for feeding us. We hadn't eaten in a long time, and we were very hungry."

Jailer and family exclaim, "We are so happy now that we know God loves us and Jesus saves us!"

Paul tells them, "Yes, and He will always be with you and help you whenever you need Him! Let's worship Him together."

All sing:

God is so good.
God is so good.
God is so good.
He's so good to me.

Jesus, our Savior,
Jesus, our Savior,
Jesus, our Savior,
We worship You.

Collect puppets. Thank children for participating in and attending the play. Clap. Pray: **Thank you, God for helping with all our problems—setting people free from evil, fear, death; for healing and feeding us; for saving us and being with us always. In Jesus' name we pray, amen.**

Explain the next activities and divide the children by letting those who did not get to be puppeteers but were most attentive choose an activity and go to it one at a time as they are called on, then those children who were less attentive, then the puppeteers may choose activities that are not filled.

Building the Theme

(30 minutes)

1. Chains. Before class prepare strips of paper about 1 1/2 inches by 8 inches, markers or crayons and glue or tape. **Children, we are going to print words of problems on these strips and make chains out of them. Tell me some words you want to use, and I will print them up here** (on chalkboard or chart tablet) **for you to copy.** (Some examples are sick, poor, mad, lonely.) **Each of you make a chain for yourself by linking at least six of these strips together like this.** Demonstrate how to put one strip through a finished loop before fastening the second loop. **Later we will show the rest of the class how Jesus sets us free from problems. We will break our chains when Group 2 sings about an earthquake's loosing Paul and Silas's bands.**

2. Song. Use the song "Paul and Silas" to review the Bible story. Have chart paper or poster board and markers. Allow the children to make a song chart of the words to the song. **After we have written the words to "Paul and Silas" on the chart, let's decorate the margins with scenes from the Bible story** (Refer to Acts 16:16-34 as needed.)

Sing the song several times with the pupils until they have learned it. This group will lead and teach the song to the rest of the class later in *Sharing in Worship.*

3. Newscast interview. (Be sure to have an adult or older teen assistant at this center. Also try to guide your better readers to this center.) The pupils in this group will present interviews with people who were involved in today's Bible story. The script is found on activity page 10A.

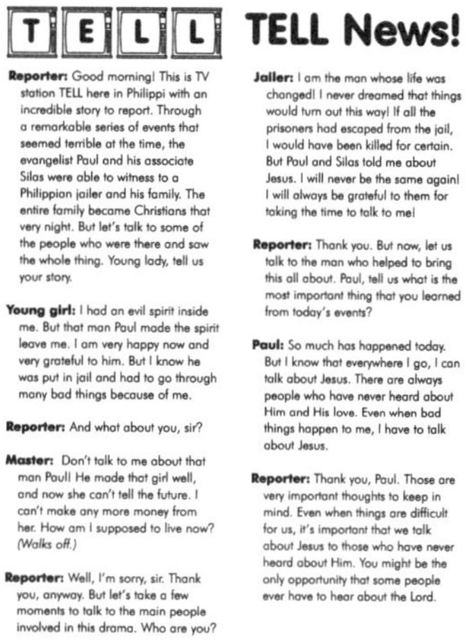
T E L L TELL News!

Reporter: Good morning! This is TV station TELL here in Philippi with an incredible story to report. Through a remarkable series of events that seemed terrible at the time, the evangelist Paul and his associate Silas were able to witness to a Philippian jailer and his family. The entire family became Christians that very night. But let's talk to some of the people who were there and saw the whole thing. Young lady, tell us your story.

Young girl: I had an evil spirit inside me. But that man Paul made the spirit leave me. I am very happy now and very grateful to him. But I know he was put in jail and had to go through many bad things because of me.

Reporter: And what about you, sir?

Master: Don't talk to me about that man Paul! He made that girl well, and now she can't tell the future. I can't make any more money from her. How am I supposed to live now? *(Walks off.)*

Reporter: Well, I'm sorry, sir. Thank you, anyway. But let's take a few moments to talk to the main people involved in this drama. Who are you?

Jailer: I am the man whose life was changed! I never dreamed that things would turn out this way! If all the prisoners had escaped from the jail, I would have been killed for certain. But Paul and Silas told me about Jesus. I will never be the same again! I will always be grateful to them for taking the time to talk to me!

Reporter: Thank you. But now, let us talk to the man who helped to bring this all about. Paul, tell us what is the most important thing that you learned from today's events?

Paul: So much has happened today. But I know that everywhere I go, I can talk about Jesus. There are always people who have never heard about Him and His love. Even when bad things happen to me, I have to talk about Jesus.

Reporter: Thank you, Paul. Those are very important thoughts to keep in mind. Even when things are difficult for us, it's important that we talk about Jesus to those who have never heard about Him. You might be the only opportunity that some people ever have to hear about the Lord.

For more emphasis use costumes and make-believe microphones. Allow pupils to add as much to the dialogue as possible. (The teacher should take the part of the reporter.) **We will present our interview during the devotional time of *Sharing in worship.***

4. Discussion group. The pupils in this group will discuss difficult situations that Primaries might have to deal with. (These ideas are presented not to be depressing but to make the pupils think about opportunities to talk about Jesus to family members, teachers, friends, and others.) How could a child witness for Jesus in these situations?

- being sick or in the hospital

- living with parents who are fighting or divorced
- dealing with unemployed parents who can't afford needs/wants
- working through trouble with school or day care or sitters
- coping with disagreements with siblings or playmates
- feeling alone or feeling like no one cares
- not being able to do things other kids can do (like tie shoes)

Tell the children the problems they suggest/discuss will be prayed for later in *Sharing in Worship*.

5. Congratulations/Thank-you cards. Provide construction paper for cards, scraps of colored paper and markers for decorating them, and glue. **Children, sometimes we celebrate happy times, such as birthdays, Christmas, and Mother's and Father's Days, by giving greeting cards. Let's celebrate the love and help we receive from Jesus with greeting cards.**

We can make thank-you cards to let Him know we appreciate His help, and we can make congratulations cards because He always does a good job—He always wins! When we're finished, we'll bring them as part of our offering and put them on our "Celebrate the Lord" bulletin board wall.

6. Memory verse. 1 Thessalonians 2:2 (ICB). Before class prepare a chart with the verse in lines as follows:

(1) We suffered in Philippi.
(2) People there insulted us.
(3) You know about that.
(4) And when we came to you,
(5) many people were against us.
(6) But our God helped us to be brave
(All) and to tell you his Good News.

We will present this verse as a chant.

Assign each line to a child and the last line for all of them to say together. (If you have fewer than six children at this center, assign more than one line to each child; if you have more, assign more than one child for each line and have these children recite their line in unison.) Line them up and point to them when it is time for them to say their line. Practice for the presentation. Encourage the children to memorize the whole verse as they recite and hear the others recite parts of the verse.

Sharing in Worship

(20-25 minutes)

Use soft music (recorded or live) to signal the pupils that the worship time is beginning.

Call to Worship (Groups 1 and 2): Ask the students from Groups 1 and 2 to come forward. Have those in Group 1 slip the end loops of their chains over their wrists. **We worship God because He sets us free from problems. The children in Group 1 made chains with words that name some of the problems we have.** (Allow Group 1 to name some of the problems they listed.) **We sometimes feel all wrapped up in, or tied down by, our problems, and we want to be free of them. While Paul and Silas were in prison they had some real problems, but what were they doing? Singing! The children in Group 2 learned a song they are going to sing for us now.** When they get to the part in the song that says "then an earthquake loosed their bands," the children in Group 1 should break their "chains"! After the children do so, invite the class to join Group 2 in singing the song, making actions with their arms as though they are breaking off chains at the appropriate time.

Devotional (Group 3): Ask the students from Group 3 to come forward. Ask these questions of the servant girl, Paul and Silas, and the jailer: **What problems did you have? Did you give your cares to Jesus? Did God solve your problem for you?** Have these students sit down, then read from the Bible, preferably the International Children's Bible, Psalm 34:19 and 1 Peter 5:7.

Prayer (Group 4): Have Group 4 come forward. Ask the children, **What problems do children have that they need Jesus to help them solve?** After they name some problems, say, **Let's pray now, giving these cares and worries to Jesus, expecting Him to help us with them.**

Offering (Group 5): **Now let's offer praise to the Lord for His help! Children who made celebration cards please bring them up.** Allow the children to share, one at a time, about their cards of thanks or congratulations to the Lord for His help. After each child shares, he can attach it to a prepared bulletin board or wall. Give the first one or two whose hands are empty the offering baskets to pass. You may want to sing "It's Time to Praise the Lord" or "Give the Lord Some Praise" as the cards are being put up and the other offerings received.

Lord, thank You that we can show our gratitude and trust to You as we bring offerings to You. May the money we bring be used to help others to know Jesus our Savior, our problem solver. In Jesus' name, amen.

Lord's Supper: When Jesus went to the cross, He wore a crown of thorns, showing that He took our troubles on himself. He was beaten and the Scriptures say that we are healed because of His wounds. Listen while I read Isaiah 53:4-6 (ICB). As we worship through the Lord's Supper, let's remember that Jesus

has already done what He needed to do to take care of all our problems. And when He rose from the dead, He proved His power to overcome even death. And now He is with the Father, and He is praying for us because He understands our problems.

Scripture (Group 6): After the Lord's Supper, have the students who learned the memory verse chant come and share it. If there is time, let members of Group 6 lead the class in saying the chant.

After the class chants the verse once or twice, close with a prayer circle. Allow any child who wishes to thank God for His help with problems. A leader should pray after all who wish to have prayed.

Closing Moments

(10-15 minutes)

Give the children activity page 10B to work on. As they work, talk with them about how Jesus helps us solve our problems (as the letters J-E-S-U-S help find the way on the maze puzzle).

You may want to give happy face stickers to the children as they successfully complete the puzzle and send stickers with those who leave before completing it. As they leave, remind them to share the good news that God sets us free from problems!

Suggested Resources

Critter County cassettes and books

deGraaf, Anne, *Family Time Bible Stories*

Miller, Marjorie, *God Is on Your Side*

TELL News!

Reporter: Good morning! This is TV station TELL here in Philippi with an incredible story to report. Through a remarkable series of events that seemed terrible at the time, the evangelist Paul and his associate Silas were able to witness to a Philippian jailer and his family. The entire family became Christians that very night. But let's talk to some of the people who were there and saw the whole thing. Young lady, tell us your story.

Young girl: I had an evil spirit inside me. But that man Paul made the spirit leave me. I am very happy now and very grateful to him. But I know he was put in jail and had to go through many bad things because of me.

Reporter: And what about you, sir?

Master: Don't talk to me about that man Paul! He made that girl well, and now she can't tell the future. I can't make any more money from her. How am I supposed to live now? *(Walks off.)*

Reporter: Well, I'm sorry, sir. Thank you, anyway. But let's take a few moments to talk to the main people involved in this drama. Who are you?

Jailer: I am the man whose life was changed! I never dreamed that things would turn out this way! If all the prisoners had escaped from the jail, I would have been killed for certain. But Paul and Silas told me about Jesus. I will never be the same again! I will always be grateful to them for taking the time to talk to me!

Reporter: Thank you. But now, let us talk to the man who helped to bring this all about. Paul, tell us what is the most important thing that you learned from today's events?

Paul: So much has happened today. But I know that everywhere I go, I can talk about Jesus. There are always people who have never heard about Him and His love. Even when bad things happen to me, I have to talk about Jesus.

Reporter: Thank you, Paul. Those are very important thoughts to keep in mind. Even when things are difficult for us, it's important that we talk about Jesus to those who have never heard about Him. You might be the only opportunity that some people ever have to hear about the Lord.

S
I
U
G
O
R
D
S
T
E
L
A
J
Y

Paul Tells a Crowd About Jesus

Worship Focus

Worship God by telling about Him, even when it is difficult.

Transition Time

(10-15 minutes)

Allow time for the pupils to use the rest room and get drinks of water.

Ask the children to help you arrange the chairs in a circle.

Telephone. Have the children sit in the circle. Explain that you are going to play "Telephone" with them, where they will try to pass a message around the circle. Put some music on a player, a little too loud for "background music." Begin the game by whispering to the first student **Today our story is about Jews from Asia, a Greek, and a Roman commander who thought Paul was an Egyptian.**

While the children are trying to pass the message, the teachers talk over them to one another: **Are all of our class members here today?**

No __________ is missing. Do you have the supplies for the craft ready?

I hope everything is ready.

Is the music too loud?

Maybe we should turn it down.

Continue in this way until the message has gotten around the circle. Ask the last child to say aloud what the message was. (It will most likely be very different from the original message.)

Turn off the music and ask everyone, especially the teachers, to be very quiet as the message is passed again. One teacher should start the message and follow it around, listening in as each child whispers it to the next, giving a nod if it was given correctly. If it was not correct, have that child ask the person who gave him the message to repeat it before trying to pass it on.

When the message gets to the last child, have him give it aloud. The message should be much more accurate this time. **If we want to get a message to someone without misunderstandings, we must try to remove distractions, use the correct words, and keep trying if someone doesn't get the message the first time.**

Launching the Theme

(10 minutes)

Stand in the middle of the circle of chairs. **I need a strong, brave volunteer to be Paul and another volunteer to be a man named Trophimus.** Choose two to join you in the middle of the circle. **I also need three Jews from Asia.** Choose three to join you. **And a Roman commander.** Choose one and tell him to stand outside of the circle until his part comes. **Now the rest of you are going to be people from Jerusalem** (indicate children on one side of the circle) **and Roman soldiers** (indicate those on the side near the commander).

I'm going to read a story to you, and I want you to act it out, but without being rough when you grab Paul and drag him outside the temple—which will be outside the circle. Remove a chair for a passageway if necessary. Other teachers, or helpers, prompt the children in actions to accompany the narration.

Read Acts 21:27b-22:2, ICB. Read the shouts of the Jews with lots of expression. At verse 34 ask the three "Jews" all to yell things at the same time. At verse 40, "Paul" stands on a chair and waves his hands (teacher nearby to steady him if needed) and everyone else gets quiet.

After the people were quiet, what did Paul talk to them about? He told them about Jesus, the Son of God, who had been crucified and arose from the dead! Do you think you would feel like sharing the good news about Jesus with people who were treating you as these people were treating Paul? Paul really had the love of God in him. And that's what we want to have too: the love of God in us, so we'll tell people about Jesus, even if they don't like us and aren't nice to us.

Explain the activity choices for today and divide the children into groups according to their ability and interest. Six activity ideas are provided.

Building the Theme

(30 minutes)

1. Song. Help the children make a song chart for "Go Everywhere." Teach the children the song. Have them practice the song until they are comfortable with it.

Discuss with the children how there are many times and places that it is difficult to tell other people about children. Talk with them about going to other countries, learning other languages, talking to other children at school who make fun of them, talking to a large group of people, and other ideas they might have. Stress that **God's good news is so good and everyone needs to know it, so we must go everywhere and tell people about Jesus.**

2. Act out the Memory Verse. At this center, teach the pupils these motions to help them memorize I Thessalonians 2:2 (ICB).

We (arm around a friend's shoulder)
suffered in Philippi (back of hand on forehead, looking sad).
People there (arms out at side)
insulted us (point and shake finger).
And when we came (fingers walking on other hand)
to you (point to someone),
many people (arms out at side)
were against us (hand pushing against imaginary object).
But our God (point up)
helped us to be brave (fists against chest)
and to tell you (hands cupped around mouth)
his Good News (hold hands like holding Bible).

Tell the children you will call on them to present this during the preparation for the Lord's Supper in *Sharing in worship*.

3. Television News Report. A big box with a hole large enough for the children's heads to show through can be used as a television. Group 4 will also show pictures through this hole. Provide copies of the script on activity page 11A. Divide the lines among the children at this center by cutting them apart or by marking them with different colors of highlight markers.

We will be presenting a television news report about the events in today's Bible lesson. Each of you is a reporter telling part of the news. Group 4 will show pictures of the actions you have described.

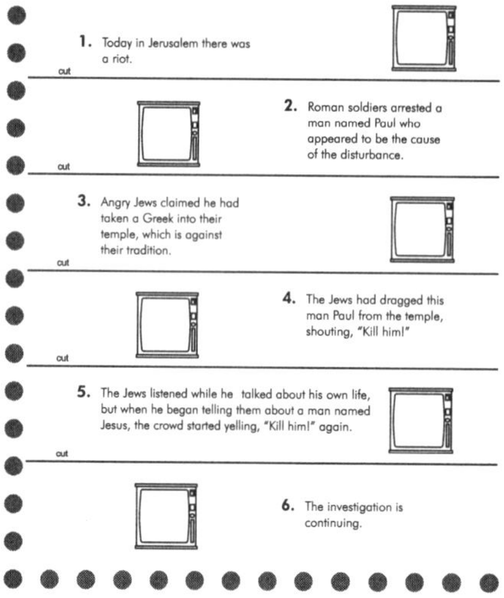
1. Today in Jerusalem there was a riot.
cut
2. Roman soldiers arrested a man named Paul who appeared to be the cause of the disturbance.
cut
3. Angry Jews claimed he had taken a Greek into their temple, which is against their tradition.
cut
4. The Jews had dragged this man Paul from the temple, shouting, "Kill him!"
cut
5. The Jews listened while he talked about his own life, but when he began telling them about a man named Jesus, the crowd started yelling, "Kill him!" again.
cut
6. The investigation is continuing.

Allow the children to practice their parts, looking out through the hole in the box so they appear "on television." After each reporter gives his report, he will move "off screen," and a child from Group 4 will display his picture on "the screen."

Five minutes before large group time, groups 3 and 4 will practice together.

4. Story Illustrations. Students will draw pictures and number them in correct order to show at the appropriate time to illustrate the television report to be presented in *Sharing in Worship*.

Have markers and drawing paper available.

Also provide each child with a copy of activity page 11A. Allow each child to choose a scene to illustrate on the drawing paper, making sure each scene in the news report is illustrated.

Group 3 is preparing a television news report based on this script. We will provide pictures to illustrate their report. After each scene is described by someone from Group 3, whoever has that scene will hold that picture so it will show through the hole in the box that is a pretend television. Then you will move so the next reporter can appear on "television."

Groups 3 and 4 will rehearse together five minutes before *Sharing in Worship* begins. This presentation will be part of the devotional.

5. Getting the Message activity. Provide each pupil with activity page 11B. Students in this center will share the message they decode during the devotional in *Sharing in Worship*.

Philippians 4:13, NIV

Cross out each symbol—everything that is not a letter, number, or punctuation mark. Then copy the message that is left onto the lines at the bottom of the page. Check your message

by looking up the verse in the Bible.

Help children find the verse in the Bible. If your children are not used to looking up Scriptures, use bookmarks to mark the page for them.

The children will tell their message during the devotional in *Sharing in Worship.*

6. **Trophies/plaques.** These will be added to the unit project "Celebrate the Lord" display. Have prepared sheets of aluminum foil about 4 x 6 inches, sheets of construction paper 5 1/2 x 8 1/2 inches, tape, permanent markers, scissors.

Isn't it wonderful how God delivered Paul from the angry mob and gave Paul the love and courage to tell the good news of Jesus to his enemies!

Wouldn't it be nice to present an award, a trophy or a plaque like you get when you win a contest or perform in a recital, to the Lord to let Him know we think He is the greatest? Let's make some trophies and plaques and present them to Him during the offering today.

Help the children cut the shapes they want for trophies and plaques and write the words they want.

Sharing in Worship

(20-25 minutes)

Use soft music (recorded or live) to signal the pupils that the worship time is beginning.

Call to Worship (Group 1): **The students from Group 1 will sing "Go Everywhere." They will sing it several times so that all of us can learn it also.**

Lord's Supper (Group 2): Ask the children who learned the memory verse with motions to come and present that. After they return to their seats, give this meditation: **As Jesus was willing to suffer for Paul's sake, Paul was willing to suffer for Jesus. And God helped Paul when he was in danger. Jesus died for us, so we live for Him and have the comfort of knowing He will help us in danger and confusion and give us peace. Let's remember the price Jesus paid for us so that we can enjoy a secure life with Him as we worship through the Lord's Supper.**

Offering (Group 6): Have the children from Group 6 bring their trophies and plaques and speak a few words of praise or thanksgiving to God as they attach them to a bulletin board or wall prepared as the "Celebrate the Lord" display. (Items from last week will also be on display.) Give offering baskets to the first to get their hands empty so that they may receive the money offerings. Dedicate the offering with prayer: **Lord, You are great—a mighty warrior and deliverer. You are stronger than the enemy. You help us tell about You, even when it is difficult. We thank You for saving us, and we gladly bring You the best offerings we can.**

Devotional (Groups 3, 4, 5): Ask the news reporters and the illustrators from Groups 3 and 4 to come forward. Let the reporters tell the news and the children show the pictures to illustrate the report. (Have a cassette tape and cassette recorder ready. Tape record the news report.)

Stand with your Bible (ICB preferably) and say, **This is Paul speaking** and read 1 Corinthians 9:16 and 17. Then say, **Paul was so excited by God's love that he couldn't keep from telling the good news about Jesus! He would tell it anywhere, any time, any way he could.**

Today we experienced many ways of sharing news: we whispered a message from one person to the next. And we learned that it is important to get rid of distractions, to use the right words, and to repeat the message if it wasn't understood the first time.

We read and acted out a story. We sang, using music to help tell our message. We put motions to a memory verse. We recorded a news report so that it can be played whenever someone wants to hear it. We used a series of pictures to tell a story. We used trophies and plaques to display messages.

One of our groups worked out a coded message. Ask those children who were in center 5 to bring up their decoded message and read it. **When these children got rid of the stuff that did not belong, they found some very important words. All people need to hear the message of God's power to save us. We can learn to talk to people about God using clear words and actions that will show His love.**

Song: Sing "Go Everywhere" again. You may also want to sing "Shout the Word" and "Who Can I Tell?"

Prayer: Dear Lord, we thank You and praise You for being a very present help in times of trouble. We thank You for hearing us when we call to you, any time, any place. Help us to tell others this good news about You. In Jesus' name, amen.

Closing Moments

(10-15 minutes)

Have the children tell you about incidents where people didn't seem to like them or were mean to them, and help them role play how they might share the love of God and the good news about Jesus with that person.

Provide copies of activity page 11B for the children to take home and decode. Those who were in Group 5 can share theirs with a friend.

Suggested Resources

deGraaf, Anne, *Family Time Bible Stories*

Miller, Marjorie, *God is on Your Side*

1. Today in Jerusalem there was a riot.

cut

2. Roman soldiers arrested a man named Paul who appeared to be the cause of the disturbance.

cut

3. Angry Jews claimed he had taken a Greek into their temple, which is against their tradition.

cut

4. The Jews had dragged this man Paul from the temple, shouting, "Kill him!"

cut

5. The Jews listened while he talked about his own life, but when he began telling them about a man named Jesus, the crowd started yelling, "Kill him!" again.

cut

6. The investigation is continuing.

■☆I❊❄❀c✎✸a❄❑n✢◆✬d✷☆o✐❍✽e◗✼❑v✄✾e❉❖r✶✯y✓✳t✼❒h▼

✻i❄❖n✶✥g✎☛❄t✺✢h✶▲r✰✼o✬✪u✎✭g❀✂h★▼✦h➔★i✉✿m✈☞

✏w✱➡h✃☞o➾❄✼g↕▼i❊✺v✥✷e✐✼s☆✔✳m✱➫e❉✳▼s✧✩t❒✱r✂⇨

e✱✺n➪✼g✰✎t➾➚h✠✐.

Philippians 4:13, *NIV*

Paul Tells Islanders About Jesus

Worship Focus

Worship God because He makes enemies to be friends.

Transition Time

(10-15 minutes)

Allow time for the pupils to use the rest room and get drinks of water. Direct them to the work tables for the following activity as they return.

Preparing Cargo. Have work tables set up so the children have easy access to them. Put empty containers (such as 48 oz. juice cans, oatmeal canisters, cereal boxes)—one for each pupil—on these tables. Also have sheets of plain newsprint or butcher paper or computer paper, glue, and markers or crayons.

As the children are seated at the tables, tell each one, **I will explain what to do with all the materials you see here when everyone is ready. Right now, why don't you use the paper to draw a picture of something you might want to take along if you were going on a long trip?** When everyone is seated, ask those who have already started to stop and listen. Ask all the children to fold their hands and put them in their laps while they listen to you.

Each of you has a container and some paper. I'd like for you to think of something you would want to take with you if you were going away from home for a long time. Draw a picture of it or print the word on your paper, and then use the paper to cover your container.

If you will suggest some things that you would need or want to have, I'll print the names up here (on marker board, chalkboard, or chart tablet) **for you to copy if you want to.** (Examples: clothes, food, bicycle, skates, books, TV, VCR, crayons, dolls, toys, pets, etc.) **We will use these containers as "cargo" later in our session.** (Help them with the project as needed.)

When time is up, ask the pupils to help you arrange chairs into two long rows to form the sides of a "boat," and have each pupil put his or her container under his/her chair.

Launching the Theme

(10 minutes)

Acting out the story. Two teachers need to take the parts of the Narrator and of Paul. They should be familiar with their parts and have in mind the actions they will prompt the children to do as they narrate. The children are seated in the chairs set up in the shape of a boat.

Narrator: **Children, we are going to act out an exciting story from the book of Acts. Listen carefully as "Paul" and I read and give you directions on what to do as shipmates.** Read Acts 27:1 and 2 as you and Paul board the ship. Continue reading verses 3 through 9, up to Paul's speech.

Paul: Speak the words from Acts 27:10.

Narrator: Read Acts 27:11-17. Guide the shipmates in pretending that they are in a storm. Turn the lights off and on, sway back and forth, duck water, etc. Continue reading verses 18 through 20, and prompt the shipmates to throw out their cargo. (A rope would make a nice prop for ship's equipment if you can provide one.)

Paul: Read Acts 27:21-26.

Narrator: Read Acts 27:27-30. Prompt the shipmates to "let down the lifeboat." A small floatation toy would be a good prop if you can provide one.

Paul: Read Acts 27:31-38. Guide the shipmates in pretending to break bread and eat it. Real bread would be fun!

Narrator: Read Acts 27:39-44. Guide the shipmates in the motions of a shipwreck and pretending to swim to shore. Read Acts 28:1 and 2. Lead the shipmates in pretending to gather firewood. Pencils and rulers might do as props. Then all gather around the pretend fire. Read Acts 28:7-10. Choose someone to be Publius and another to be his father and lead Paul to them.

Paul: Put hands on head of Publius' father and pray for his healing.

Narrator and Paul: Lead the children in a prayer of

thanksgiving to God for bringing them safely through the shipwreck and for healing Publius' father.

Clap for the children and thank them for their attention and participation. Explain the activity choices and assign pupils to groups according to their interests and abilities. Ask them to take their chairs with them back to the tables or activity areas.

Building the Theme

(30 minutes)

1. Audio Newscast. Have ready a tape recorder and tape, a marker board or chalkboard or chart tablet, and a marker or piece of chalk.

Children, you will play the part of radio announcers telling all about the shipwreck. To begin, let's think of all the important parts of the story that would need to go into a good news report.

As the children mention parts, make a list, using a few simple words and/or pictures. After they have mentioned everything they can think of, you fill in any necessary missing parts. Then ask the children to help you put them in order as to what happened first, next, and so on until you come to the last thing that happened. Number the items in order; then assign parts to each child.

Let the children practice telling their parts in order, then record. Remind them that their newscast will be "aired" for the class later in the session.

2. Crayon Resist Picture. Before class, obtain manila paper (old file folders work well), crayons, blue watercolor paint, brushes, cups of water, and paper towels. (You might also want to have colored construction paper on hand to use as frames.) You will want to put newspapers down to protect the table. It would also be a good idea to provide old shirts or large garbage bags for the children to wear as painting smocks.

Ask the pupils to draw and color a picture of Paul's ship out on the stormy sea. Tell them to bear down hard with the crayons. Then show them how to brush over their papers with the blue watercolor paint. The paint should be watery. The crayon on the paper will "resist" the paint, creating an interesting effect. For an added touch, you may want the pupils to frame their pictures with colored construction paper.

Inform the children that these pictures will be shown to the class later during *Sharing in Worship*.

3. Shipwreck Song. These words, to the tune of "Row, Row, Row Your Boat," should be written on a chalkboard or chart ahead of time so the children can see and learn them. They might also be recorded ahead of time to help pupils. This activity is one the students should be able to accomplish independently.

Paul said, "Don't sail your boat
Out into the storm.
If you do, I tell you true,
We will come to harm."

But the master of the boat
To Paul refused to listen.
They had to throw the cargo
 out
For the boat to lighten.

Then an angel came to Paul
To say no one would drown.
They grabbed ahold of planks
 and boards,
And floated to dry ground.

Then the people from the ship,
And those upon the land,
Decided they were glad that
 God
Sent Paul to be their friend.

Tell the pupils that they will share this song with the class later in *Sharing in Worship*.

4. "Let's Talk About It" Group. Tell the pupils in this group about a time someone didn't like you or didn't trust you or wouldn't listen to you, but later changed his mind about you. Share the Scripture, "A person should live so that he pleases the Lord. If he does, even his enemies will make peace with him" (Proverbs 16:7, ICB).

Remember, God expects us to love our enemies. (Ask a couple of good readers to read Matthew 5:44 and Luke 6:27, 35.) **Remember how Jesus treated His enemies? He was always good to them, wasn't He?**

Invite the children to share about times they've had trouble getting along with others and talk about how they can behave in a way that pleases the Lord in each situation and how they can trust God to work it out for them. Tell the pupils that the difficulties they share will be prayed for later in *Sharing in Worship*.

5. Activity pages. These pages will be most beneficial if an adult works with the children.

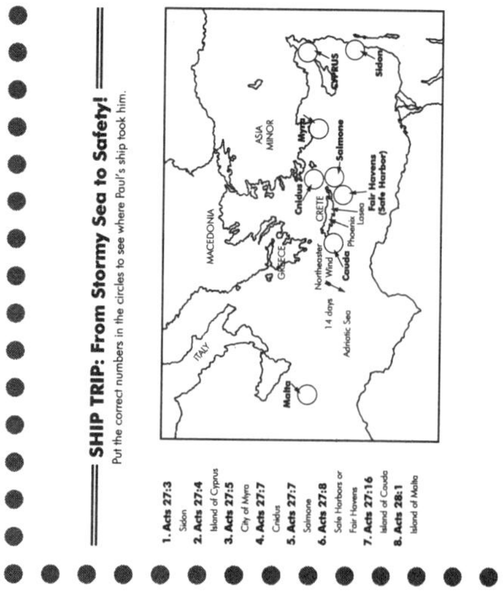

SHIP TRIP: From Stormy Sea to Safety! (Activity page 12A). **Have you ever gone on a long trip?** (Let the children who say yes tell about what it was like to be away from home, going to strange places and meeting strange people.) **Paul went on a long trip. He traveled with soldiers, sailors, and other passengers whom he had never met before. Some of them did not like Paul—they thought he was a bad man who had been arrested and was on his way to prison. Actually, he was arrested because some people told lies about him.**

Let's look at some of the places Paul traveled. Read the key verses (they are listed on the activity sheet) from the ICB or Living Bible while pointing out the places mentioned on a wall map. Talk about the fourteen days they were in a storm at sea. Relate fourteen days to how long it has been since the children did something two weeks ago, or how long it will take until they get to do something in two weeks. Ask them to think about what it would be like to be in a thunder and lightning storm that lasted two weeks!

This must have been a frightening trip. Think about traveling with all those strange people, going to strange places, and then a two-week storm! Remember how the storm got so bad that those on the ship threw their stuff overboard, and did not eat during this time? But Paul was not afraid. He trusted God, and finally God got all the passengers onto the island and to safety. Help the children trace the journey on their activity pages.

God Changes Enemies Into Friends (Activity page 12B). Distribute copies of this page. **The sentences on the right tell about enemies. See the word *enemy* down that side? But the sentences on the left are different. If you can match the correct sentences from the left to the ones on the right, you will see how God changes enemies to friends.**

Help the children cut the page in half vertically on the center cutting line. Leave the right side intact. Cut each puzzle shape apart on the left-hand side (including the jagged puzzle edges).

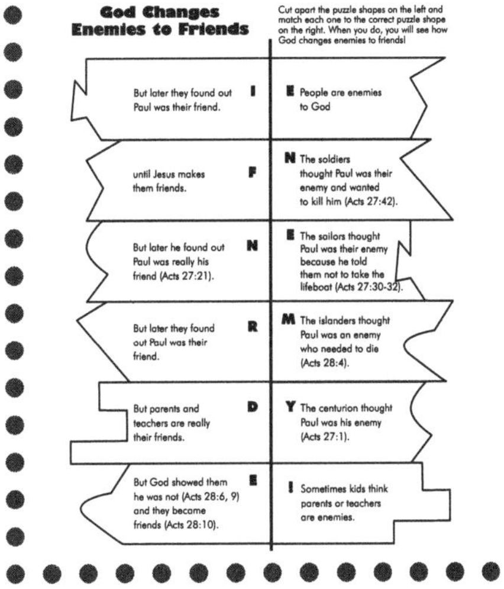

What new word is spelled on the right when the pictures are correctly matched? *(Friend)*

6. "Fireworks!" (for the unit project, "Celebrate the Lord" display). Have available black or dark blue construction paper, glue and glitter (or glitter glue), and sequins.

Do you like to celebrate with fireworks? When have you seen a fireworks display? (Allow some children to raise their hands and respond.) **What was being celebrated?** (Let children explain what they know.) **Yes, we celebrate our free country on Independence Day, the Fourth of July, with fireworks displays.**

Wouldn't it be good if we could have a fireworks display to celebrate God's love and Jesus our Savior? Wouldn't it be fun to see the sparkly word *Jesus* in the sky? (Write JESUS on the board).

Sometimes fireworks displays have music to go with them. Wouldn't it be great to have praises to God going up with the fireworks? Here is a good praise word: *Hallelujah*! (Write HALLELUJAH on the board.)

Let's make some fireworks display pictures to honor God and thank Jesus for setting us free from sin. We will offer these celebration pictures to the Lord at offering time during *Sharing in Worship* and add them to our "Celebrate the Lord" wall display.

Sharing in Worship

(20-25 minutes)

Have a musical signal (recorded or live) to lead the pupils into the worship time. (Omit any of the following sections if you did not offer the corresponding activity.)

Call to Worship: Read 1 Corinthians 2:1-5 and explain that this was written by Paul, and it tells how he felt when he told strangers about Jesus. Ask, **When Paul talked to the sailor and soldiers on the ship, did they listen to him at first? How do you think he felt?** Pause and let them consider. **Part of our class has prepared a song that tells about this. Let's all listen and see what happens.**

Song (Group 3): Introduce the group and have them sing their "Shipwreck Song." After they sing, say the words once to make sure the other children understand what is being sung; then invite the entire class to join in as Group 3 leads them in singing the song.

Lord's Supper: When Jesus came to earth, there were many people who did not want to listen to or believe Him. But He was their friend anyway. He died in *their* place. As we share the Lord's Supper, let's remember how He loves us, even though we don't listen to Him as we should. And let's ask Him to become so alive in us that we will listen and trust Him more and more.

Offering (Group 6): Ask Group

6 to bring their celebration pictures and put them on the wall display. As they do, explain to the class, **These children were thinking of praising God with fireworks displays! There are many ways to express our love and thanks to God. One way is by giving Him back part of the money He gives us. That shows Him that we trust Him to always give us what we need. Let's give our *money* offering now.**

Appoint two children to pass the basket(s) among the children.

Devotional (Groups 1, 2, and 5): **Children, we are going to hear a newscast of an exciting story! Will those who prepared this newscast please stand and take a bow.** Clap for them. **As we listen, we will see some pictures and maps that show what happened.** Invite Groups 2 and 5 to come to the front and hold up their pictures and maps.

After listening to the newscast, collect the pictures and maps and have the children sit down. Use one of the activity pages (12B) and read the words and show the pictures as you talk about how God changes enemies into friends. Lead into the following song.

Song: "Jesus, I Love You," from the song pages in the back of the book.

Prayer time (Group 4): Have the "Let's Talk About It" group share some times when it is hard to be friends and pray about those situations.

Closing Moments

(10-15 minutes)

Bookmarkers. Beforehand, cut one-inch by six-inch pieces of poster board. Write on them the words, "'A friend loves at all times' (Proverbs 17:17)," or, "'God is love' (I John 4:8)." Provide appropriate stickers and ask the pupils to decorate them as bookmarkers. (For more durability, you may want to cover them with clear adhesive-backed paper.)

As the pupils finish the bookmarkers, ask each one to give his or her bookmarker to someone and share something from the Bible story with that person. Children of this age may be timid about talking to others and may be afraid they won't be able to tell the story right. Encourage them to go ahead and do their best and trust God to bless their efforts.

Suggested Resources

Now You Can Read Bible Stories: The Journeys of St. Paul, retold by Leonard Matthews, Rourke Publications, 1984.

SHIP TRIP: From Stormy Sea to Safety!

Put the correct numbers in the circles to see where Paul's ship took him.

1. Acts 27:3
Sidon

2. Acts 27:4
Island of Cyprus

3. Acts 27:5
City of Myra

4. Acts 27:7
Cnidus

5. Acts 27:7
Salmone

6. Acts 27:8
Safe Harbors or
Fair Havens

7. Acts 27:16
Island of Cauda

8. Acts 28:1
Island of Malta

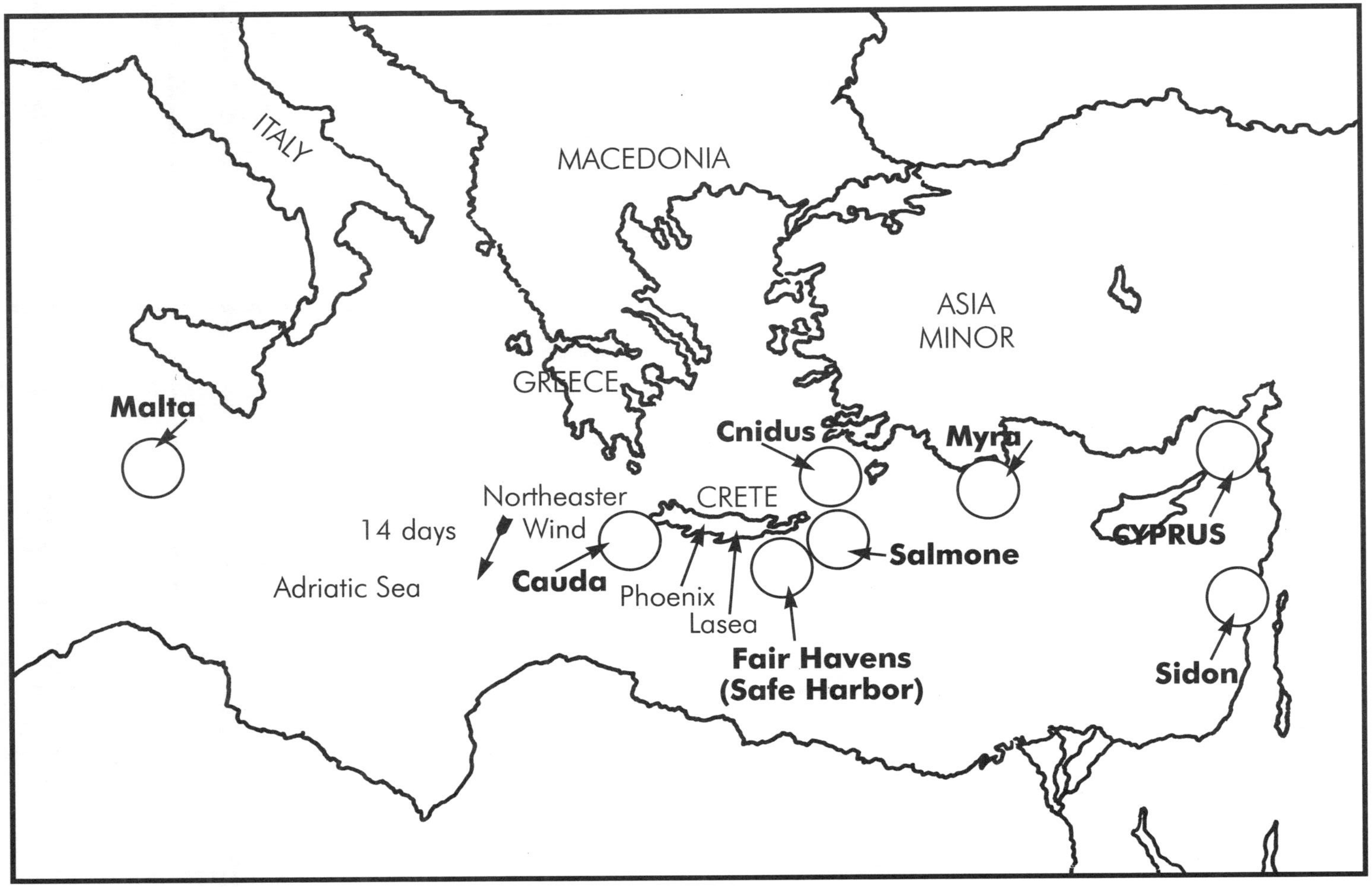

God Changes Enemies to Friends

Cut apart the puzzle shapes on the left and match each one to the correct puzzle shape on the right. When you do, you will see how God changes enemies to friends!

But later they found out Paul was their friend. **I**	**E** People are enemies to God
until Jesus makes them friends. **F**	**N** The soldiers thought Paul was their enemy and wanted to kill him (Acts 27:42).
But later he found out Paul was really his friend (Acts 27:21). **N**	**E** The sailors thought Paul was their enemy because he told them not to take the lifeboat (Acts 27:30-32).
But later they found out Paul was their friend. **R**	**M** The islanders thought Paul was an enemy who needed to die (Acts 28:4).
But parents and teachers are really their friends. **D**	**Y** The centurion thought Paul was his enemy (Acts 27:1).
But God showed them he was not (Acts 28:6, 9) and they became friends (Acts 28:10). **E**	**!** Sometimes kids think parents or teachers are enemies.

Paul Tells People in Rome About Jesus

Worship Focus

Worship God because He wants all people to receive the good news of salvation through Jesus Christ.

Transition Time

(10-15 minutes)

Allow time for the pupils to use the rest room and get drinks of water. As they return, involve them immediately in the following activity.

All Kinds of People Collage: Have on hand a magazine for each pupil. Ask the students to look for and cut out pictures of different kinds of people: people in clothing that shows they are from different countries; people in clothing that shows different kinds of work; people of different ages and races. If you have the "People with Problems" collage from lesson 10, you may want to take it apart and reuse some of those pictures.

Have an area of the wall where these pictures can be put up with Plasti-tak, or a large paper background where they can be taped, or a large cork board where they can be tacked. Over the area, have the heading: "GOD WANTS ALL PEOPLE EVERYWHERE TO BE SAVED."

Be sure to recognize and thank each child as he makes his contributions to the collage. This will increase the children's interest in the project.

When time is up, ask the children to move to the teaching area and sit facing the visuals board.

Launching the Theme

(10 minutes)

Write on a chalk or marker board or on a chart tablet, from top to bottom, the numerals 11 through 17. As children are watching to see what you are up to, say, **Children, remember Paul's SHIP TRIP that we learned about last Sunday?** Review the story of Paul's shipwreck at Malta very briefly, giving the main points for those children who might not have been present.

Now I'm going to read to you about where he went after that. Listen carefully for different people Paul might have talked to about Jesus.

Read Acts 28:11, preferably from the ICB, and ask whom Paul might have talked to. If someone responds "Sailors," ask that person to come stand by you. If no one responds, choose someone to come represent sailors. Print next to numeral 11: SAILORS.

Read verse 12 and ask the same question. Again, ask the one who answers to come up front, or chose someone, and next to numeral 12 print: PEOPLE OF SYRACUSE.

Read verse 13 and ask the question. Invite the one who answers, and another pupil, or any two pupils to join you in front. Print PEOPLE OF RHEGIUM AND PUTEOLI.

Read verse 14 and follow the same routine, printing: ROMANS. Verse 15: PEOPLE AT THE MARKET OF APPIUS AND THE THREE INNS. Verse 16: SOLDIERS. (And put "also verse 16" next to "14: ROMANS.") Verse 17: JEWISH LEADERS.

Read verses 23 and 24 without the routine follow-up. Then put the numeral 30 on the list and read verse 30, asking for a response, and printing: ALL VISITORS.

Invite the remainder of the pupils to join the group up front (if this will not create any problems) and read verse 31 to them all.

Describe the activity choices for the day and let the "sailors" choose a center, then let "people of Syracuse" choose, and so on, and then let the "visitors" one at a time go to a center. Try to have the groups equal in number.

Building the Theme

(30 minutes)

1. Choral reading. Tell the children in this group that they will prepare Romans 10:14, 15 for a choral reading during the call to worship part of *Sharing in Worship*. (The following is from the ICB.) You may want to prepare an audio tape for the children to practice with so that this center can be done independently.

Boys: But before people can trust in the Lord for help,

Girls: they must believe in Him.

Boys: And before they can believe in the Lord,

Girls: they must hear about Him.

Boys: And for them to hear about the Lord,

Girls: someone must tell them.

Boys: And before someone can go and tell them,

Girls: he must be sent. It is written,

All: "How beautiful is the person who comes to bring good news."

If your girls are more mature than your boys (not unusual at this age), you might want to switch the parts. Also, you can help the children remember the order by having them hold up the fingers of one hand and point to them in order as you say "trust," "believe," "hear," "tell," "be sent," and then use the hand to point to the "beautiful person."

2. Reversible booklet (Activity pages): Tear out Activity pages 13A and B and photocopy enough for each pupil and for you to make a model. You can make two-sided (one paper) copies or glue the back of 13A to the back of 13B. Assemble one booklet in advance to show the children. (Follow the instructions below, the same ones you will give the children.)

This page will become a sixteen-page booklet that is actually two eight-page books in one. One is called *Paul Travels and Tells About Jesus.* The other is called *Places I Can Go and Say, "Jesus Loves You!"* This second one is the fun one because you get to write it yourself!

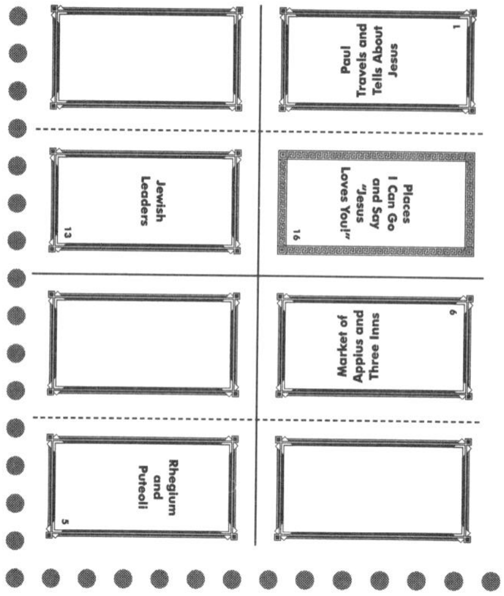

To begin, cut the page into quarters by cutting along the solid lines. Fold on the dotted lines and stack the folded pieces together by inserting them into each other. Then staple the folded edge. Make sure the title, *Paul Travels and Tells About Jesus*, is on the outside and each of the places Paul visited and people he talked to are on the right-hand pages before you staple the folded edges together.

Now flip the booklet over. You will see the book has a new title: *Places I Can Go and Say, "Jesus Loves You!"* When you open the booklet, you will find a blank page on each right-hand side. Think of some places you can go and tell people Jesus loves them, and print them on these pages. In fact, let's think of some together. If you will call out some places you go, I will write them up here (on a chalkboard or tablet). **If any of them is a place you can say, "Jesus loves you," then you can copy that into your booklets, one on each page.** (Examples: playground, park, grocery store, toy store, day care, school, sitter's home, grandparents' home, neighbor's home, yard, yard sales, museum, etc.) Put a happy face sticker on each page after a child prints a place where he or she can say, "Jesus loves you" to someone. This will encourage them to keep working, even if printing is not easy for them.

3. Songs. Have the words to "I Love to Tell About Jesus" and "Who Can I Tell?" (from the song section of this book) on a chart tablet. Record the songs on a cassette so that the pupils in this group may learn the songs independently. Encourage them to do their best as they will be presenting these songs during *Sharing in Worship*.

4. Good News Group. Have available a chart tablet or a chalk- or marker board. Say, **Children, since God wants all people to receive the good news about Jesus, those who know about Jesus can please God by telling those who don't know. Let's think of some things we could tell a person who doesn't know about Jesus.** Take the children's suggestions and print a list of brief phrases. Be sure to thank and compliment each child for his or her suggestion. Remind the children that their pieces of good news will be used in *Sharing in Worship*.

5. Scrambled Scripture Verse. You will need colored index cards or light-colored construction paper cut into two-inch by three-inch rectangles, a piece of poster board (or as many posters as you have small groups; see below), and some glue. Write the words of Philippians 1:12 and 13 from the ICB on the cards, one word on each card. You can make one set and let the children all work together to unscramble the text, or make two or three sets (using a different color set of cards for each one) and let the students work individually or in smaller groups. Put the cards into an envelope (or each set in a different envelope). Tell the children, **The words of an important Bible passage are included in this envelope. See whether you can arrange them in order without looking it up in your Bibles. When you have arranged them properly, glue the cards to the poster board for display later.** (If after fifteen minutes they have not been able to arrange the words, tell them where to find the passage.)

6. "Celebrate the Lord" wall display. *Gifts*: Have available a small empty box for each pupil, wrapping paper, bows, marker, tacks (for a corkboard display) or rubber cement (for a paper backed display area). If you use rubber cement, apply a thin coat to the display area and a thin coat to the gift box and let them dry until they feel tacky and then press them together.)

Tell the children, **We sometimes celebrate special occasions by giving presents. Let's wrap some boxes and label them to show what kind of presents we can give to the Lord. We'll attach the gift boxes to our "Celebrate the Lord" wall display after we present them as part of our offering.**

After the children wrap their boxes, help each one print on one side of his or her box a gift for the Lord: songs, praises, obeying, kindness, thanks, money, helping the poor, etc.

Sharing in Worship

(20-25 minutes)

Omit any of the following sections if you did not offer the corresponding activity. Use a musical signal to draw the children to the area.

Call to Worship (Group 1): Invite Group 1 to the front to share the choral presentation of Romans 10:14, 15. Have them lead the entire class in repeating the choral reading after they have done it once.

Songs (Group 3): Ask the group to come to the front and share the two songs they learned. Encourage the class to join them in singing as they become familiar with the songs.

Offering (Groups 2 and 6): Invite Group 6 to bring their gift boxes and share what gift to the Lord each one stands for as they are attached to the "Celebrate the Lord" wall display.

Children, there are many things we can offer to God in worship. And when we offer our money, we help all kinds of people, in places all over the world, to hear the good news about Jesus. This pleases the Lord very much.

Invite children from Group 6 to pray over the offering and pass the baskets. As the baskets are being passed, say,

We give money to help preachers, evangelists, and missionaries take the good news of Jesus to places we can't go. But there are lots of places where we can share the good news ourselves. Invite Group 2 to come forward with their reversible booklets and share some places where they can say, "Jesus loves you!"

The Lord's Supper: Read 1 Corinthians 11:23b-26. Say, **Did you know that eating the Lord's Supper was one way of telling others the good news about Jesus?** Read verse 26 again. **What if someone asked you, "Why do you eat bread and drink juice in church?" You could explain that the bread reminds us of how Jesus gave His body and the juice reminds us of how He gave His blood when He died in our place. Then you could say, "After Jesus died to pay for our sins, He came back to life, giving us the promise of coming back to life after our bodies die, too!" That sure is good news, isn't it? Let's think about that while we share in the Lord's Supper.**

Devotional (Groups 4 and 5): Have the members of Group 5 display their poster(s). Read the words aloud and say, **Paul's example of telling anyone anywhere the good news about Jesus encouraged other believers to be brave in sharing the good news, too.** Invite Group 4 to join you at the "All Kinds of People" collage. Demonstrate how the children can tell others about Jesus by pointing to one person on the collage and telling that "person" something about Jesus. Then let each person from group 4 point to someone on the collage and tell that person something about Jesus. (Remind them of something they put on their list earlier if they get stuck.) Thank them for their participation and let them sit down.

Prayer: Thank You, God, for giving Your Son to be our Savior and Friend. Help us to be brave and excited about sharing the good news with anyone, anywhere, just like Paul.

Closing Moments

(10-15 minutes)

Go to Game: Cut sixteen pieces of posterboard into rectangles 5 1/2 inches by 7 inches. (Poster board sheets are 22 X 28 inches, so divide one into four equal sections each way.) On each of eight of the rectangles print one place Paul went (use a wide marker and print as big as will fit on the card.): SHIP, SYRACUSE, RHEGIUM, PUTEOLI, ROME,

MARKET, INN, HOUSE PRISON. On each of the remaining eight cards, print places children go: HOME, YARD, NEXT DOOR, SITTERS', STORE, PARK, SCHOOL, GRANDPARENTS.

Have the children line up in one or two lines (depending upon the size of the class). Tell them to watch closely where in the room you put each card and try to remember, because they are going to be upside down and you are going to ask them to go to a certain place! Begin by putting down only three or four of the places Paul went, announcing plainly what they are as you put them printed side down on the floor in different parts of the room. Then tell the first person in the line(s), "Paul went to _____." (Name one of the places.) Ask the student to go to the card that names that place. If he does go to the correct card, let him remain there. If he went to the wrong card, have him go to the back of the line. Call another place for the second person in the line(s). If this one goes to the correct card, allow him to stay there; if not, he returns to the back of the line. When you have two cards occupied, add the remainder of the cards before you continue the game. After children have gone to each of these eight cards, applaud for them, have them get back into the line(s), and repeat the game using the "places we go" cards. This time have each child announce, "Jesus loves you!" when he gets to the place card. Mix the cards up and play again if time permits.

Suggested Resources

Now You Can Read Bible Stories: The Journeys of St. Paul, retold by Leonard Matthews, Rourke Publications, 1984.

Paul Travels and Tells About Jesus

1

Jewish Leaders

13

Places I Can Go and Say "Jesus Loves You!"

16

Market of Appius and Three Inns

9

Rhegium and Puteoli

5

Syracuse

3

All
Visitors

15

Soldiers

11

Rome

7

Joshua Chooses to Obey God

Worship Focus

We worship God because He gives us leaders to help us choose what is right.

Transition Time

(10-15 minutes)

Allow time for the children to use the rest room and get drinks of water. Welcome them and involve them in the following activity.

Relay Race. Divide the class into two teams and ask them to form two lines. Set a chair in an open area across the room from the two lines of children. The first person in each line pretends to be Moses. Provide a ruler or dowel rod for a staff for each "Moses."

When you give the signal to begin, each "Moses" walks (emphasize, **No running**) to the chair, goes around it, and walks back to the next person in line, who pretends to be Joshua. "Moses" hands the "rod" to "Joshua," saying, "Lead the people for God." "Joshua" says, "I obey God," and takes the rod and becomes the next "Moses." Repeat this sequence until the first person in each line is again at the front.

Play this again if time allows. Use recorded music to signal the beginning of *Launching the Theme.* Have the children gather in the large group area.

Launching the Theme

(10 minutes)

Flannelgraph Story: You will need figures to represent old Moses, younger Joshua, the river (may be a strip of flannel), the meeting tent (may be a triangle of flannel), cloud (may be a scalloped oval of flannel), mountain top (may be of flannel), and Activity page 14A (one copy for each child).

As the children gather to sit in front of the flannel board, give those who come quickly and quietly the figures. If you use paper figures, give them to the children least likely to bend or tear them.

Children, I want you to help me with this story. Sometimes I will need you to give me a missing word or a short answer to a question. And when it is time for the figures, I will motion for you to come put them on the board.

You remember that Moses had led the Israelites out of slavery in the land of. . . . (Pause and wait for a child to fill in the missing word: Egypt.) **They had been traveling around in the desert for years. Do you know how many years?** (40) **Moses was an old man. Do you know how old he was?** (120. Ask the pupil with the figure of old Moses to bring it up and put it on the board.) **The Lord told Moses that he could not cross the river to go into the Promised Land.** (Put the river on the board.) **Do you know the name of that river?** (Jordan) **Why couldn't Moses go into the Promised Land?** (He had disobeyed God.) **The Lord said another man would be the new leader to take the people into the Promised Land. Do you know who that man was?** (Joshua. Have the pupil with the Joshua figure put it up.)

The Lord told Joshua He would destroy the nations and give the land to the Israelites. He told Joshua to obey Him, to be strong and brave, and not to be afraid of the enemies. What three things did God tell Joshua? (Obey Him, be strong and brave, don't be afraid.) **Let's say those three things together: obey God, be strong and brave, don't be afraid. Let's say them together again: obey God, be strong and brave, don't be afraid.**

Then the Lord told Moses and Joshua to come to the Meeting Tent. (Have the pupil with the "tent" bring it up and put it on the board.) **And then the Lord appeared to them in a cloud!** (Have the pupil with the "cloud" place it over the "tent.") **The Lord told them that when the people disobeyed Him, terrible things would happen to them.**

After this, Moses went up on a mountain. Do you know what the name of that mountain was? (Mt. Nebo. Have a pupil bring the "mountain" as you remove the "tent," "cloud," and "Joshua.") **There the Lord showed Moses the Promised Land. Moses could see from Gilead to Dan.** (Show the children Mt. Nebo, Gilead, and Dan on the activity page.) **He could see from Naphtali to Ephraim and Manasseh.** (Point out these places on the map.) **He could see all the land of Judah to the Mediterranean Sea.** (Point to these on the map.) **He could see the southern desert and valley of Jericho clear to Zoar.** (Point to map.)

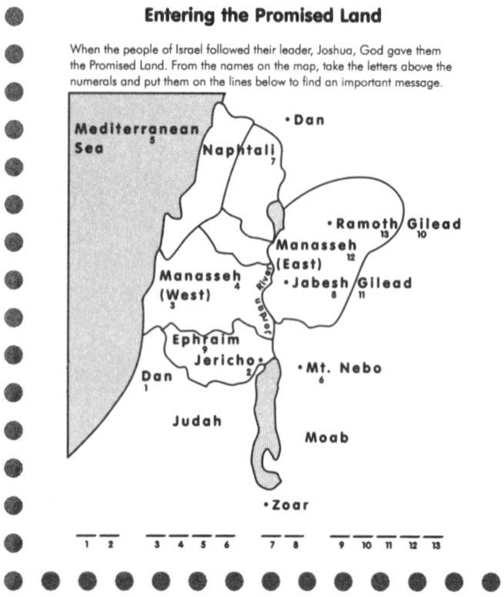

There the Lord said, "This is the land I promised to Abraham, Isaac, and Jacob."

Then Moses died, there in Moab. (Show on map.) **But no one knows where his grave is.** (Remove the figure of Moses.) **Does anyone put flowers on Moses' grave?** (No) **The Israelites cried about Moses, leaving them. But then they listened to Joshua** (put up his figure) **because God had given Joshua the wisdom to be their leader and to help them do what is right. What was Joshua going to do for the people?** (Lead them; help them do what is right.)

And God promised Joshua He would never leave him. And Joshua took the children of Israel across the Jordan River. (Move "Joshua" from right, east, of river to left, West.) **They were in the land God had promised to give them!** (Everybody clap.)

Give the children time to complete the activity page and find the secret message. ("Do what is right.") Allow each pupil to choose an activity center as he or she finishes the map activity.

Building the Theme

(30 minutes)

1. Song. "He Promises Love" from the song section at the back of this book. Have a chart or tablet with the words of the song ready. Introduce the song: **Children, you will be our song leaders in worship later this morning. Let's see whether you can learn to sing this song with two parts—won't that be pretty?** Assign the children to the two parts and help them practice it a time or two. Then they may be able to continue practicing independently with the cassette, with a teacher checking on them and encouraging them occasionally.

2. Devotional. This group will prepare the devotional for *Sharing in Worship*. Provide drawing paper, crayons, pencils, a lunch sack and slips of paper with the following questions written on them about choices your pupils make every day:

What shall I eat for breakfast?

What clothes do I want to wear?

What games do I want to play today?

With whom do I want to play?

Will I go outside today or stay indoors?

Will I share my toys today?

Put the questions in the lunch sack.

Begin the activity by asking the children, **What choices do you make every day?** Write their suggestions on slips of paper and put them into the bag with your others to save for the large group.

What choices do we make to obey God? It's pretty easy to choose which cereal to eat for breakfast, or to choose to wear jeans and a T-shirt. How do we choose to obey God? (Write their ideas on the chalkboard.)

Suggestions: I choose to obey God by being kind. I choose to obey God by reading the Bible. I choose to obey God by sharing my things. I choose to obey God by telling the truth.

Ask the pupils to illustrate one way they can obey God on the drawing paper provided. Encourage each pupil to choose a different idea to illustrate. Then ask them to **Write on the back of your picture how this shows you obey God. Write, "I choose to obey God by—" and then write what action you have chosen to draw on the other side of your paper.**

3. Activity page. "Choose What Is Right." For non-readers the teacher can read the directions: **Cross out the picture in each pair that is not right. Then discuss with the others in the group why the right choice is better.** Inform the pupils that they will be sharing with the large group in *Sharing in Worship* why these choices are better than the ones they marked out. This activity may be done independently.

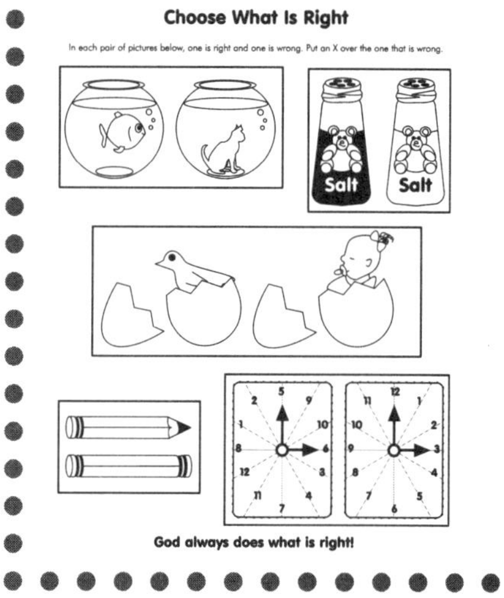

Encourage the children to draw their own examples of good and bad choices on the back of the activity page.

4. "Let's Think About It" Group. Have prepared a chart tablet or other large sheet of paper with LEADERS written in large, fat letters at the top. And have a supply of stars to stick on the letters.

Children, we are going to think about leaders (point to word on **chart) that God gives us, and how they help us to do right. Each time you raise your hand and tell me a leader, I will write it on this chart and give you a star to stick on these big letters that say "Leaders" here at the top. And each time you raise your hand and tell me how one of these leaders helps us to do right, I will give you a star to stick on the letters. Do you think we can fill these letters with stars? That would be a lot of good thinking! I need a long list of leaders for us to use later in *Sharing in Worship*.**

If this group runs out of ideas early, let them work on Activity page 14B.

5. Craft. A picture of when God met with Moses and Joshua at the Tent of Meeting to give them instructions.

Have ready for each pupil in this center: full sheet of manilla art paper, a sheet of brown art paper, a half-sheet of white art paper, some fine-point washable markers in dark colors, glue, and scissors

Remind the children of the story of God's meeting with Moses and Joshua in the tabernacle (Tent of Meeting). Explain that they will use the full sheet of manila art paper as the "desert" background; they will cut a "tent" shape out of the brown art paper; tear a cloud shape out of the white art paper. If you don't have too many children in this center and you have time, print, "I will never leave you" in each cloud. Have the children glue the "tent" and "cloud" onto the background; then draw two stick figures with the markers to represent Moses and Joshua.

Tell them they will share their pictures with the class at offering time.

6. Unit project mural. Have a wall covered with blank paper. Have available pencils and washable markers. Review the story covered in the *Launching the Theme* flannelgraph presentation. Explain the concept of a mural: **Children, we have a large section of our wall covered with blank paper. Each Sunday this quarter we will draw a picture that shows what happened in our Bible story to make a mural. Today we will make a picture of something from our Bible story. What shall we put on the mural?** (Take suggestions. They should include: (1) old Moses, (2) younger Joshua, (3) Tent of Meeting, (4) cloud, (5) mountain, and (6) river. If you have an extra activity page of the map, you might want to cut it out and paste it next to the mountain.

Show the children how much of the mural they can use and help them decide what section of the area and what part of the picture each of them will work on. It would be best not to have more than five children in this center.

As they work, have them practice saying "The Lord does what is right, Psalm 129:4." to use in the Call to Worship.

Sharing in Worship

(20-25 minutes)

Omit any of the following sections if you did not offer the corresponding activity. You may want to use a musical signal to draw the children to the area.

Call to Worship (Group 6): **It looks as if you've been having a good time in your centers this morning. Group 6 has begun a wall mural for us that we will add to the next three Sundays. They also have prepared a verse of Scripture to share with us.** Invite the group to come up and say the verse together. Thank them and have them sit down.

Song (Group 1): **Yes, the Lord does what is right, and He helps us do what is right, and then He promises blessings when we do what is right. Group 1 has a song to share with us about the blessings of doing right and obeying God.** Invite group 1 up to sing, "He Promises Love." You may want to divide the class into two groups and assign parts and see if they can sing along.

Offering (Group 5): Invite the children from Group 5 to bring up their pictures. **God gave the children of Israel leaders, instructions, and promises. He gave them a new land for their new home. He gives us our homes and all that we have. We give back to Him by giving to others.** Have Group 5 put their pictures down and return to their seats and invite children from Group 2 to pray for the offering and pass the baskets.

Devotional (Groups 2, 3, and 4): Ask Group 3 to come to the front with their activity pages, and provide a copy for each child in the large group as well. Allow each member of Group 3 to tell about one choice—why the good choice is better than the other—taking turns until each one has been mentioned. Ask the rest of the children to mark their pages as the "leaders" explain the correct choices. To conclude, ask all the members of Group 3 to read the statement at the bottom of the page together: "God always does what is right."

Thank the children and have them sit down. **Yes, God always does what is right doesn't He? And He wants us to choose what is right, too. Let's think about**

choices for a while. Ask volunteers in the large group to choose slips of paper from the sack. Have each one read the question on the slip and to explain how he might make the choice indicated. This will introduce the devotional. Ask Group 2 to stand in front of the large group and to bring their illustrations, but tell them not to show the pictures yet.

Every day we have to make choices. Some are easy, like which clothes to wear or which cereal to eat for breakfast. Some are hard, like whether to clean my room without being asked or to play until Mom has to tell me to clean it up. Some choices do not matter much, like which toy to play with, but some choices are very important and matter a lot. Choosing to obey God is one of the important choices. Group 2 is going to tell us some ways to help us make that important choice. Ask the children of Group 2 to display their illustrations, one at a time, and to read what they wrote on the back of the drawings.

One way God helps us to make the right choice about obeying Him is by giving us good leaders, just as He gave the Israelites a good leader in Joshua. He tells us to obey the leaders He gives us because they will help us do what is right. Group 4 is going to tell us about leaders. Invite Group 4 to come up and give them the opportunity to share about the leaders they put on their Leaders Chart.

Lord's Supper: God does what is right and keeps His word. He led the Israelites out of Egypt and into the land He had promised them. He has promised to give us a new home in Heaven, when we obey Him, and when we accept forgiveness through Jesus for when we don't obey Him. God will keep His promise. Let's think about the hope that we have through Jesus and remember the price Jesus paid for us to have that hope as we share in the Lord's Supper. Invite children from Group 3 to help pray and pass the bread and juice.

Prayer: Thank You, God, for giving your children leaders to help them do what is right. Thank You that the children of Israel had Moses and Joshua. And thank You that we have parents and teachers. Remind us always to do what is right. In Jesus' name. Amen.

Closing Moments

(10-15 minutes)

Game: "Crossing into the Promised Land." Have two lengths of yarn, or a strip of cloth, on the floor to represent the Jordan River. Let one teacher be "Moses" and another "Joshua." "Moses" can sit off to the side of the game. "Joshua" will give the instructions for crossing the "Jordan." When "Joshua" gives an instruction that *is* obeying God, all the children cross the "Jordan." When Joshua gives an instruction that is *not* obeying God, they stay where they are. If a child crosses the Jordan when he should not have, that child goes to sit with Moses. Allow the children sitting with Moses to return to the game after a few turns.

Joshua says: "Tell the truth" (cross).

"Tell a lie" (don't cross).

"Tell your mother you washed your hands when you didn't" (don't cross).

"Put your toys away" (cross).

"Shove your toys under your bed" (don't cross).

"Sneak a cookie" (don't cross).

"Share the last cookie" (cross).

"Tease your pet" (don't cross).

"Be kind to your pet" (cross).

"Help fold the laundry" (cross).

"Knock the clean laundry on the floor and walk over it" (don't cross).

"Hog all the crayons" (don't cross).

"Share the crayons" (cross).

"Turn book pages carefully" (cross).

"Scribble on and tear pages of books" (don't cross).

"Bother Mother while she's talking on the phone" (don't cross).

"Wait until Mother gets off the phone before asking her something" (cross).

"Go to bed when your parents say it's time" (cross).

"Keep playing after your parents say it's time for bed" (don't cross).

"Draw or color on the wall" (don't cross).

"Draw or color only on paper or coloring books" (cross).

"Listen to your parents and teachers" (cross).

"Don't pay attention to your parents and teachers" (don't cross).

Entering the Promised Land

When the people of Israel followed their leader, Joshua, God gave them the Promised Land. From the names on the map, take the letters above the numerals and put them on the lines below to find an important message.

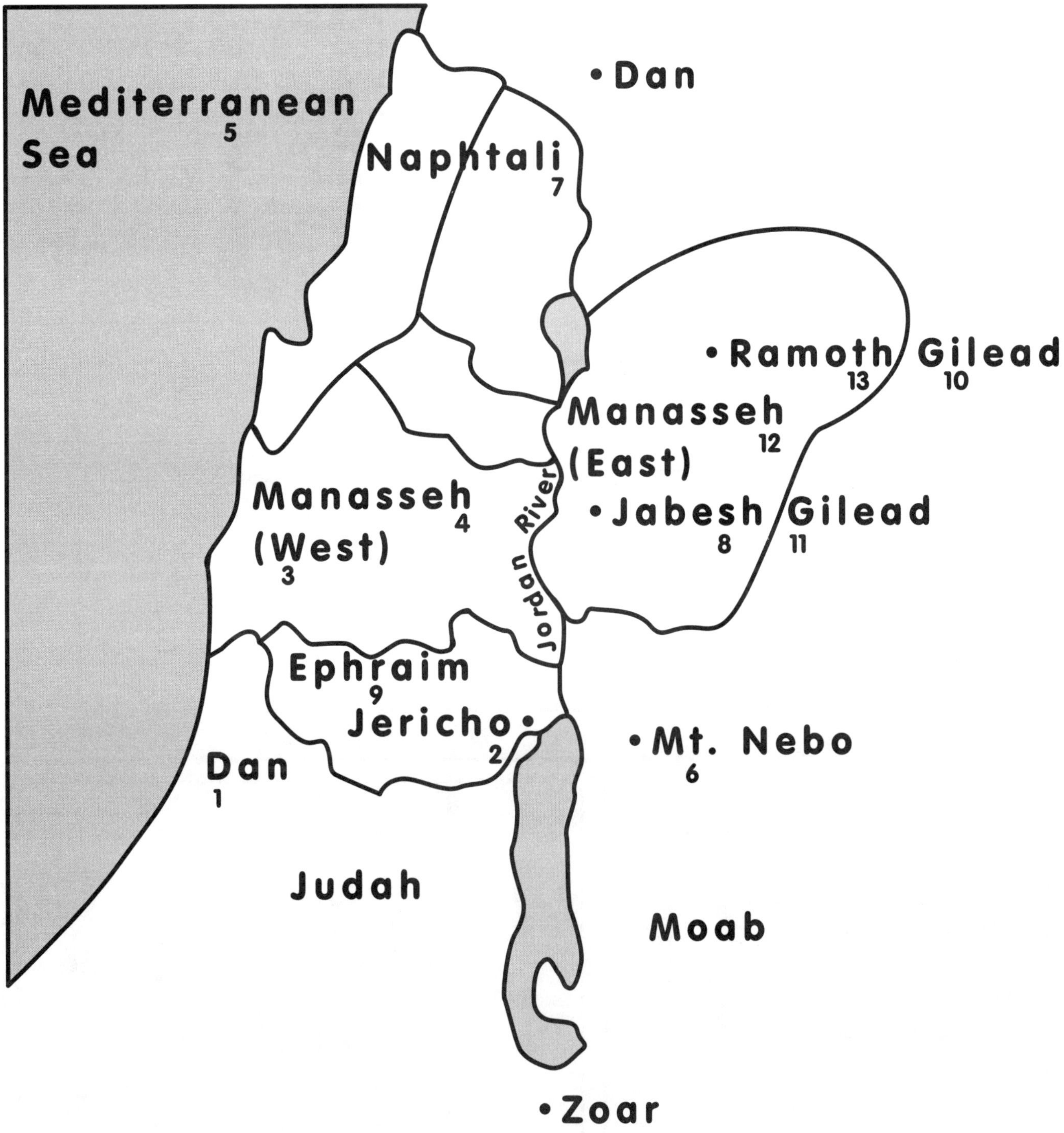

__ __   __ __ __ __   __ __   __ __ __ __ __

1 2   3 4 5 6   7 8   9 10 11 12 13

Choose What Is Right

In each pair of pictures below, one is right and one is wrong. Put an X over the one that is wrong.

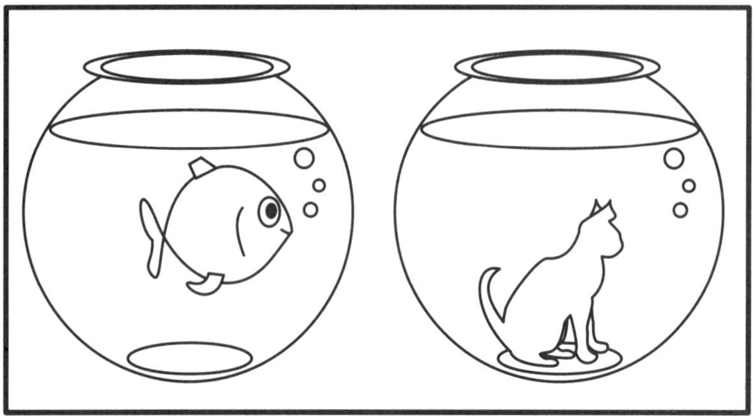

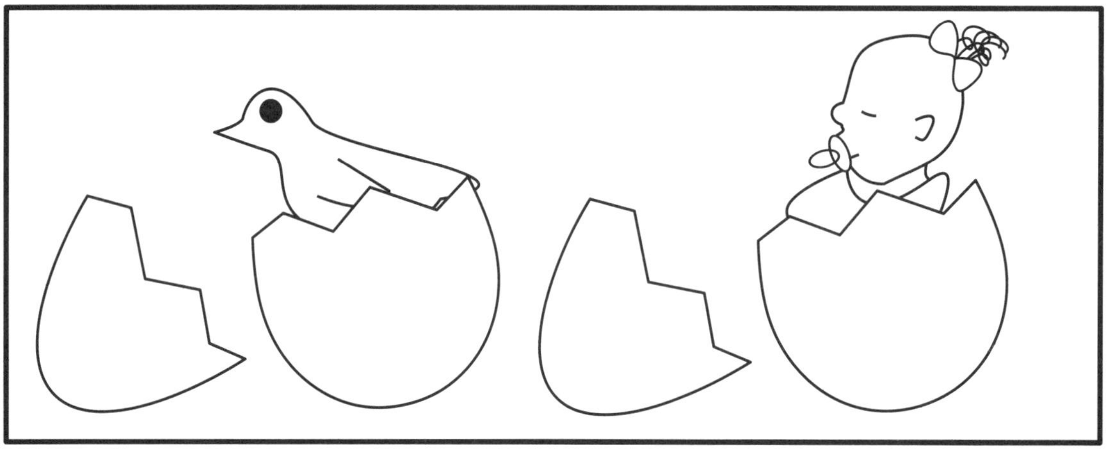

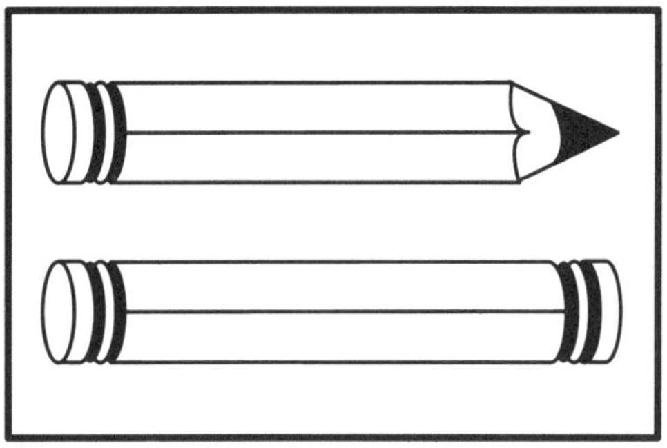

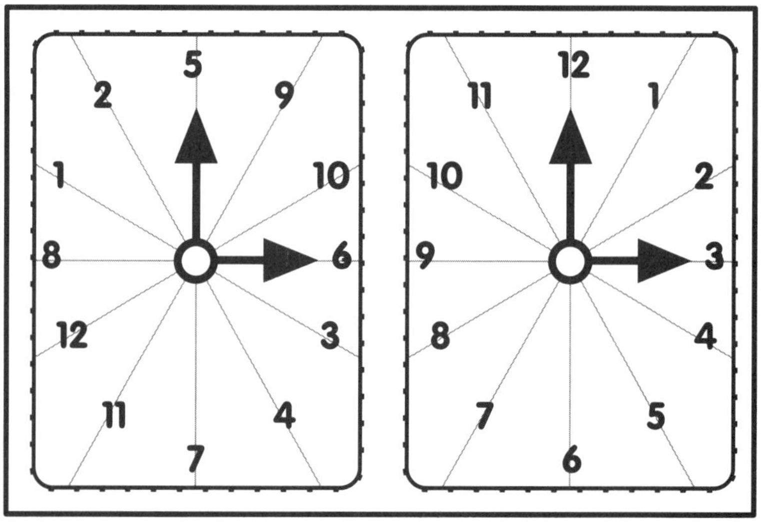

God always does what is right!

Joshua and Caleb Tell the Truth

Worship Focus

Worship God because He makes us strong and brave when we trust Him.

Transition Time

(10-15 minutes)

Allow time for the children to use the rest room and get drinks of water. Welcome them and involve them in the following activity.

Character Groupings: Have prepared sets of name slips: "Moses" "Caleb," "Joshua," and "fearful spy." Be sure to have one slip for each pupil. (If your class size is not a multiple of four, make the number of each character as even as possible—i.e., for a class of twenty-two, you might have six of Moses, six of Joshua, five of Caleb, and five of the fearful spies.)

As the children come in, give each one a slip. (For children who can't read, whisper the names on the slips.) Tell the children to keep their character names a secret, and give the following instructions:

We are going to play a little game. The idea is to get into one of four groups, one for the "Moseses," one for the "Joshuas," one for the "Calebs," and one for the "fearful spies." But you cannot tell anyone which one you are! In fact, you can't say anything except what I am going to tell you right now. If you are a "Moses," you will say, "Be strong and brave" and will say nothing else. The "Calebs" will always say, "Go take the land" and will say nothing else. The "Joshuas" will always say, "Don't be afraid of giants" and will say nothing else. The "fearful spies" will always say, "We can't do it" and will say nothing else.

When I say, "Begin," you may walk around the room. Go up to another pupil, and you will each say your phrase. If you are the same character, take each other's hands and stay together as you walk up to another pupil. Say your phrases to each other. If the new person has a different line, you can't hook up together, but if you have the same phrase, you may hook up. When everyone is in one of the four groups, each group will stand in a circle, holding hands and raising your hands together.

Remember, you are not to let other players see your slip. And you cannot say anything but the special phrases I told you. Now, think about which character you are—raise your hand if you don't remember who you are to be. (An aide can go to those who raise their hands and whisper their character names to them.) **Think about what phrase you will be saying as I repeat the phrases.** (Repeat instructions.) **Begin.**

As the children play, circulate among them, prompting them as needed.When all groups are formed, applaud.

Ask the group of "Moseses" to come to one area, the "Calebs" and "Joshuas" to another, and the "fearful spies" to another. Have them sit in their groups for *Launching the Theme*.

Launching the Theme

(10 minutes)

Bible Story Review. Have available a calendar, some grapes, pomegranates, and figs, and a picture of the spies carrying a huge bunch of grapes on a pole.

Children, I want you to help me with this story from the book of Numbers in the Bible. It's about the time God told Moses to send men to explore the land of Canaan, which He was giving to the Israelites after He had set them free from their slavery in Egypt. I will tell you what to say, and you repeat after me.

First, raise your hands if you are playing the part of Moses. Okay, now "Moseses," you look at the "Joshuas," "Calebs," and "fearful spies" and say after me: "Go explore Canaan." Pause for them to repeat. **"See what the land looks like."** Pause for repeat. **"Are the people there strong or weak?"** Pause. **"Are there a few people or many?"** Pause. **"Is the land good or bad?"** Pause for repeat. **"Do the towns have walls?"** Pause. **"Bring back some fruit from that land."** Pause.

Thank you, "Moseses." Now

you just listen. So the spies went and explored the land. They cut off a branch of a grapevine and carried it on a pole between two of them. Show picture. **They also got some pomegranates and figs.** Show. Pass out fruit to eat. **After forty days of exploring the land, the men returned.** Show forty days on a calendar and try to relate it to something the children did forty days ago or will be doing in forty days. **The spies brought their report and showed the fruit to Moses and the Israelites.**

Now, "Joshuas" and "Calebs" and "fearful spies," you look at the "Moseses" and repeat after me: "We went to explore the land." Pause for repeat. **"It is a land that grows much food."** Pause. **"But the people who live there are strong."** Pause. **"Their cities are large and have walls."** Pause.

Thank you, "spies." Now only the "Calebs" will talk. Calebs, repeat after me: "We should go up and take the land." Pause. **"We can do it."** Pause for repeat. **Thank you, "Calebs."**

Now, "fearful spies," repeat after me: "We can't attack those people." Pause. **"They are stronger than we are."** Pause. **"All the people are very tall."** Pause. **"We felt like grasshoppers."** Pause. **"They would eat us up."** Pause.

Okay, "fearful spies." You just listen now. Joshuas and Calebs, you repeat after me: "The land is very good." Pause for repeat. **"If the Lord is pleased with us, He will lead us into that land."** Pause. **"He will give us that land where much food grows."** Pause. **"Don't turn against the Lord!"** Pause. **"Don't be afraid of the people in that land!"** Pause. **"We will chew them up!"** Pause. **"We have the Lord!"** Pause. **"So don't be afraid of them!"** Pause.

Thank you "Joshuas" and "Calebs." Now just listen. The Lord said, "Only Caleb and Joshua will go into the land I promised. For forty years you others will suffer for your sins. That is a year for each of the forty days you explored the land."

Joshua and Caleb knew God had promised them the land, so they knew they could take it. The fearful spies weren't thinking about what God had said, and they were afraid. When we put our trust in God, He makes us strong and brave.

Explain the activity choices available and then ask the "Moseses" to go to the centers of their choice, then the "Joshuas," then the "fearful spies," then the "Calebs."

Building the Theme

(30 minutes)

If the children in any of the following groups finish early, have them work on activity page 15A, coloring the pictures and tracing their way through the maze. This is an easy activity that can be done independently, so the teacher/leaders can be available to help elsewhere.

1. Song. Use the tune "God Wants Me to Do Right." Write the following words on a chart tablet and record them on a cassette before the session:

Trust God and He'll make you strong to do right.
Trust God and He'll make you be brave to do what's right.

Tell the pupils they will share this song later in *Sharing in Worship*.

2. Letter Writing. This is a challenge activity that will require a bit more writing skill than many of your children will possess. Be careful about selecting children who will not be discouraged by such an activity.

Imagine you are writing a letter to a friend or a relative who does not know about how the spies were sent into the Promised Land and how they were to trust the Lord to keep His promise to give them the land even though its people were big and bold and their cities had strong stone walls around them. Write a letter and tell your friend what happened—but don't stop there. Tell your friend why this story is so important. It teaches us to trust God, doesn't it?

Tell your friend about something in your own life that makes you afraid sometimes, and how this story will help you trust God. Maybe you have a hard class at school, and you are afraid of the teacher or of the tests. Or perhaps your friend is afraid of something or does not go to church or trust the Lord. Could you use this story to tell your friend not to be afraid but to trust the Lord? Give it a try.

We will share these letters later in our worship time.

3. Skit. This group will act out the Bible story. Have them practice it now for use later as the devotional for *Sharing in Worship*. You will need the following characters: Moses, Joshua, Caleb, three or four other spies (tell the children you'll pretend there are others), and a few others to be the rest of the Israelites. You can copy Activity page 15B and distribute it so everyone has a copy. When you pass out the scripts, tell each child which character he or she will play and point out the appropriate lines. (This is especially important for the spies: be sure to tell the children which spies will be carrying the fruit and will say the lines assigned to "two spies."

Note: the teacher's lines at the

end are not included on the activity page. Be sure you have this page or have written down the words so you can say them at the end of the skit.

Moses (to the spies, including Joshua and Caleb): Go and spy out the land that the Lord is giving to us. See what kind of land it is and how strong its people are. Check out their cities—do they have strong walls around them? And bring back some of the fruit to show the people how great a land the Lord has promised us.

Spies: Yes, sir! (They exit.)

Teacher: **Forty days later, the spies returned.** (Spies return. If possible give two of them a broomstick with a bag of fruit suspended from it to carry.)

Moses: Tell us. What did you find? Is it a fruitful land?

Two spies (with fruit): Oh, yes! It is a wonderful land. Look at the fruit we have brought back. And there's plenty more even bigger.

Joshua: It is just as the Lord promised us. The Lord has truly been good to us!

Caleb: Yes! Let's go up and take the land, where we will be able to live and prosper as the Lord has said.

People: Hurray! Let's go!

Fearful spy #1: Wait a minute! You didn't mention the people. They are giants. We look like grasshoppers next to them!

Fearful spy #2: Yes, and their cities have strong stone walls. We will never be able to break through them.

Fearful spy #3: What have you done to us, Moses? Why did you lead us out here to be killed by these giant Canaanites?

People: Oh, no! We will all be killed!

Joshua: That's not so! God has given us this land. It is ours. We can take it.

Caleb: That's right. All we have to do is trust God. He will keep His promise.

Fearful spies: No! It's too hard. We can't do it.

Teacher: So the people believed the fearful spies instead of trusting the Lord. Because of that, they were not allowed to enter the land for forty years. Of the men who were there when the spies came back with their report, only Joshua and Caleb lived long enough to enter the land because only they trusted the Lord and believed His promises.

4. Scripture Response. You may want to have this script printed on a chalkboard so that you can erase one word out of each response line each time the children rehearse it. You may want to choose a different child to erase the words each time you go through it, choosing children who are being very attentive, as a means of increasing their concentration.

Leader: If the Lord is pleased with us,

Response: He will lead us into that land.

Leader: He will give us that land

Response: where much food grows.

Leader: Don't turn against the Lord!

Response: Don't be afraid of the people of that land!

All: We will chew them up.

Leader: They have no protection,

Response: But we have the Lord.

All: So don't be afraid of them.

All: Numbers 14 verses 8 and 9. (ICB)

5. Play Dough Fruit. Set out reusable play dough, or mix up a recipe that will harden, if you want to let the children take them home. (See recipe on page 110.) Good colors to use would be green, red, orange, brown. It would be nice to have a basket, or a place mat, to arrange them in/on. Encourage the children to make good looking fruit and tell them they will present their fruit as offering later.

6. Unit Project Wall Mural. Today the pupils may add fruit trees and vines, walled cities, giants. Help section off an area for each child to stay within. Remind them that there will be two more Sundays for adding to the mural so it is important that they stay within the area you mark off for them. See page 97 for more information about the mural.

As the children work, have them practice saying, "When I am afraid, I will trust you, Psalm 56:3" (ICB) to use in the Call to Worship. Have them write the verse over the picture on the mural.

Sharing in Worship

(20-25 minutes)

Use soft music (recorded or live) to signal the pupils that the worship time is beginning.

Call to Worship (Group 6): Display the mural and have the children recite the verse. Then have all the children repeat it. Follow with a short prayer (or ask one of the children from Group 6 to lead in prayer).

Song (Group 1): Invite the children from Group 1 to come and sing the song they learned. If time permits, you may want them to repeat it and teach it to the rest of the class.

Offering (Group 5): Invite the children from Group 5 to bring their fruit and arrange it in a basket or on a place mat. **The Lord has so many good things to give His children, like fruit. He had given the children of Israel His promise—that He would give them a good land where much fruit grew. He wanted**

them to believe Him, to give Him their trust. When they didn't give Him their trust, He couldn't give them the land.

God has promised to provide all our needs. But if we don't put our trust in Him, we cannot receive or enjoy all He has to give us. As we give back part of the money He gives us, we show that we trust Him, to give us what we need.

Scripture (Group 4): Invite the children from Group 4 to come and share the Scripture response.

Lord's Supper. Do you think Jesus might have felt afraid when He was about to be crucified? We know He was not happy about what was going to happen to Him because He prayed and asked His Father not to make Him do it if it was not necessary, and He sweat great drops like blood—He was praying so hard. But He put His trust in God and did what He needed to do. He needed to do that for us. He died for our sins. Let's think about that as we share in the Lord's Supper.

Devotional (Group 3): Introduce the skit by Group 3 and allow them to present it. Follow up the skit with the following:

Sometimes we are afraid and forget to trust God to keep His promises, don't we? What makes you afraid? Allow some of the children to answer. **When we are afraid, we need to be like Joshua and Caleb. We need to trust God to keep His promises. Let's think of some of His promises. You mention some of them, and I will write them up here** (on a chalkboard, marker board, or some other display). Give the children time to mention several promises, adding some yourself to help get them started or to pick things up if they lag.

Do you remember our Call to Worship? Ask one of the children from Group 6 to recite Psalm 56:3 again. **King David, one of Israel's greatest kings, said that. "When I am afraid, I will trust you." If someone like David was sometimes afraid and needed to remember to trust God, then so do we, don't we? Let's repeat that verse together so we will remember it.** Repeat the verse three or four times together.

Follow up (Group 2): **One of our groups wrote letters to tell a friend how this story helps us not to be afraid but to trust God. Group 2, come up and share your letters with us.** Have each one in the group read his or her letter. Make appropriate comments to point out to the rest of the children how the ideas in the letters might be used by all of them.

Option: If time is short, you might read the letters yourself or choose just one or two (at random) as an example. Post the letters on a bulletin board so all the children can see them later.

Prayer: Lord God, thank You for showing us that when Caleb and Joshua trusted You, You made them strong and brave. Thank You for teaching us that even when we are afraid we can trust You, and that You will help us to be strong and brave to do the things that You want us to do. Amen.

Closing Moments

(10-15 minutes)

Have the children come to an open area. Designate one side of the area as "The Promised Land." Designate the other side as "The Desert of Wanderings." Have the children stand in the middle. Tell them, **The leader will make a statement and, if it is a true statement, one that honors God and shows faith in His Word, you may go into "The Promised Land." But if the statement is untrue or shows a lack of faith in God, you must go walk around in "The Desert of Wanderings" while the leader counts to forty. The count to forty will remind us of the forty years the children of Israel had to wander in the desert because they did not put their trust in God."**

Write each of the following statements on an index card. Choose one of the children to be the leader, and give him a card. After the statement is read and the children respond, choose another leader for the next statement. Allow the leader to make up a statement or to take a card. Continue in this way, one leader per statement, until all the cards are used and no one else wants to think up a statement to use.

The Lord will never leave us or forsake us. (P.L.)

I don't think God can hear all of our prayers. (D.W.)

The Lord gives us all things to enjoy. (P.L.)

Christians don't have any fun. (D.W.)

God will reward us for obeying our parents. (P.L.)

If you seek the Lord, you will find Him. (P.L.)

Learning about God makes people unhappy. (D.W.)

The Lord will rescue us from danger. (P.L.)

God won't help you if you get into trouble. (D.W.)

God doesn't want you to have friends. (D.W.)

God will help you to learn what you need to know. (P.L.)

God is a father to those without earthly fathers. (P.L.)

Sometimes it's okay to tell little lies. (D.W.)

Spy Out the Land

You are one of Joshua's spies. Find your way through the maze (the promised land), passing by each picture on your way from "Start" to "Finish." Then color the pictures.

Moses (to the spies, including Joshua and Caleb): Go and spy out the land that the Lord is giving to us. See what kind of land it is and how strong its people are. Check out their cities—do they have strong walls around them? And bring back some of the fruit to show the people how great a land the Lord has promised us.

Spies: Yes, sir! (They exit.)

Teacher: Forty days later, the spies returned. (Spies return. Two carry a huge bunch of grapes on a stick.)

Moses: Tell us. What did you find? Is it a fruitful land?

Two spies (with fruit): Oh, yes! It is a wonderful land. Look at the fruit we have brought back. And there's plenty more even bigger.

Joshua: It is just as the Lord promised us. The Lord has truly been good to us!

Caleb: Yes! Let's go up and take the land, where we will be able to live and prosper as the Lord has said.

People: Hurray! Let's go!

Fearful spy #1: Wait a minute! You didn't mention the people. They are giants. We look like grasshoppers next to them!

Fearful spy #2: Yes, and their cities have strong stone walls. We will never be able to break through them.

Fearful spy #3: What have you done to us, Moses? Why did you lead us out here to be killed by these giant Canaanites?

People: Oh, no! We will all be killed!

Joshua: That's not so! God has given us this land. It is ours. We can take it.

Caleb: That's right. All we have to do is trust God. He will keep His promise.

Fearful spies: No! It's too hard. We can't do it.

Joshua Follows God's Instructions

Worship Focus

Worship God because He gives perfect instructions that we can follow to do what is right.

Transition Time

(10-15 minutes)

Allow time for the children to use the rest room and get drinks of water. Welcome them and involve them in the following activity.

Walls of Jericho Bricks. Have available four egg cartons or a shoe box and a brown paper grocery bag for each pupil. In addition, have plenty of masking tape on hand. If your class is small, have enough materials for each child to make two or three "bricks." Have a copy of activity page 16A for each child.

As the children come in, show them how to stack the four egg cartons two high and two across, wrap them with a couple of pieces of masking tape, and then cover them with the brown paper. (See the illustration on activity page 16A.) The shoe boxes need only be covered with paper.

As they finish assembling "bricks," have them stack them against a wall or under a table for use during *Closing Moments.*

Launching the Theme

(10 minutes)

Have the following instructions printed on four cards, and give each card to one of the pupils. Have the four pupils with cards stand up in front of the class. Address the class and say, **Each of these children has a card with some instructions on it. As each one reads what is on the card, you try to figure out what the result would be if you followed the instructions. Raise your hand when you think you know.**

Tell your readers, **Read the card (except for the answer at the bottom) and then call on someone whose hand is raised. See if that person guesses right. If not, call on someone else until you get the right answer. When someone guesses correctly, give the card back to me and go sit down. Okay, reader 1, begin.**

1. Pull up the sheet. Smooth out the wrinkles. Fold the top back. Pull up the bedspread. Be sure it is straight and not crooked. Fold back the top. Fluff up the pillow. Lay it on the bed. Pull the bedspread over the pillow and smooth out the wrinkles.

Answer: Make a bed.

2. Scoop out one or two dips of vanilla ice cream. Pour hot fudge, butterscotch, or caramel syrup on the ice cream. Squirt or spoon whipped cream over the ice cream and syrup, and put one cherry on the top.

Answer: Make an ice cream sundae.

3. Mix together butter, sugar, milk, flour, salt, and baking powder to make a batter. Heat a griddle until it is very hot. Pour batter onto the griddle to form a circle of batter. Fry it until it bubbles on one side. Flip it over. Fry it until it is light brown. Flip it onto a plate. Put butter and syrup on it.

Answer: Make a pancake.

4. Lay enough plates for each member of your family around the edge of the table. Fold napkins. Put a napkin on the left side of each plate. Put a fork on each napkin. Place a knife and spoon on the right side of each plate. Put a glass above each plate on the right.

Answer: Set a table.

Thank you, readers. And thank you, class, for guessing so well. How did you guess what was being described? How did you learn to do those things? (Parents explained, teachers showed them, etc.)

If I said, "Be kind, tell the truth, obey your parents," whose instructions are those, really? (God's.) **How do we know what is the right thing for us to do?** (God gives us instructions in His Word.)

God gave instructions to Joshua about how to defeat the city of Jericho. Let's look at those instructions. Read Joshua 5:13-15, ICB. **What was the first instruction you heard Joshua receive here?** Take off your sandals. **Now, listen for the next instruction, and when you hear it, raise your hand.** Read Joshua 6:1-3. If no child raises his hand, prompt them. March around the city with your army one time every day for six days. Read verse 4. Seven priests carry trumpets made from horns of male sheep—rams' horns. March in front of the Ark of the Agreement. On the seventh day march around the city seven times. On the seventh day priests blow trumpets as they march. Read verse 5. When people hear the long blast of the trumpets, they give a loud shout. When the walls of city fall, the people go straight into the city. Read verses 6 and 7.

What new instruction did you hear? Soldiers with weapons were to march in front of the Ark of the Agreement. **Now listen to see if the instructions were followed.** Read verses 8 and 9. Children should note that the instructions were followed. Read verses 10-16. **Now listen for a new instruction.** Read verses 17-19. The city and everything in it were to be destroyed as an offering to the Lord. Only Rahab and the people in her house were to be saved. The Israelites were not to take anything. Silver, gold, bronze, and iron things were to be saved for the Lord. **What did God say would happen if anyone took anything that was supposed to be destroyed?** They would be destroyed. Read verse 20. **They obeyed God's instructions and the city was defeated as God had promised. What do you think would have happened if they had not obeyed God's instructions?** The city would not have been defeated.

We worship God because He gives us instructions that, when we follow them, will cause us to succeed, to do a good job of whatever it is God wants us to do.

Now I am going to describe the activity centers we have today, and then I am going to give instructions on how to choose and go to the centers. Let's see if everyone can follow the instructions. Describe the center activities.

If you have on something blue, stand up, and take baby steps to the center of your choice. Wait for them to do so. Compliment those who follow instructions well. **If you have on something red, stand up, hold your arms above your heads, and take giant steps to the center of your choice.** Again, compliment those who do well. If any centers are filled, advise the remaining children that they can no longer choose these. **If you have on something green, stand up and hop to the center of your choice.** After they have moved to their centers, allow any remaining children to skip to any centers that have room for them.

Building the Theme

(30 minutes)

1. Song. Use the song "Samuel Pleased the Lord" (in the back of this book), but call it "Joshua Chose to Serve the Lord" or just "Choose to Serve the Lord." Use the name Joshua instead of Samuel on the third verse. Write the words on a poster board or chart tablet, and record it on a cassette tape before the worship session.

Listen to this song, and read the words. Then play it again and sing along. Keep playing it and singing it until you have learned it. You will teach it to the rest of the class during our worship time later.

2. Hidden Message. Give this group copies of activity page 16B. **Color all the spaces with even numbers blue. Color all the spaces with odd numbers yellow. Add different colors to the shapes without numbers. Then find the hidden message.** Depending upon the maturity of your pupils, this may be an independent activity.

3. Scripture. Psalm 19:7-11. Use the *International Children's Bible* if you have access to one. It would be good to have the verses printed on a chart tablet or chalk/marker board so that you could point to the words as you read them. Read through the passage once, pointing to the words as you do. Then go through it line by line and have the children say in their own words what each line means.

Read it again, inviting the children to read aloud along with you. Tell them this Scripture passage will be used during *Sharing in Worship* and you would like them to say it with you. Practice reading the passage until the children do it smoothly. If you have any exceptionally good readers, you may let them take over the leadership of this activity.

4. Craft. Provide light brown construction paper for the children. Allow each child to roll a piece of the paper into a cone shape. Then the children should tape the outside edge of the cones so that they will stay cone-shaped. Encourage the children to curve their horns gently so that they seem to resemble rams' horns. If the children work carefully, they can shape the paper horn slightly without crushing it.

We are making pretend rams' horns this morning. The rams' horns used in Bible days were

real horns taken from male sheep. The horns were hollowed out and used as trumpets. These were very important at Jericho because they were included in the instructions God gave to Joshua. Can someone tell me the instructions that mentioned the rams' horns? Allow a child to reply that the priests were to blow the horns on the seventh day after the people had marched around the city seven times.

God doesn't tell us to blow rams' horns today, but He has given us instructions in the Bible, and He has given us parents and teachers to give more instructions. Why is it so important to follow the instructions? What would have happened if the priests had not blown the rams' horns at Jericho? Defeat. **That's right. Can you think of times today when it is very important to follow instructions or rules, and what happens when people do not follow them?**

Lead a discussion of the importance of following the instructions/rules. If the children are not able to think of situations, you might suggest one or more of the following examples: putting together a model, playing by the rules in sports, obeying the rules at home and at school, following a recipe when cooking, traffic rules, or laws about stealing—e.g., shoplifting.

5. Lord's Supper. This group will learn God's instructions about the Lord's Supper to present during *Sharing in Worship.*

What are some of the things we do as parts of our worship? (We sing, read the Bible, bring offerings, have the Lord's Supper, and so on.) **How do we know to do these things?** (God has given us instructions to do these things in our worship of Him.) **Today we will think about the instructions He has given concerning the Lord's Supper.**

Listen to what the Bible says about the Lord's Supper. Read Matthew 26:26-29 from the *International Children's Bible.* Then hold up a piece or cracker or wafer. **What does Jesus tell us to do with this bread?** Eat it to remember Him. **Of what does this bread remind us?** Jesus' body. Hold up a cup of grape juice. **What does Jesus tell us to do with the cup?** Drink it to remember Him. **Of what does the cup remind us?** Jesus' blood; that He died to forgive us for the wrong things we do.

Let's work together to write a couple of sentences about the bread and the juice. I'll write them up here (on a chart tablet or other display), **and then we can use them later in our worship time.** Some examples of sentences your class might come up with are as follows: We are to eat this bread to remember Jesus. It reminds us of His body. We are to drink this juice to remember Jesus. It reminds us of His blood and of how He died on the cross for us. Take the children's suggestions and then write them in such a way as to be useful for leading in the Communion service later.

Assign one member of the group to read the sentences about the bread during *Sharing in Worship.* Assign another to read about the cup. Choose one or two others to read the Scripture, Matthew 26:26-29. Other group members can be assigned the task of passing the trays. If there is time, have the readers practice reading their assigned parts (Scripture or sentences) while the others draw pictures of Jesus having the Last Supper with His disciples.

6. Unit Project Mural. Today the children in this center will want to add the walls of Jericho with the priests carrying horns, the Holy Box of Agreement with the Lord, and the soldiers marching around. Assign spaces for each child to work within. See page 97 for more information about the mural.

Have them write the words of Psalm 19:8 on the mural and to learn to recite the verse as they work. Once again, this group will lead the Call to Worship.

Sharing in Worship

(20-25 minutes)

Use soft music (recorded or live) to signal the pupils that the worship time is beginning.

Call to Worship (Group 6): Invite Group 6 to come and recite Psalm 19:8. Ask the entire class to repeat the verse. Then lead in prayer.

Song (Group 1): Display the words to "Joshua Chose to Serve the Lord" and have Group 1 lead the class in singing it. (Have the group sing it once for the class; then have the class sing it together.)

Offering: The Lord told the Israelites not to keep anything from Jericho for themselves, that all of it was to be an offering to God. Since God had done such great things for the Israelites in bringing them out of Egypt and defeating the city of Jericho, this giving of everything back to Him was the way the Israelites could show that they knew He was taking care of them.

All through the Bible God has asked His people to give Him back the first or best of what He has given them. When we know that God gives us all things, we are glad to do this. Let's clap our hands after we give our offering this morning to show that we are glad to give back to the Lord. Ask two of the children to pass the offering baskets and another to lead the clapping.

Lord's Supper (Group 5): **As we have the Lord's Supper this**

morning, it is important to follow the instructions Jesus has given us. Group 5 will lead us.

Have all of Group 5 come to the front. Those who drew pictures will hold them up so the rest of the children can see them while the student or students assigned to read the Scripture do so. Then have the Group sit down except for the ones reading the sentences and the ones passing the trays. After a prayer, have the first reader read about the bread; then have the servers pass the bread trays. Then have the second reader read about the cup and have the servers pass those trays.

After those partaking have shared in the Communion, say, **After the disciples and Jesus had this supper, they sang a hymn, so let's sing this song.** Display the words to "Jesus, I Love You" (at the back of this book) prominently so the children can see them and sing. (If you don't have a piano in your room, or if you don't have a helper who plays, you could have the church pianist record the song and use the recording for accompaniment.)

Scripture (Group 3). Invite Group 3 to come and help the leader present Psalm 19:7-11. Ask the entire class to repeat verse 11.

Devotional (Group 4): **Today we have been talking about the instructions God gives us and how important it is to follow them. When we follow them, we are successful, we are winners, we know we are doing the right thing and pleasing God. Who can tell us something that God wants us to do?** You should get responses such as "obey parents and teachers," "be kind," "share," "tell the truth," and the like. Discuss the good that comes from following these instructions and the harm that comes from not following them.

Our craft group thought of instructions from everyday life that help us to succeed and do a good job when we follow them and cause problems when we don't follow them. Let's listen to some of those kinds of rules and guidelines. Have the children from Group 4 come to the front and recall some of the ideas they discussed, such as instructions for playing a game or a sport, traffic rules, guidelines for home and school.

Application (Group 2): **God gives us instructions to help us and we will be most happy and successful when we follow them. One of our groups found a special message in their work today. That message is just what we have been talking about. Group 2, come up and show us what you found.**

Have the members of Group 2 stand in front of the class and show their activity pages. Have them say the message in unison or choose one of them to say it.

Prayer. As we pray today, let's ask God to help us to follow His instructions, and to help us follow instructions that parents and teachers give us. Invite children to lead out in sentence prayers if they want to. You close with **Thank You, Lord, that you have given us instructions so we can know how to do what is right. Thank You for sending the Holy Spirit to help us to follow your instructions. Thank You for Jesus, who made the way for us to be forgiven when we mess up and don't follow Your instructions. In Jesus' name we pray. Amen.**

Closing Moments

(10-15 minutes)

Allow the children to get the "bricks" they made during *Transition Time* and build a wall to march around. Sing, or play a recording of, the following song:

Joshua marched around
Jericho,
Marched seven times around
the town.
Joshua marched around
Jericho,
And the walls came tumbling
down.
The people of the Lord gave a
shout,
The trumpet of the Lord
sounded out,
Joshua marched around
Jericho,
And the walls came tumbling
down.

Tell the children they cannot knock the wall down until the last line of the song, Then they can shout and knock it down. The children who made "trumpets" will want to pretend to blow them at the right place in the song. They may rebuild the wall and do the song again until it is time for them to leave.

Play Dough Recipe

Mix 1 cup flour, 1/2 cup salt, and 2 teaspoons cream of tartar in a saucepan. (Do not omit the cream of tartar.) Add 1 cup water, 1 tablespoon cooking oil, and food coloring. Cook, stirring for three minutes or until mixture pulls away from pan. Knead immediately. Store in an airtight container. This recipe makes enough dough for about six children.

Walls of Jericho Bricks

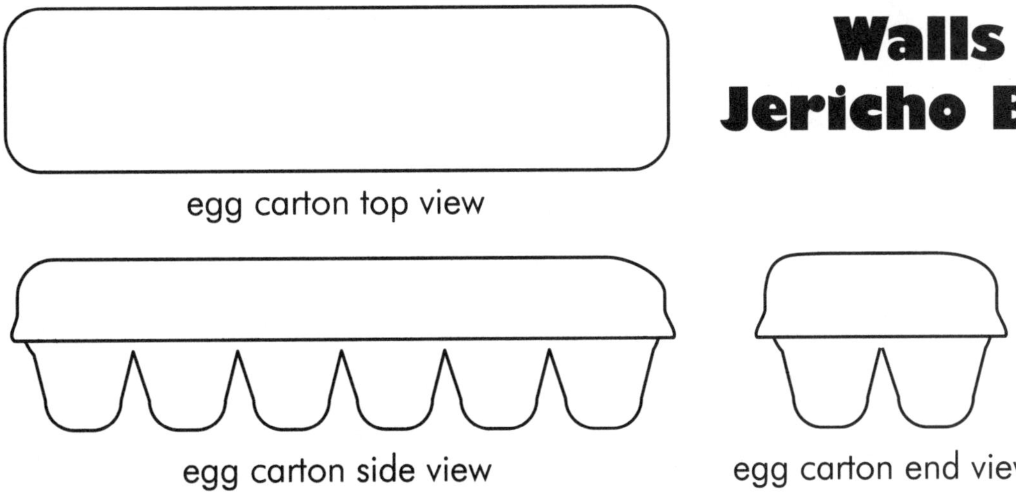

1. Place two egg cartons side by side.

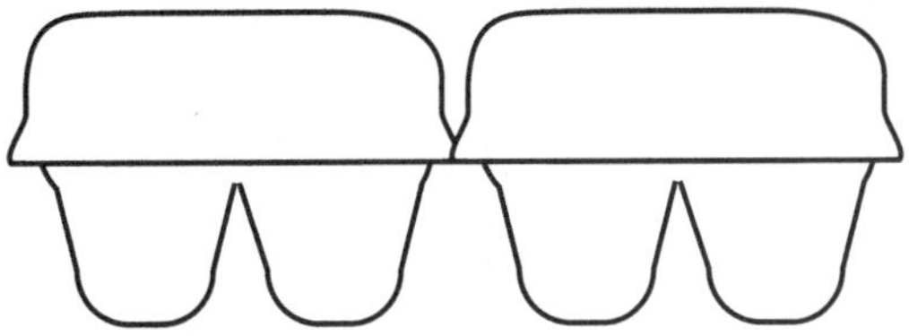

2. Then place another egg carton on top of each one. Tape these together with masking tape.

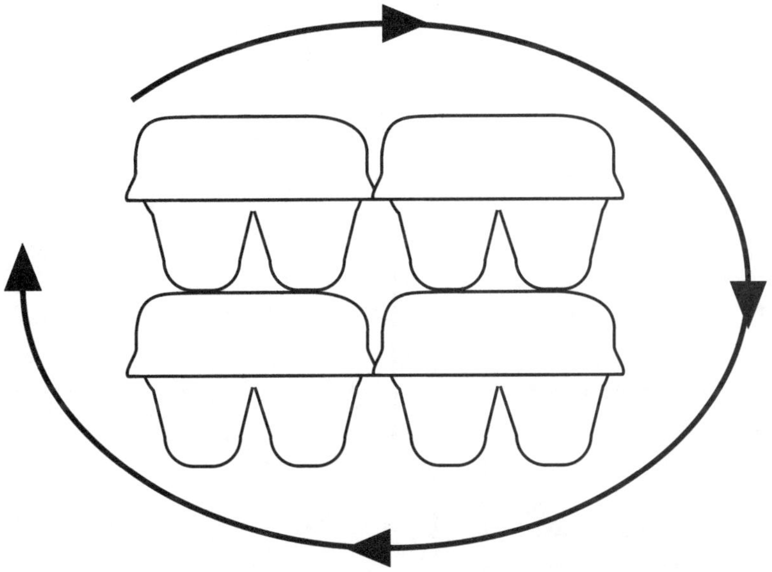

3. Put the assembly on a piece of brown paper and pull the paper up around the egg cartons. Tape it in place. Square off the corners and tape securely.

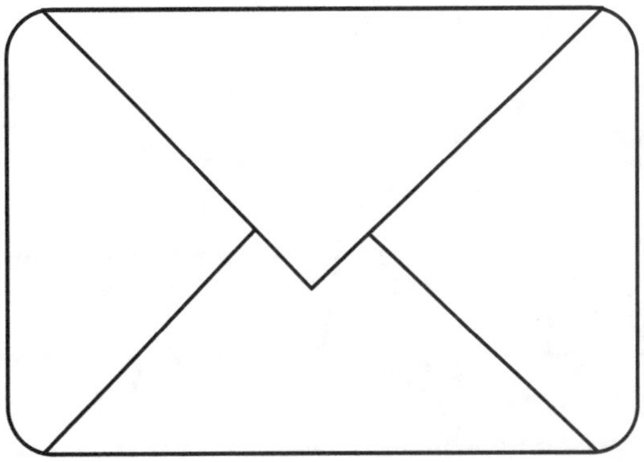

God's People Choose to Do Right

Worship Focus

Worship God because He is the only true God and He is greater than all enemies.

Transition Time

(10-15 minutes)

Allow time for the children to use the rest room and get drinks of water. Welcome them and involve them in the following activity.

Bowling Game. Obtain a child's plastic bowling pin set and ball, or make your own set of pins out of quart-size plastic jugs.

Label the bowling pins "Egyptians," "Amorites," "Moabites," "people of Jericho," "Perizzites," "Canaanites," "Hittites," "Girgashites," "Hivites," and "Jebusites." Label the ball GOD/JOSHUA. Mark a spot on the floor (with a sticker or piece of masking tape) for each bowling pin.

As the children come in, let them line up for a turn rolling the ball to see how many pins they can knock over. Read the labels on the pins and the ball and explain, **These bowling pins stand for the enemies that God and Joshua defeated so that God could give the promised land to the people of Israel. Each of you will have a turn rolling the ball to knock over as many pins as you can. When it is your turn, stand here** (indicate a particular place for them to stand from which to roll the ball; a strip of masking tape would make a good "foul line" that can be removed later) **and roll the ball toward the pins. Count how many fall down, and then go set them all up so the next person can have a turn. Mark your score on the chart and then go to the end of the line. If there's time, maybe you can all get two turns.**

For scoring, have a chart with the numerals 1-10 at the top and allow each child, after setting up the pins, to make a tally mark under the numeral that shows the number of pins that were knocked over. This seems like "keeping score" without ranking the children in a competitive way

If your class is large, it might be good to have more than one game going.

Launching the Theme

(10 minutes)

Use a sports or military musical theme to draw the children's attention. Stand near the set up of bowling pins. Read loudly, from the *International Children's Bible,* Joshua 24:1 and motion for the children to come to you. But if any of them sit down, reread **"these men *stood* before God"** and motion for them to stand.

Then continue reading loudly, as though you are Joshua speaking to a huge crowd. Use lots of vocal expression and body movements as you read.

When you get to verse 4, pick up the bowling pin that's labeled "Egyptians" and hold it over your head. Move it to look like chasing as you read verse 6. When you read in verse 7, **"I caused the sea to cover them,"** toss the pin to an assistant who will take it and drop it into a clean empty trash can. (It can be retrieved later.)

As you read verse 8, pick up the pin labeled "Amorites" and move it back and forth as you read, **"They fought against you."** As you read, **"I destroyed them before you,"** throw that pin to your assistant to put into the trash can.

Continue reading. As you read verse 9, pick up the "Moabites" and hand that pin to a child, telling him or her to hold it. As you read "people of Jericho" in verse 11, hand that pin to another child.

Continue reading and passing out pins until all the pins are distributed. When you get to the end of verse 11, have the children throw all the pins into the trash can.

Read loudly the first part of verse 12, **"While your army**

traveled forward," and begin marching around the room, motioning the children to follow you. As you read, **"I sent hornets ahead of them"** make loud buzzing noises and motion for the children to do the same. After buzzing for a while, motion for the children to be quiet and then read loudly, **"These hornets made the people leave before you came. So you took the land without using swords and bows."** Continue reading verse 13. Pantomime eating from trees and encourage the children to do the same.

Read verse 14. When you get to **"Throw away the false gods,"** make violent throwing motions and encourage the children to do the same.

Read verse 15 forcefully. Say to the children, **Now listen because you have a part to say.**

Read verse 16 and ask the children to repeat it loudly. Coach them. Repeat it once or twice until the children are responding boldly.

Read verses 17 and 18 with much conviction.

Read verses 19 and 20. Then say, **Okay children, you have another part to say, so listen!** Read verse 21 and have the children respond "No! We will serve the Lord."

Read verse 22 and have the children repeat "Yes, it's true! We all see that we have chosen to serve the Lord."

Read the first part of verse 23 with throwing motions. Read loudly and slowly the second part of the verse

Have the children repeat verse 24 after you.

Read verses 25 and 26. Pretend to be writing in a book and putting a large stone under a tree. (Props would be good to have.)

Look sternly at the children as you read verse 27.

Say **Amen!** and clap, encouraging the children to do the same.

Have the children sit down and have a few moments of quietness and relaxation. Then describe the activity centers for the day and help them make their choices and go to the areas in an orderly manner.

Building the Theme

(30 minutes)

1. Song. Have the words to "My Offering" (see the last section of this book) ready in this center. Explain to the children in this group that they will share this song at offering time during *Sharing in Worship*. If they finish learning the song early, they may work on the activity pages.

2. Special Music. The children in this center will be celebrating according to the songs written in Exodus 15. It would be fun to have some dress-up robes and long skirts for them to wear. It would also be good to have at least one tambourine. You may want to make tambourines for this group by attaching bells to the edges of stiff paper plates: use a hole punch to make holes and use twist ties to attach the bells. You may want to use other rhythm instruments that you have available also.

Explain to the children that, as you read the songs, they are to look at you and listen, holding their instruments quietly until you give them the signal to rejoice (a nod of the head, a lifting of a hand) and then they may dance, play their instruments, and shout "Hallelujah," or, "Praise the Lord," for a minute and then at your signal (finger over lips, lowering of hand) they are to be still while you read until the next signal to rejoice.

Read Exodus 15:19-21 (ICB) and then give them the signal to rejoice. After a minute, give them the signal to get quiet and listen. Then read Exodus 15:1 and 2 and give the signal to rejoice. After a minute, give the signal to listen. Read verses 3-7, let them rejoice, get quiet. Read verses 11-13 give the signal to rejoice.

Explain to the children that they will celebrate these during *Sharing in Worship* later.

3. Memorization. Joshua 24:15, from the ICB, the last sentence only. Use Activity page 17A and have the children color in the letters with colored pencils while they practice saying the verse. Then have them paste the colored page onto a heavy paper backing and glue yarn or art paper around the edges for a frame. You might also provide flower stickers for them to place in a few empty spots to make a pretty plaque for their home. Explain to this group that they will recite the verse later in *Sharing in Worship*.

4. Reminder Rock. Give the children in this group copies of Activity page 17B. There are two separate activities that can be done from this page. Have the children cut off the bottom section, containing the "rock" with the words "OBEY GOD" and the heart. Then have them cut out the rock and heart. Set aside the heart. Have the children color the tree trunk, adding leaves, and the tent; they should try to avoid coloring the circle where the "rock" will be. Have them color the rock. Give each child one layer of a facial tissue. Show the children how to put glue in the circle and then crumple up the tissue and press it onto this glued area. Then have them put glue on the back side of the "rock" and press this lightly over the tissue and firmly around the edges of the rock.

As you work, talk with the children about the meaning of the rock under the tree: **Children, why did Joshua put a big rock under the oak tree near the Lord's Holy Tent?** Pause for response. **Yes, he put it there to remind them that they had chosen to serve the Lord. Sometimes God's enemy tries to get us more interested in other things than we are in God. We need to be reminded that we know God is the greatest and most important and He alone is worthy of our worship.**

What are some things that we have in our lives that remind us that we have decided to worship and serve the one true God? Pause for responses, such as Bibles, church buildings, Scripture plaques. **Those are excellent answers. There is one more that we need to think about. We have a special reminder today just as the people of Israel did. No, it's not a rock under a tree. It's our Communion service. Jesus served the bread and juice to His disciples just before He died and told them to remember His death on the cross every time they had Communion. We still do today, just as Jesus said.**

If there is time, the children may color the heart and paste it on a white lacy doily backing or a larger heart cut out of art paper. You may want to punch a hole in the top center, string a piece of yarn through it and allow them to wear it as a necklace. As they work on this project, talk with them about the words on the heart, "Love the Lord with all your heart," and how they can do this.

5. Craft. Provide copies of the mobile pattern from page 16. Have the children cut only the dark lines, then fold on the dotted lines. Have them put paste on the inside surfaces after they have folded the pieces. Help them make hole punches where the little circles indicate. Make a circle of the piece with the words, "THE ONE TRUE GOD" and tape the ends together. Hang the pieces with the words "love," "worship," "serve," and "obey," using yarn or string. Put yarn through the three holes in the top of the circle piece to hang the mobile up.

6. Unit project mural. Have the children add pictures of Joshua talking to the people, the tree near the Holy Tent with the large rock under it. Add the words, "Worship only the one true God." See page 97 for more information about the unit project mural.

Sharing in Worship

(20-25 minutes)

Omit any of the following sections if you did not offer the corresponding activity. You may want to use a musical signal to draw the children to the area. (Sports, military theme.)

Call to Worship (Group 6): Invite the children from Group 6 to display their mural. **Children, our mural is finally complete. Look at all the stories it displays.** Review the mural, asking children to recall the stories each section displays and reciting the verses. **Today's section reminds us that only the one true God is worthy of our worship. We're going to worship Him right now!**

Song. Sing a song about our great, victorious God. There is a Scripture song from Exodus 15:11, KJV, that you might use if your group knows it; or the song with the words, "How great is our God, how great is His name, He's the greatest one, forever the same. He rolled back the waters of the mighty Red Sea. And He said, 'I'll lead you, put your trust in Me."' If you don't know either of these songs, try to find one the children know along this theme

Offering (Group 1): Invite Group 1 to come to share their song. After they sing it once, have them remain standing in front while you say, **The more we learn about God and the great things He does for His people, the more glad we are to worship and serve Him. One way we do this is by giving money to Him for His work here on earth. Let's listen to the song again as we give our offerings.** Choose as many children as you need to pass the offering baskets.

Special Music (Group 2): **Today we learned about how God overcame all of the enemies of His people. His people were very happy when God gave them the victory over enemies. Group 2 is going to present some celebration songs that God's people sang after He defeated their enemies.** Invite the children from Group 2 to come share their celebration song from Exodus 15. Follow the same outline they practiced in their center, but this time invite the entire class to join in the rejoicing after the last portion of Scripture reading.

Scripture (Group 3): Have the children from Group 3 come to the front and display their plaques. Have them recite their verse together. **These words are from Joshua 24:15. Let's read that whole verse together.** Encourage the children to look up the verse in their own Bibles. Then read it aloud from the *International Children's Bible.*

Devotional (Group 5): **Sometimes people wonder why God helped Joshua defeat all those enemies instead of just letting them all live together in the land. They think it seems mean for God to allow the Israelites to have wars with these other people and to destroy them.**

But there is a very good reason God did not want these people living with His people. These other people did not worship

God; they worshiped idols, or false gods. Many of the things they called "worship" were very evil and mean. They would even kill some of their children because they thought that pleased their "gods."

God knew He could not let such wicked people live with the people who worshiped Him. If He did, they would convince some of His people to worship their idols instead of the one true God. That is the reason God defeated the enemies of Israel.

Invite Group 5 to come forward and display their mobiles. **Group 5 has made some reminders for us to worship, serve, obey, and love the one true God. We don't have people around us who would try to get us to worship idols, today. But we still have to be careful. Many of the people around us think the things they can buy with money are more important than God. That's just like worshiping idols. I suppose God could help us defeat people like that in a war, as He did for Joshua, But, instead, He has chosen a better way. He has a secret weapon He wants us to use to show people they should worship the one true God. Do you know what it is?** Allow the children to respond.

That secret weapon is love! Have you heard that Jesus told people to love their enemies? Jesus said if we would love our enemies and do good to them, we would be like our Father in Heaven. (Read Matthew 5:44, 45.)

The Bible tells us that God does not want anyone to be destroyed, but He wants all people to be saved. Listen to this. (Read 2 Peter 3:9.) **In His Word, God tells us that when we please Him, He can make even our enemies be at peace with us. It is not our job to fight our enemies. We are to love them and let God fight our enemies for us. One way we can love our enemies is to tell them not to be God's enemies, but to love God and be saved! And when they're not God's enemies anymore, then they won't be our enemies anymore!**

Lord's Supper (Group 4): Invite Group 4 to bring their activity pages to the front of the group and display them. Address the following questions (or similar ones, depending on the exact answers you get) to the members of this group:

What do your pages show? How Joshua put the large rock under the tree near the Holy Tent to remind the people what He had done for them.

Why was it important to remember that? So they would always love and serve only the one true God.

What reminders do we have today to help us remember what God has done for us? Let the children mention several.

What special thing did Jesus tell His disciples to do to remember that He died for them? The Lord's Supper.

Thank you, Group 4. You may sit down now.

Children, when we eat the Lord's Supper, we are reminded that Jesus loved us and died for us. That is the reason this part of our worship is so important. Jesus told us to do it, and we want to obey Him and remember Him. We want to worship Him in this special way.

Offer a prayer and serve the Lord's Supper. Involve the children in as much of this (praying and/or serving) as they are able.

Prayer: **Lord, You are the one true God, and You are greater than all enemies. Thank You that because of Jesus we are no longer Your enemies. Help us to always love, obey, serve and worship You with all our hearts. In Jesus' name we pray. Amen.**

Closing Moments

(10-15 minutes)

Relay Response Game. Line the children up in two teams. Explain that you will take turns making a statement to one team and then the other. Each team must decide whether the statement is the right thing to do. If it is, the person at the front of that team must say, "We will serve the Lord. We will obey Him." If it is not the right thing to do, the person in front must say "No! We will serve the Lord." Each team may help the person in front with the response. If the person responds properly, give him a sticker and let him go to the back of the line and then give a statement to the other team. If the response is incorrect, the person stays at the front and the statement goes to the other team. Each child will stay in the front until he or she answers a statement correctly.

Some sample statements and responses:

Stay home from Sunday school to read the funny paper.

No! We will serve the Lord.

Pay attention to the Bible school teacher.

We will serve the Lord. We will obey Him.

Complain when it's time for family devotions.

No! We will serve the Lord.

Thank God for food when you have a snack with friends.

We will serve the Lord. We will obey Him.

Give a nice toy to a child who doesn't have any nice toys.

We will serve the Lord. We will obey Him.

Ignore mother when she says to turn off the TV.

No! We will serve the Lord.

Hide your offering money and keep it to buy candy.

No! We will serve the Lord.

Memory Verse

Fill in the letters with colored pencils, crayons, or pieces of yarn. Cut on the line. Then glue the page on to heavy paper or cardboard to make it stiff.

Glue yarn or strips of art paper around the edges to make a pretty border. Put a hole at the top in the center if you want to hang it on a wall.

t here.

As for me
and
my family,
we will
serve
the Lord!

(Joshua 24:15, *ICB*)

Reminder Rock

Joshua 24:26, 27

Cut here.

Deborah Helps Barak Do a Hard Job

Worship Focus

Worship God because He gives us strength to do difficult jobs.

Transition Time

(10-15 minutes)

Helping Match Game. Before today's session, obtain index cards, stickers, and markers to make a matching game. Put a helping situation on one half of the card and the kind of help needed on the other half of the card. Cut the card into two puzzle pieces. Also make two signs, "Hard Job" and "Easy Job." Post one sign on one side of the room and the other on the other side.

Give one half of the card to each student as you greet him when he arrives. Then, at a signal, have students move around the room to find their partners. After they have found them, the student pairs must sit on the appropriate side of the room, either "Hard Job" or "Easy Job." Play continues until all partners are together. Use the following suggestions to help you get started. Make appropriate ones for your students.

*My mom is doing the laundry/so I will pick up my clothes.

*My sister needs help on her math/so I will help her with math.

*There is trash all over the ground/so I will help pick it up.

Launching the Theme

(10 minutes)

Ask each pair of students to remain seated in the "Hard Job" or "Easy Job" section of the room. Take time to discuss why the pairs thought it was an easy or hard job. There should be some discussion and hopefully some difference of opinion. Stress that jobs may be considered difficult because they take our time, money, or giving of ourselves.

There were different opinions on whether these were easy or hard jobs. Easy jobs seem that way because they don't take much time or effort. Hard jobs usually take more of our time and effort or even our money. It may involve a longer period of time or it may involve our giving up something we really want. The job may be hard because some people might get angry or upset with us. It could be a hard job because we can't always have help—sometimes we have to do the job ourselves.

But you're not alone when you do these hard jobs. There is Someone who is always ready to help us do the hard jobs—God. Since God always does what is best and right, He will be there to help us do the right thing too—even when it is difficult. Today we will worship and praise God because He helps us by giving us strength to do the hard jobs.

Summarize the available activities for *Building the Theme* and allow students to choose the group in which they would like to participate. Try to have an equal number of children in each group.

Building the Theme

(30 minutes)

1. Call to Worship. This group will lead the Call to Worship during *Sharing in Worship*.

Help the students find Psalm 28:6 in their Bibles. Read the verse together. Print the verse on the chalkboard or a piece of poster board. Ask the students to name times when God has helped them. Encourage the pupils to name at least as many situations when God helped them as the number of students in the group. Write these on the chalkboard or poster board. Assign one situation to each student. (Suggestions: God helped me feel better when I was ill; God helped me remember what I learned for my spelling test; God helped me tell my friend about Jesus.)

During *Sharing in Worship* we will lead the large group in a responsive reading. That means that the large group will say something and then we will give a response. We will need one of you to lead the large group. Then after our group responds together, one of you will tell something that fits with our response. Here is an example:

The large group will say, "Praise the Lord."

Our group might say, "He heard my prayer for help."

Then Drew might say, "God helped me not to be afraid of the dark."

The large group and our group will repeat what they said the first time and someone else will tell another situation where God helped him.

Practice this with the volunteer who will lead the large group saying the first part, the group saying the second part, and volunteers telling situations.

2. Scripture Reading. This activity is for older or gifted students. You will need activity page 18A.

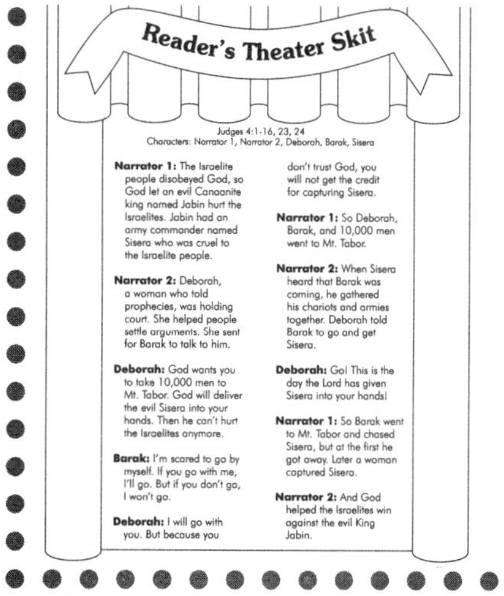

Reader's Theater Skit

Judges 4:1-16, 23, 24

Characters: Narrator 1, Narrator 2, Deborah, Barak, Sisera

Narrator 1: The Israelite people disobeyed God, so God let an evil Canaanite king named Jabin hurt the Israelites. Jabin had an army commander named Sisera who was cruel to the Israelite people.

Narrator 2: Deborah, a woman who told prophecies, was holding court. She helped people settle arguments. She sent for Barak to talk to him.

Deborah: God wants you to take 10,000 men to Mt. Tabor. God will deliver the evil Sisera into your hands. Then he can't hurt the Israelites anymore.

Barak: I'm scared to go by myself. If you go with me, I'll go. But if you don't go, I won't go.

Deborah: I will go with you. But because you don't trust God, you will not get the credit for capturing Sisera.

Narrator 1: So Deborah, Barak, and 10,000 men went to Mt. Tabor.

Narrator 2: When Sisera heard that Barak was coming, he gathered his chariots and armies together. Deborah told Barak to go and get Sisera.

Deborah: Go! This is the day the Lord has given Sisera into your hands!

Narrator 1: So Barak went to Mt. Tabor and chased Sisera, but at the first he got away. Later a woman captured Sisera.

Narrator 2: And God helped the Israelites win against the evil King Jabin.

You will need to assign parts to the students and have them go over their lines two or three times. Help with words and characterization as necessary. You will need two narrators, Deborah, Barak, and Sisera (a nonspeaking part).

We will present a version of today's Bible story. This is a play where we will read our parts. This will be part of our devotional during our worship.

Practice the play several times until it goes smoothly. If you have younger students who can't read, record this ahead of time with adults or teens reading the part. Then let the children pantomime the parts of Deborah, Barak, and Sisera. Extra children can be either Israelites or Canaanites.

3. Offering. This group will make offering containers for all of the pupils and will give the offering prayer during *Sharing in Worship.* Provide one empty container (such as a gelatin box or juice can) for each student in the large group, construction paper cut to a size slightly larger than the container, crayons or markers, scissors, stickers, and glue.

As students cover the cans with construction paper and decorate them, lead the following discussion.

Today we are worshiping God because He helps us do hard jobs. Sometimes we are the people that God wants to use to help other people do their jobs. One group of people who does a hard job and needs our help is missionaries. Our offering money helps missionaries do their jobs. What do missionaries do? Allow response. Be sure to emphasize that missionaries might live in a different culture, teach other people about Jesus, work in churches and Bible schools. **Can you name one missionary that our church helps with our offerings?**

If you have the resources and support, you might want to take a few moments each week during this unit's offering time to tell more about the missionaries your church supports. It would be helpful to bring pictures and items for students to see. Be sure to have a map marked with the location where the missionary serves. If someone is close to that particular missionary, he could come speak for a few moments.

Help this group of students to write a prayer to be said before the offering is taken. Focus the prayer on these ideas: thanking God for helping us do hard jobs, thanking God that we can help Him by helping others do hard jobs, asking God to bless the money given to help missionaries do their jobs.

Print the prayer on poster board or the chalkboard. Ask the group to say their prayer together during *Sharing in Worship.*

4. Special Music. This group will present a song before the devotional during *Sharing in Worship.*

Help the students find Psalm 68:19 and Psalm 28:6 in their Bibles. Give these instructions: **Find the Old Testament book of Psalms. It is near the middle of your Bible. Find the large number 68** (or 28). **Then find the small 19** (or 6). **We will read these verses together as a group.**

Encourage the students to put the words of these verses to the tune of "London Bridge."

Song of Praise

Praise the Lord day by day,
Day by day, day by day.
Praise the Lord day by day.
God our Savior helps us.

Praise the Lord, He heard my prayer,
Heard my prayer, heard my prayer.
Praise the Lord, He heard my prayer.
He heard my prayer for help.

Practice the song so students will feel comfortable in leading the song. Before practicing, remind students again to remember times that God has helped them do difficult jobs.

5. Devotional. This group will present the devotional during *Sharing in Worship.* Provide large sheets of paper, two pieces of poster board, and crayons or markers.

Write these words on a chalkboard: Bible verses, prayer, friends, parents, teachers.

How does the Bible help us do hard jobs? It reminds us to do what is right, tells us about God's help for us, encourages us. **How does prayer help us do difficult things?** God hears our prayers and gives us help, strength, and encouragement. **How do our friends help us?** They sometimes assist us in our jobs or encourage us or give us advice. **How do parents and teachers help us do a difficult job?** They tell us how to do a job and sometimes assist us. They can give us examples of people who have done these kinds of jobs before.

Beside each word on the board, ask students to name specific situations where each of these groups could help us in a difficult job. For example: Bible verses remind us of the hard jobs we have to do; God answers our prayers for help in doing hard jobs; friends may help us do a difficult job, such as cleaning up a yard; parents and teachers may teach us how to do a difficult job, such as learning math facts.

Divide each piece of paper in half with a diagonal line. One one side, a picture of the situation or job will be drawn. On the other side, the way God gives help will be drawn. After each student has drawn one situation and the way God will helps, put the sheets together in a big book format. Use the poster board as the front and back covers of the book. Title the book, "God Helps Us Do Hard Jobs."

Older students could create a big book of Bible people who did difficult jobs, such as Abraham, Moses, David, Elijah, and Jesus. Each student should draw a picture of the Bible character and write a sentence or two about how God helped that person do his difficult job.

During *Sharing in Worship,* present the big book to the large group. Ask members to show their part of the book and explain their pictures.

6. Prayer. This group will brainstorm difficult things that they think most students will have to do. Use activity page 18B to help get started on prayer ideas. Have one older student act as the secretary and list the items on the chalkboard or a piece of poster board. You might want to divide the board up into sections, such as "Difficult things we do at home," "Difficult things we do at school," or "Difficult things we do when we're out somewhere." Students can fill out the page to help them lead in prayer.

During our worship time, we will lead in prayer to ask God to help us do these difficult things. I need volunteers to lead in prayer for one or two specific items. You will need to say a short prayer—one or two sentences—about each idea that you have chosen. Allow each child to choose for what he will pray, based on the charts the group made. Try not to allow repetition so that all areas will be included in the prayer.

Sharing in Worship

(20-25 minutes)

Omit any of the following sections if you did not offer the corresponding activity.

Call to Worship (Group 1): **God gives us help when we must do hard jobs. Today we will worship Him for His help. Group 1 will lead us in a responsive reading now.**

Scripture Reading (Group 2): **God's Word, the Bible, tells us the true story of how Deborah showed Barak that God would help him in the difficult job he had to do. Our Scripture readers will present a short readers' theater presentation to review the Bible story.**

Lord's Supper: Each week at this time we remember Jesus and the difficult job He did for us. He died for us, enduring all the pain and suffering for our sins. He loved us so much that He was willing to die for us. Be sure to give a short explanation of the Lord's Supper for any visitors you may have.

Offering (Group 3): **We worship God because He helps us do difficult jobs. Sometimes we can help other people do their hard jobs too. Missionaries have a difficult job to do, and we can help them. Group 3 will give each of you an offering container that they made. Take this home and put money in it to give to the missionaries supported by our church. Bring your offering each week to our worship time.**

At this time, review the short talk about a missionary your church supports. You could ask students in Group 3 to present the material they learned about the missionaries. Ask a student from this group to have the offering prayer and have two students take up the offering.

Special Music (Group 4): **Group 4 will sing "Song of Praise" for us.** Let the group sing the song twice. Ask the large group to sing it through the second time.

Devotional (Group 5): **Sometimes we have to do hard jobs. They may take lots of time or some of our money, or maybe we're afraid that people will laugh at us or make fun of us if we do this job.**

But God has given us help in doing hard things. One way He helps us is by giving us the Bible. Group 5 shows the appropriate book pages at this time. **God gave us the Bible to remind us to do what's right and encourage us to do what is right. There are all kinds of stories of people who did the right thing, even when it was difficult. Think about people like Abraham, Moses, David, Elijah, even Jesus. When you need help or have questions about a hard job, the Bible can be a source of strength and answers.** If you did the alternate project, have that group show their big book and explain the pictures at this time.

Another way God helps us is by hearing our prayers. We don't have to work alone at these hard jobs. God listens to us and helps us by giving us strength. When we don't feel like we can do a hard job or feel like we're strong enough to pull it off, God can help. He doesn't want us to have to do it alone. Have the group show the appropriate pictures from the book at this time.

Since God wants to help us, He also gives us friends. Show the appropriate pages from the big book at this time. **Friends can help us do a hard job like raking leaves or cleaning a garage or studying for a test. They can help us get the job done quicker, and we'll probably have a lot more fun.**

And God gives us parents and teachers to help us with hard jobs. Show appropriate pictures at this time. **Parents and teachers can teach us how to do a difficult job quicker and easier. They can help us with difficult jobs and support us.**

We worship God for His wonderful help for us. He knows that we have jobs that are hard for us to do. He knows our strengths—what we're good at—and our weaknesses—what we need lots of help with. He knows exactly what kinds of help we need and when we will need it. We need to remember that when we are in a hard situation and ask God for help right then. He does not want us to have to work alone. That's why He has given us some resources or helpers.

Prayer (Group 6): **Let's thank God for all the ways He helps us. We can also say thank you to people who help us. Our prayer group will help lead us in a special prayer now.** Ask Group 6 to come at this point to show the list that they brainstormed together. Use activity page 18B for the entire group for ideas. Ask Group 6 to lead in prayer like this with each situation:

"For all of those students who need help in school . . ." and the large group would say, "Help us, God."

Closing Moments

(10-15 minutes)

Make sure the room is clean and everything is put away. Play "Eraser Tag" with Deborah and Barak. Use two chalkboard erasers. Put one on top of a child's head. This child, "Deborah," must walk around the room and try to tag "Barak" (who also has an eraser on his head). If the eraser falls off, the person is out, and another is chosen. The idea is for Deborah to try to tag Barak and say, "God will help you." Continue as long as there is interest until the end of the session. Try to make sure that all students get a chance to participate.

Reader's Theater Skit

Judges 4:1-16, 23, 24
Characters: Narrator 1, Narrator 2, Deborah, Barak, Sisera

Narrator 1: The Israelite people disobeyed God, so God let an evil Canaanite king named Jabin hurt the Israelites. Jabin had an army commander named Sisera who was cruel to the Israelite people.

Narrator 2: Deborah, a woman who told prophecies, was holding court. She helped people settle arguments. She sent for Barak to talk to him.

Deborah: God wants you to take 10,000 men to Mt. Tabor. God will deliver the evil Sisera into your hands. Then he can't hurt the Israelites anymore.

Barak: I'm scared to go by myself. If you go with me, I'll go. But if you don't go, I won't go.

Deborah: I will go with you. But because you don't trust God, you will not get the credit for capturing Sisera.

Narrator 1: So Deborah, Barak, and 10,000 men went to Mt. Tabor.

Narrator 2: When Sisera heard that Barak was coming, he gathered his chariots and armies together. Deborah told Barak to go and get Sisera.

Deborah: Go! This is the day the Lord has given Sisera into your hands!

Narrator 1: So Barak went to Mt. Tabor and chased Sisera, but at the first he got away. Later a woman captured Sisera.

Narrator 2: And God helped the Israelites win against the evil King Jabin.

God will give me strength to do difficult things.

Gideon Chooses To Be Brave

Worship Focus

Worship God because He always does right and He helps us do what is right.

Transition Time

(10-15 minutes)

Greet each child as he comes into the room. Allow time for the children to use the rest room and get drinks of water. Welcome newcomers and involve everyone in the following activity.

Upset the Midianites. Arrange the chairs in a circle with one less chair than there are pupils. Go around the circle and whisper to each student whether he is a trumpet-blower, a shouter, or a torchbearer. Appoint one student to stand in the middle of the circle and be Gideon. When Gideon calls out one of those groups, those pupils must run to a different chair. Gideon must try to sit on one of the empty chairs. The pupil left without a chair becomes the next Gideon. As the pupils move, they must act out their parts—torchbearers hold their left hands high; trumpet-blowers hold their hands to their mouths and make a trumpet sound; shouters shout, "A sword for the Lord and for Gideon."

Play this game as long as time allows.

Launching the Theme

(10 minutes)

Let's see how much you can remember about some brave men in the Bible. I'll tell you something about each one, and you tell me whether it's right:

1. Joshua led God's people around the city of Jericho for six days. On the seventh day, Joshua said, "I've had enough. Let's quit!"

2. One night, Gideon and his men sneaked down to the edge of the Midianite camp with their torches, empty jars, and trumpets. When they go to the edge of the camp, Gideon said, "Don't make a sound. Turn around, and let's get out of here!"

3. David looked at the five small stones he had gathered for his sling. Then he looked at the giant Goliath and said, "There is no way I can best him."

4. Daniel knew King Darius had commanded that anyone who prayed to any god or man besides the king for thirty days would be thrown into the lion's den. Daniel said, "I don't want to be a lion's meal. I'll wait thirty days and then I'll pray."

How many of you have marched around an enemy city? How many of you have faced a giant? How many of you have fought with only a trumpet and a torch? How many of you have faced a den of hungry lions? Probably none of us have had any of these things happen to us.

But how many of you have been in a scary storm? Or a car accident? How many of you have had to stay in the hospital? How many of you have had to stay home alone at night? How many of you have had to help at home when your parents or brothers or sisters were sick? How did you feel when you did that? Were you really scared? Did you think you could do it by yourself? But we don't have to be alone; God will help us just as He helped Joshua, Gideon, David, and Daniel. And today we will worship God because He helps us to be brave.

Summarize the activities for *Building the Theme* and allow children to choose the groups in which they would like to participate. Try to have an equal number of students in each group.

Building the Theme

(30 minutes)

1. Call to Worship. This group will make "Psalm Mobiles" to present during *Sharing in Worship.* Provide enough copies of activity page 19A, crayons or markers, scissors, and yarn.

Have students find Psalm 46:1-3 in their Bibles. Read the Scripture together and discuss it.

We've talked today about how God helped Joshua, Gideon, David, and Daniel be brave. What do these verses say God

will do for us? Help us in times of trouble, be our protection and strength. **God will be with us even if what terrible things happen?** Earth shakes; mountains fall into the sea.

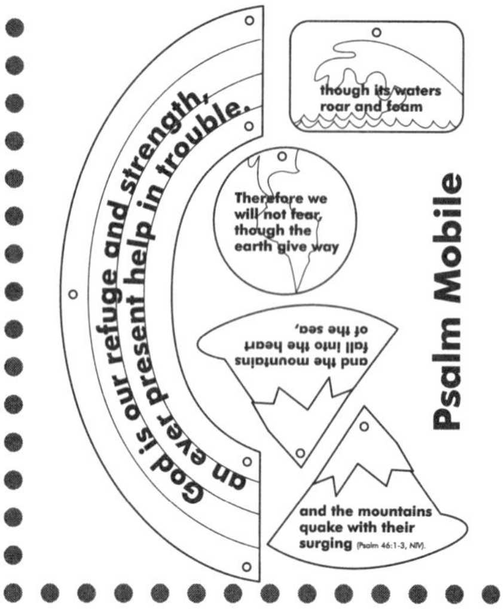

Pupils should color the mobile shapes. Then they cut the shapes out and arrange the shapes in the correct order of the verses. Then they tie the mobile shapes onto the rainbow and hang with a string from the top. As the children present the mobiles to the group, they will recite the Scripture or one child can read the Scripture aloud.

2. Scripture. Older students might make a clothesline time line now. Provide copies of activity page 19B, Bibles, paper, crayons, clothespins, and string.

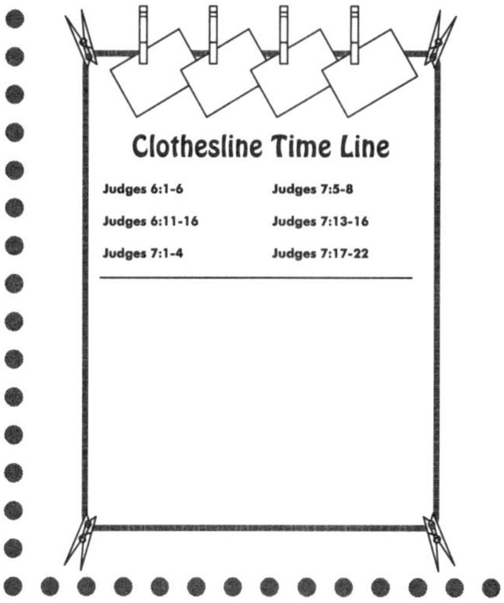

Read the Bible story again and divide the group up into five parts. Assign one or two students to draw each picture and write a short statement about it.

After you have completed your picture, hang it on our string. Make sure the pictures are in the order in which they happened in the story. We will show and explain our time line during *Sharing in Worship*.

If you have younger students, give more guidance and help in making the time line.

3. Offering. If you are using this time to teach students more about the missionaries your church supports, have a speaker talk to this group about that. You may talk about a different missionary each week or continue the thoughts from last week, and show slides or pictures if you have them available. Be sure to show a map with the location of the missionary marked on it. Make sure these students are familiar with the information because they will be presenting it during the offering portion of *Sharing in Worship.*

Missionaries have to be brave too. They are away from their homes and their friends and their families sometimes. The people might live differently than the missionaries are used to. The people may speak a different language. If the people don't believe in God, it may be difficult.

We can worship God by giving our money to help missionaries do their hard jobs.

4. Special Music. This group will present a song for *Sharing in Worship.* Read Psalm 56:3 with the students. Sing the song "God Is So Good" with the new words, "When I'm afraid, I will trust in You."

When are some times that you are afraid? List responses on the chalkboard. **What does this verse tell us we are to do when we are afraid?** Trust in God. **What does it mean to "trust"?** Allow pupil responses. **To "trust" God means to believe what He tells us in His Word. We believe that He is always with us, and that He will help us to be brave and do what is right.**

Use the pupils' responses on the chalkboard to write new stanzas for the song. Substitute different phrases for "when I'm afraid." (Suggestions: when I'm alone, when I am scared, when there's a storm, when it is night, when I could cry, when I need help.) Choose several of the stanzas to present during *Sharing in Worship.* Practice the song and verses several times. If you have time during *Sharing in Worship,* teach it to the large group.

5. Devotional. This group will prepare skits for the devotional for *Sharing in Worship.*

Ask the pupils to name times when God helps them be brave. Read the following situation to help them get started.

Steve asked his brother if he could borrow his bike. Accidentally, the bike got dented when Steve ran into a tree. What does Steve need to do?

While taking a spelling test at school, Sarah saw Emily cheating from a page in her desk. What does Sarah need to do?

A new boy moved next door to Eric. At school the next day, Eric sees the boy who looks as though he's lost. What could Eric do?

Ask the group to come up with other situations where students need to be brave. For each situation, ask them to write a prayer the student could say and an action the child could take. (For instance, Steve needs to ask for courage to tell his brother the truth and then do it.)

Divide the group into pairs and assign one situation to each group. Each pair will discuss, write, and act out a situation.

Then they will need to practice acting out their situation several times to present as the devotional. Help with dialogue, spelling, and writing as needed.

6 Prayer. This group will lead the prayer during *Sharing in Worship.* **God asked Joshua to march around Jericho. God asked Gideon to lead an army of only 300 men into battle. God asked Deborah to go with Barak to do a hard job. What are some hard things God asks us to do?** Take time to list specific ones the students suggest.

God told Joshua, "I will be with you." God told Gideon, "I will be with you." What does God say He will do for us? Help us in times of trouble. **Do you believe that? How do you know? Can you see that just as God helped those men, He will help you too?**

Ask students to choose one thing God asks them to do and illustrate it through a picture (either on paper or on acetate to be shown on the overhead projector). Each student will show his illustration and say a sentence prayer, such as "Help me, God, to be kind to a friend that no one else likes." "Help me to be quiet when I want to talk in a mean way about someone."

Sharing in Worship

(20-25 minutes)

Omit any of the following sections if you did not offer the corresponding activity.

Call to Worship (Group 1): **We worship God because He always does the right thing. He helps us to be brave and He will always be there for us as "an ever present help in trouble." That means God's help is always available—you don't have to wait for it.** Have Group 1 show the Psalm mobiles and go over Psalm 46:1-3 with the entire group.

Scripture Reading (Group 2): Have two or three good readers read the Scripture passages while students show their pictures on the clothesline time line. **God's Word, the Bible, tells us how God gave strength to Gideon. Our Scripture readers will review the story of Gideon with us just now.**

Lord's Supper: Just as God promised to be with Gideon, God promises to be with us as we do difficult jobs for Him. God did a very difficult thing when He let His Son come to earth and die for us. Can you imagine how difficult that was for God, knowing the outcome, that Jesus would be hurt and killed? Let's take time now to thank God for loving us so much that He sent Jesus.

Offering (Group 3): At this time, present the new information about the missionaries your church supports. Let students show pictures or slides if you have them. Point out the location on a map. Ask students in this group to give a prayer for the offering and take it up. Make sure to take the money that students have been saving in their offering containers at home.

Special Music (Group 4): Have Group 4 sing "God Is So Good" with the new words. If time permits, let them teach the large group the new verses.

Devotional (Group 5): **Being brave takes lots of things. It takes thinking, praying, and trusting God. When we think about courage and being brave, we think about heroes—Bible heroes and people we know who have done very great things, such as saving people from fires or feeding many hungry people or big things like that. But every day, in big and small ways, you have to be brave and have courage. You might not think of these things as being brave, but they are. As the people in Group 5 present their skits, think about a situation that you might have been in that's similar to one of their situations.**

Ask the pairs of children from Group 5 to present their skits one at a time. After each skit, take a few moments for any discussion.

Prayer (Group 6): Ask the students in this group to present their individual prayer pictures at this time. To involve everyone in praying, take a moment to pray individually for each student who is present. Or include everyone in a sentence prayer when they ask God to help them with a difficult task they have this week.

Closing Moments

(10-15 minutes)

Brook. Play the game of "Brook." Put a rope down on the floor. Make it straight. Students line up along it. They jump over the rope brook if you say a word that has to do with bravery, courage, or worshiping God. They don't jump if you say other words. The object is to go quickly and say the words to get students to jump. If they jump on a wrong word or step on the rope, they are "wet" and have to get out of the game.

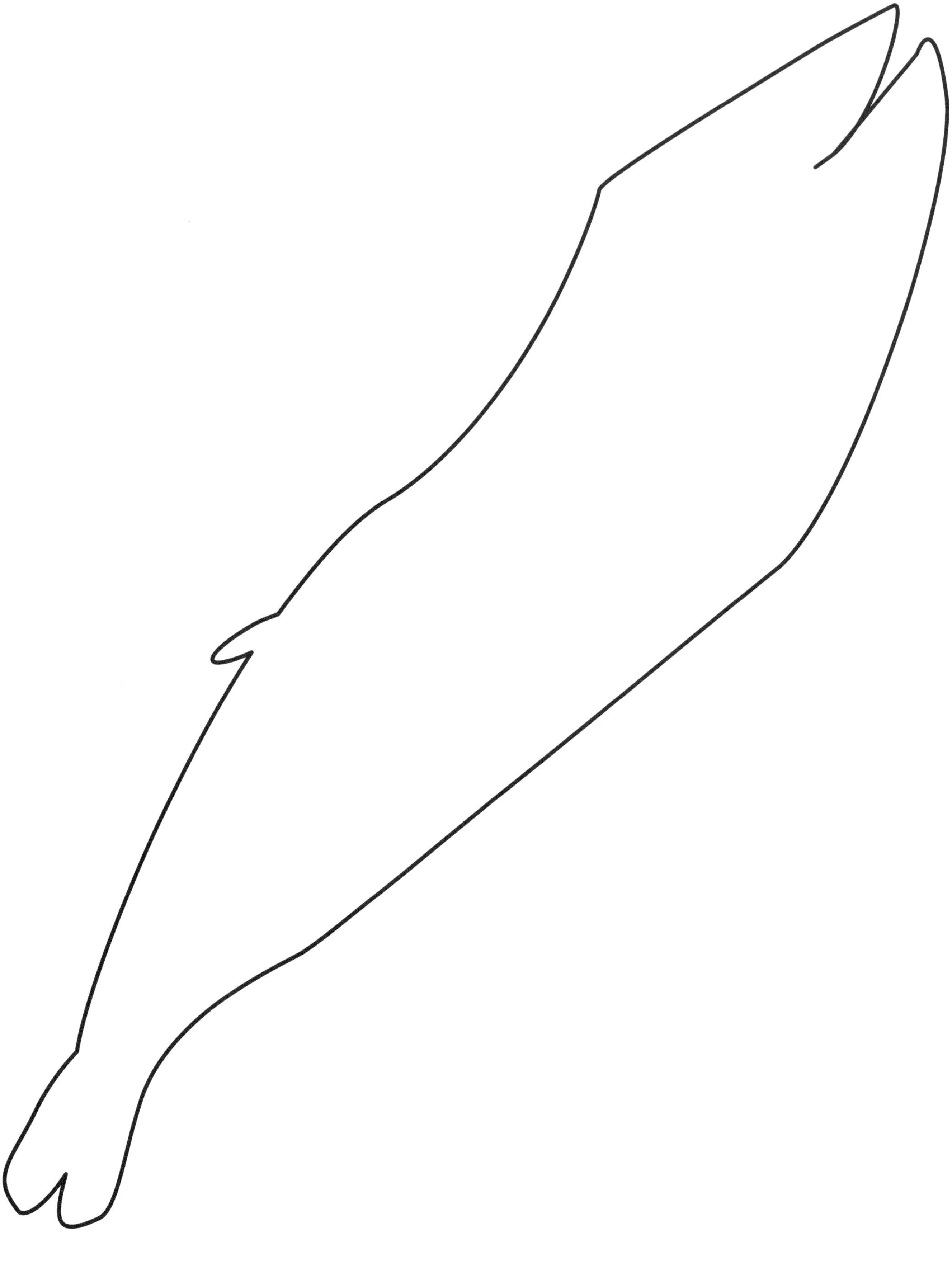

Psalm Mobile

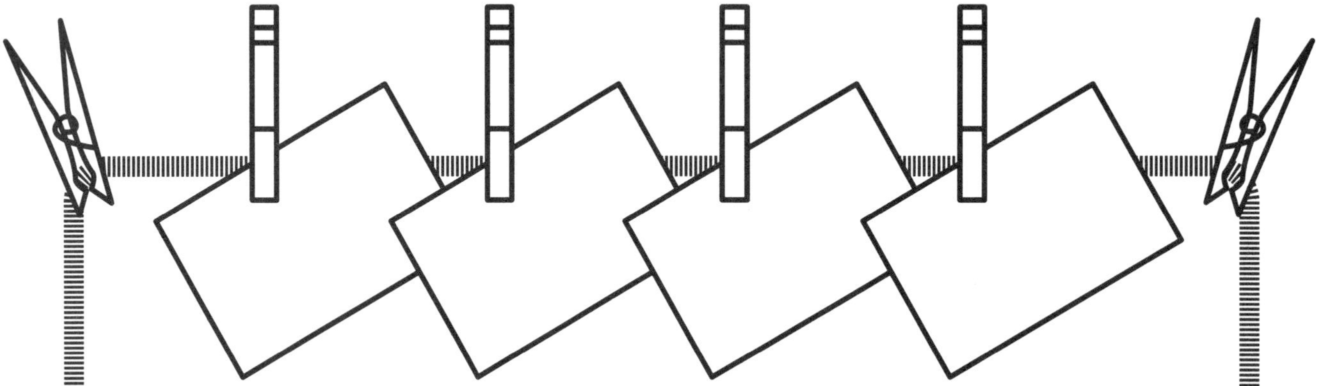

Clothesline Time Line

Judges 6:1-6

Judges 6:11-16

Judges 7:1-4

Judges 7:5-8

Judges 7:13-16

Judges 7:17-22

Ruth Works Hard

Worship Focus

Worship God because He always does what is right.

Transition Time

(10-15 minutes)

Occupation Concentration. Play a memory game to help students relax. Before class, get index cards and different colored markers. Make matching cards with an occupation on one card, and what the occupation does on the other card. Include a variety of jobs, such as computer programmer, carpenter, medical technician, farmer, real estate salesman. Make at least ten match pairs. If you have a large class, make more than one set. (Sets may be identical. You may wish to use a different color of index card or a different color of marker for each set to make it easier to keep a complete set together.) Mix up all cards and then turn them over on the table. Students must turn over an occupation and the matching description to keep the cards.

Ruth, Ruth, Orpah. Play this game with younger children. Ask all students to form a circle. Appoint a pupil to be "Naomi." (Use "Boaz" when "It" is a boy.) "Naomi" walks around the outside of the circle, patting each pupil on the head, and saying, "Ruth" with each pat. At "Naomi's" discretion, she suddenly says, "Orpah," and "Orpah" must chase and tag "Naomi" before she gets around the circle back to the empty space.

Launching the Theme

(10 minutes)

Before Sunday, ask other adult leaders or guest adults to present the following riddles about the following occupations: a parent, mail carrier, police officer, grocery clerk, trash collector. If you have adult speakers, let them say more about their occupation, but still keep it in the form of a riddle. If you cannot get enough adults to present, either ask older students to read the riddles aloud or ask a teacher to present them to the group. Students can raise their hands to guess at any time during the riddle.

There are people who help us every day. Listen and see whether you guess who some of these people are by the clue that you hear. If you know the answer, raise your hand. Be prepared to tell one thing that person does for you each day.

I work in your city.
I walk around the city a lot!
I often drive a truck to carry everything.
I bring things to your house.
Sometimes I bring special things just for you.
Who am I? (mail carrier)

I try to help you find you what you need.
I work in a store.
I usually work with your parent, but I can help you.
I put new food on the shelves for you to see.
Sometimes you need to pay me money for things you get.
Who am I? (grocery clerk)

I work in your city.
Sometimes I walk, and sometimes I drive around.
I try to keep you and your friends safe.
I want you to think of me as your friend.
Sometimes I direct traffic.
Who am I? (police officer)

I drive a truck and I walk around.
I keep picking up things that you leave behind.
I work to keep your city clean.
I often wear a uniform.
Who am I? (trash collector)

I care for you a great deal.
I work to take care of you in many different ways.
Sometimes I work outside the house, and sometimes I work in the house.
I help you get clothes, and I feed you.
I want you to grow up healthy and strong, and I love you!
Who am I? (parent)

The people we've mentioned do many things for us. They help

us get things we need and want. You probably see most of these people every day, and they help to make your life better. But there is Someone who does things for us that no one else can do. Who is that? God! Today we will spend time worshiping Him because of all the good things He does for us.

Summarize the activities for *Building the Theme* and allow children to choose the groups in which they would like to participate. Try to have an equal number of children in each group.

Building the Theme

(30 minutes)

1. Call to Worship. This group will lead the Call to Worship during *Sharing in Worship.*

Psalm 33:1-9, *ICB*

1 Sing to the Lord, you who do what is right. Honest people should praise him.
2 Praise the Lord on the harp. Make music for him on the ten-stringed lyre.
3 Sing a new song to him. Play well and joyfully.
4 God's word is true.
Everything he does is right.
5 He loves what is right and fair.
The Lord's love fills the earth.
6 The sky was made at the Lord's command.
By the breath from his mouth, he made all the stars.
7 He gathered the water in the sea into a heap.
He made the great ocean stay in its place.
8 All the earth should worship the Lord.
The whole world should fear him.
9 He spoke, and it happened.
He commanded, and it appeared.

Help students find Psalm 33:1-9 in their Bibles. Have the pupils listen as you read these verses. Help them decide on motions and movement to express each idea in the different verses. Do not limit the pupils to illustrating every happening literally. Rather, let there also be movement for entire sections of verses. Distribute activity page 20A to the children. Let the children see the suggested motions, but encourage them to use these just as a starting place.

You may wish to use fewer verses, depending upon the ability of your pupils. After deciding what will be done, practice many times so that the pupils feel comfortable doing the motions and movements as you read the verses.

Or make a videotape to illustrate the verses. Ask a student or pair of students to illustrate each of the verses through a picture. Then use the video camera to record the still pictures as the students read their verses. If you desire, play a taped song while the students are reading. Then show the video during the Call to Worship portion of *Sharing in Worship.*

2. Scripture. You'll need copies of activity page 20B, pencils, and markers or crayons. **To review the story of Ruth, let's look at the activity page. You need to find all the hidden bundles of wheat that Ruth gathered. While you're working, let's take a few moments to review the story.**

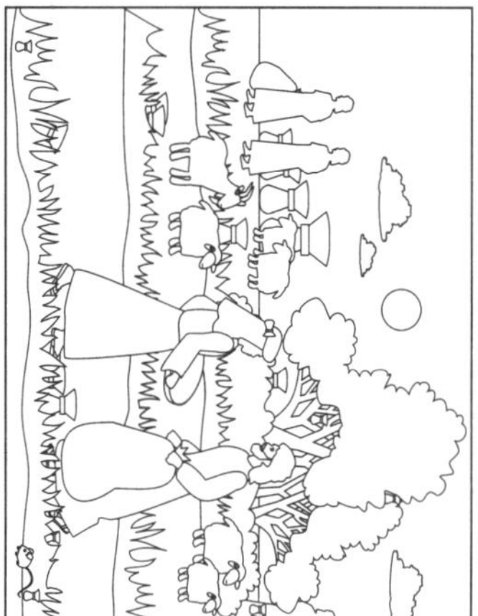

Put some review questions on pieces of paper. Wrap each question around a piece of real or imitation wheat or grass. Have each student come up, draw out a piece of wheat or grass, and answer the question. Use the following questions and add some of your own: Why did Naomi, Ruth, and Orpah travel toward the land of Judah? Why did Ruth go into the fields? Why was Boaz so good to Ruth?

If the children are unable to answer the questions, refer them to Ruth 1 and 2.

This activity could be done by the students without adult supervision. Make a poster with the instructions. The children will show their pictures and review the Bible story during the Scripture portion of *Sharing in Worship.*

3. Offering. This group will lead during the offering portion of *Sharing in Worship.* If you are giving information about different missionaries your church supports, you need to present this material to the students now. Be sure they are familiar enough with it to present during the actual worship time. If you have slides, pictures, or artifacts, it will help the students' presentations. Be sure to have a map marked with the location where the missionary serves. If someone is close to that particular missionary, he could come speak for a few moments.

The group will be creating an *ABC Book of Good Things From God.* Before class, obtain two large sheets of poster board, large sheets of paper, crayons, markers, magazines for pictures, scissors, and glue, yarn, or staples to attach the book together. You can either design the book with twenty-six pages or with two letters per page.

Beforehand, letter the words of Psalm 116:17 on the poster board cover of the book. In class, help students find Psalm 116:12 in their Bibles. Read the verse aloud. Let pupils dictate to you a list of good things from God. Each good thing should begin with a different letter of the alphabet. Act as scribe to list each item on the chalkboard by each letter of the alphabet. Students will need to choose three or four things to illustrate. You could also have students cut items from magazines to illustrate the letters. While students work, spend time memorizing Psalm 116:12 together.

At offering time during *Sharing in Worship,* this group will recite Psalm 116:12 and then show their book. Appoint children who will pray the offering prayer and collect the offering.

4. Special Music. This group will present and teach the song "The Lord Has Done Great Things," sung to the tune of "The Farmer in the Dell."

The first stanza is taken from Psalm 126:3. The second stanza comes from Psalm 66:5.

The Lord has done great things.
The Lord has done great things.
The Lord has done great things
for us.
And we are very glad.

Come see what God has done.
Come see what God has done.
He has done amazing things.
Come see what God has done.

Use echo singing to teach the song to the students. You sing a phrase and the pupils repeat the same phrase. Practice singing the song a couple of times. let different students lead each time as they become familiar with the words.

During *Sharing in Worship,* have the small group sing the song for the large group. Then spend a few minutes teaching the song to the large group to sing as a part of their worship.

5. Devotional. This group will present the devotional during *Sharing in Worship.*

Help students find the following verses in their Bibles. Read each verse together, and write down what the students determine God does for us: Psalm 65:2 (hears our prayers); Psalm 86:5 (forgives us); Psalm 89:11 (made our world); Psalm 100:5 (loves us); Psalm 121:2 (helps us); and John 3:16 (gave us Jesus).

You can choose to present this in two ways. If you have an overhead projector, ask students to illustrate and write their verses to show during worship time. Use blank overhead transparencies and washable markers. Or ask students to use crayons and paper to draw their illustrations.

Or if you have older students, use a cassette tape recorder. Record their reading each verse and their thoughts about what gifts God gives to us. Play the tape during the devotional time of *Sharing in Worship.*

6. Prayer. This group of older students will make a prayer chart of people from the Bible who prayed difficult prayers and how the prayers were answered. Each student can research and investigate one Scripture passage: 1 Samuel 1:10-20; 2 Kings 19:14-19, 35, 36; Jonah 2; Luke 22:39-46; and Acts 16:22-28.

Stress the following: **God does many good things for us. He always does what is right and He helps us to do what is right. Let's see how God answered these Bible people who prayed difficult prayers.**

Help the group prepare a chart on a piece of poster board with the following categories: Scripture, person, prayer, reason for prayer, how answered. The pupil who researches the prayer should report to the group.

Sharing in Worship

(20-25 minutes)

Omit any of the following sections if you did not offer the corresponding activity. The devotional and closing prayer may be completed with out Groups 5 and 6.

Call to Worship (Group 1): **God does many good things for us. Group 1 will present their interpretation of Psalm 33:1-9.** Ask Group 1 to present their dramatic movements or their video.

Scripture (Group 2)**: God's Word, the Bible, tells us how God helped Ruth to do the right thing, even when it was hard. Group 2 did a hidden picture to review the story.** Ask Group 2 to show their pictures and review the story.

Lord's Supper: Each week we have a special time to remember what Jesus did for us. It's called the Lord's Supper or Communion. We take this time to think about Jesus and how He suffered and died for us, even though it was hard for Him. Include more explanation as needed for your group.

Offering (Group 3)**: There are many ways to worship God and thank Him for always doing right. One way to worship is by helping missionaries do their hard jobs of telling others about Jesus.** Take up the mission and regular offering at this time if you are presenting information about your church's missionaries.

Otherwise, ask the group to present their *ABC Book of Good Things From God.* Ask the students who designed the pages to read their own words. Then ask for volunteers to suggest other good things God gives that start with the different letters of the alphabet. Group 3 will recite Psalm 116:12. Then lead the whole group in reading Psalm 116:17 from the cover of the book. Ask the students you appointed ahead of time to pray the offering prayer and collect the offering.

Special Music (Group 4): Ask Group 4 to sing "The Lord Has Done Great Things" and then lead the entire group in singing it.

Devotional (Group 5): **It's hard to really understand how much God loves us. We can know our parents and families love us—they're right here with us and we can see and hear them. You know when your friends love you because they do nice things for you.**

And that's one way we can know that God loves us. He has given us so many wonderful gifts. We've already heard about a few of them, but Group 5 wants to present some of God's gifts that are very important to us. Have Group 5 present in order. After each one, make a few short comments to lead the worship. If you did not offer this activity, read a Scripture and then make the appropriate comments.

God hears our prayers. He listens to us, and He's always available to hear us. We don't have to wait until He calls us or until He's finished with someone else.

God forgives us. Let's face it, we're not perfect people, either children or us adults. But God forgives us and helps us to go on and keep going. Since we have that gift from God, we need to have that gift of forgiveness for others from us.

God made our world. There are many, many reasons to thank God every time you walk outside. You can pray short prayers to God each time you see a lightning bug or a flower or the beach.

God loves us, truly loves us. And He doesn't just love us when we are good. His love helps us to keep going and keep getting better. And He loves us for who we are—His children—not just for what we can do or what we are good at.

God's best gift of all was Jesus. God came down in the form of His Son to live here on earth. God knows what we're going through each day. He knows what it's like. That's why we can worship Him now.

Prayer (Group 6): **We know that prayer is important because of all the examples in the Bible. Group 6 investigated people who had to pray difficult prayers and how their prayers were answered.** Ask Group 6 to present now. If you did not do this activity, just have a closing prayer thanking God for all of His wonderful gifts to us.

Closing Moments

(10-15 minutes)

Provide jump ropes and see whether students can design raps or jump rope rhymes about today's lesson. Here are a couple of examples to get you started:

Ruth worked hard to do God's work and from her duties she did not shirk.

ABCDEFG—God gives good gifts to me.
HIJKLMNO—He gives good gifts, did you know?
PQRSTUV—God gives good gifts to me.
WXYZ—These are things God does for me.

(Then let students jump in and say one of God's gifts and jump out again. Do this activity outside if you can arrange it.)

If you prefer a quieter activity, sing "The Lord Has Done Great Things" again. Encourage the children to write new stanzas to the song, such as the following stanza.

God's given us His Son.
God's given us His Son.
The Lord has done great things for us.
He's given us His Son.

Psalm 33:1-9, *ICB*

1Sing to the Lord, you who do what
is right. Honest people should
praise him.
2Praise the Lord on the harp. Make
music for him on the ten-stringed
lyre.
3Sing a new song to him. Play well
and joyfully.
4God's word is true.
Everything he does is right.
5He loves what is right and fair.
The Lord's love fills the earth.
6The sky was made at the Lord's
command.
By the breath from his mouth, he
made all the stars.
7He gathered the water in the sea
into a heap.
He made the great ocean stay in its
place.
8All the earth should worship the
Lord.
The whole world should fear him.
9He spoke, and it happened.
He commanded, and it appeared.

Circle the hidden bundles of wheat. Color the picture.

Jonah Changes His Mind

Worship Focus

Worship God because He always does right, and He forgives us.

Transition Time

(10-15 minutes)

Ahead of the session, make up ten paper fish according to the pattern of the big fish printed on page 128. Write a Scripture about forgiveness on each fish. (Use the following Scriptures: 1 John 1:9; Psalm 86:5; Mark 11:25, 26; Ephesians 1:7; Acts 5:31; Matthew 6:12; Matthew 6:14, 15; Luke 6:37; Acts 13:38; and Psalm 130:3, 4.)

While students are getting a drink or going to the rest room, hide the fish in the room. When students return, ask them to look for the fish. When a child finds one fish, ask him to sit down. After all the fish have been found, take time to have the children read their Scriptures aloud. Ask students to tell you what these verses have in common.

Activity 2
page 138

Launching the Theme

(10 minutes)

Provide an overhead projector, one overhead transparency, permanent and water-soluble felt pens, water, and a soft cloth. This activity can be adapted for a chalkboard if necessary.

What are some ways we choose to do right? Take time to ask pupils to suggest things at different places, such as how to choose right at school, how to choose right at home, how to choose right when you're with your friends. Get the children started by a couple of suggestions, such as not giving an answer on a test when someone asks you for it; cleaning your room when you're supposed to; and not making fun of someone else even when everyone else is. Let pupils respond with their own suggestions. Use the permanent pen to write them at different places on the transparency.

Is it always easy to do right? No, sometimes it can be very difficult. When everybody else is doing something different, it can be hard to do the right thing. Sometimes it is hard because we want to do what WE want, not what GOD wants. Sometimes it takes more time or trouble to do the right thing than it does to do the wrong thing.

Tell me some ways we choose to do wrong. Let pupils respond. Guide suggestions if necessary: when we do what we want instead of what God wants, when we hurt someone in getting something for ourselves, and when we disobey our parents. Write these suggestions with the water-soluble pen among the answers on the transparency.

When we do wrong, what can we do? Pray and ask God for forgiveness. **What does it mean to forgive?** Allow ideas. **It means God forgets that the event ever happened. God forgives us when we ask Him to and when we want to do right again. He forgives us and forgets that the event ever happened.** Take a damp cloth and wipe the transparency. All the wrong things should erase, and the good things should remain. **Isn't it wonderful for God to forgive us? He can forgive all the wrong things that we do. It's as if we never did anything wrong at all. We will take time today to worship God because He forgives us.**

Explain the activity options to the children. Dismiss the children to the groups of their choice. Try to have an equal number of children in all groups.

Building the Theme

(30 minutes)

1. Call to Worship. This activity could be for older or more-advanced students. this group will prepare the Scripture to be used for the call to worship during *Sharing in Worship*. Provide activity page 21A, pencils, and three Bibles (KJV, NIV, AND ICB). The Scriptures are printed on the activity page also, but it is important for the children to know where these Scriptures come from originally.

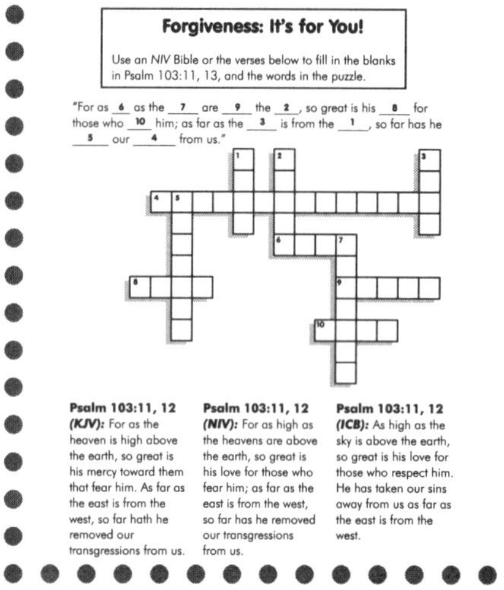
Forgiveness: It's for You!

Use an *NIV* Bible or the verses below to fill in the blanks in Psalm 103:11, 13, and the words in the puzzle.

"For as _6_ as the _7_ are _9_ the _2_, so great is his _8_ for those who _10_ him; as far as the _3_ is from the _1_, so far has he _5_ our _4_ from us."

Psalm 103:11, 12 *(KJV):* For as the heaven is high above the earth, so great is his mercy toward them that fear him. As far as the east is from the west, so far hath he removed our transgressions from us.

Psalm 103:11, 12 *(NIV):* For as high as the heavens are above the earth, so great is his love for those who fear him; as far as the east is from the west, so far has he removed our transgressions from us.

Psalm 103:11, 12 *(ICB):* As high as the sky is above the earth, so great is his love for those who respect him. He has taken our sins away from us as far as the east is from the west.

Help the pupils find and read Psalm 103:11, 12 from their Bibles. Work the puzzle on activity page 21A to fill in the blanks of the verses. Select four good readers to read verses 11 and 12 from the King James Version and the New International Version. There is a hard word: "transgressions." Help the readers pronounce it and then explain its meaning. Let these students practice reading several times. Ask two other good readers to read the verses from the *International Children's Bible*. If your pupils are all first-graders, you may need to read the verses ahead of time to the children to help them read or read the verses yourself.

How much do you think God loves us? Does God forgive the wrong things we do? How do you know that? How far is the east from the west? Allow time for answers. **God says He will forgive us in the Bible. The east and west are two opposite directions; the east will never meet the west. That means the wrong things we do are gone forever when God forgives us.**

To present the call to worship, ask the readers to read the different translations (KJV, NIV, ICB). Then end by asking the large group the same questions that you asked of the small group.

2. Scripture. This group will make a craft and review the lesson Scripture during *Sharing in Worship.*

To make the wave bottles, collect the following materials (enough for each student): one two-liter bottle (or other plastic bottle) with cap, enough mineral or baby oil to fill 1/3 of each bottle; blue food coloring; enough water to fill 2/3 of each bottle; funnels; small flat sponges that can be cut with scissors. You will also need markers and poster board for fish patterns.

Each student should cut a small fish shape from one sponge. (Trace the outline on page 137. Make several poster board patterns so the children can trace them on their sponges.) Put the sponge fish in the bottles. Then fill the bottles 2/3 full of water, add a few drops of blue food coloring, and fill the other 1/3 full of mineral oil. Then close the top tightly. (You may wish to put glue around the edge of the top before you screw on the cap. This will help seal the bottle shut.) When the bottle is moved from side to side, the combination of oil and water causes waves to occur.

While the students are working, read aloud the Bible story from Jonah 1:1-17; 2:1, 10; 3:1-3a. Students will give a story review and show their wave bottles during *Sharing in Worship.* Use the following questions to help them get started:

Why did God ask Jonah to go to Nineveh?

What did Jonah do when God asked him to go? Why do you think he did that?

What did God cause to happen while Jonah was on the boat?

What did the sailors on the boat do when the storm came up?

What was Jonah doing while he was in the fish?

What did he do after he came out of the fish?

3. Offering. This group will prepare the offering presentation. If you're using this time to give information about missionaries your church supports, work with the students about that at this time. If you have pictures or slides, use those in the group's presentation.

Gather the following materials: scissors, nature magazines (or crayons, markers, and paper for drawing), glue, and poster board. Begin by writing the words to the first stanza of the song "This Is My Father's World" on a piece of poster board or on the chalkboard.

This is my Father's world,
And to my list'ning ears
All nature sings and round me rings
The music of the spheres.
This is my Father's world,
I rest me in the thought
Of rocks and trees, of skies and seas.
His hand the wonders wrought

Leave space between the lines and around the outside of the stanza.

Let's read the words of this song together. Do so. **Let's look for or draw pictures that can talk about some of the wonderful things that God's hand has made—that's what it means when it says, "His hand the wonders wrought." These pictures can be things we see, hear, smell, taste, and feel. Look for pictures of birds, lakes, skies, trees, flowers, anything God has made.**

God always does right, even in His creation. God worked out everything so that all of creation works together. Even when Jonah didn't do right, God

worked everything out all right. God used a big fish from nature to help Jonah learn a lesson, and God forgave Jonah.

Have the children cut out magazine pictures or draw nature pictures to illustrate the stanza. Glue those around the outside of the poster board around the first stanza.

During *Sharing in Worship,* this group will help teach the song and show their poster. Then a member of the group will have the offering prayer. Other members will collect the offering.

4. Special Music. This group will prepare music for the worship time. Before the session begins, write the words for this song on poster board or a chalkboard.

Lord, You love us. (Repeat.)
You are kind. (Repeat.)
And You will forgive us.
(Repeat.)
We praise You! (Repeat.)

When we do wrong. (Repeat.)
We will pray. (Repeat.)
And You will forgive us.
(Repeat.)
We praise You! (Repeat.)

Read Psalm 86:5 from the *International Children's Bible* (or from the New International Version). **What does the verse tell us about God?** Allow answers. **He's kind, forgiving, and loving toward us. What does it mean to forgive?** To act as though something wrong never happened.

Look at the words on the poster board (chalkboard). The first stanza is taken from Psalm 86:5. Let's sing this song to the tune of "Are You Sleeping?" The first time I will sing the words and you will repeat them. Later we will divide into groups to sing this song.

Sing the song several times. Divide the group into two parts. Group A will begin; Group B will repeat the phrases. Sing the song this way for *Sharing in Worship.* Then let the small group sing as Group A and the large group repeat the phrases.

5. Devotional. This group will present the devotional during *Sharing in Worship.* You will need to alert an adult or teen ahead of time to take the part of David. Also before the session, prepare the following questions, one each on an index card. The answers are in parentheses. Do not put them on the index cards. (Prepare a list of question and answers for "David.")

1. David, you were the king of Israel. What made you such a powerful king? (God chose me to be the king, and He helped me to be a good one.)
2. Did you always choose to do right? (I tried to choose right, but everyone makes some wrong choices. Once in a while, I did wrong things too.)
3. How was God able to help you, especially in the area of forgiveness? (Because I was truly sorry for what I did, I asked God to forgive me, and He did. He forgives better than anyone else. Only God can truly forgive and then really forget that it ever happened.)
4. David, you wrote many songs of praise to God. Can you tell us why you wrote them? (That's easy. Only God always does what is right. Only God loves us no matter what we do. Only God is holy and perfect and forgiving.)
5. Could you tell us one of your songs about God's forgiveness? (Sure. *Read Psalm 103:1-3a, 8-12.*)
6. David, what advice can you give to us about God and forgiveness? (Worship and praise God only. God is perfect, but God can forgive us when we are not. Try to be as much like God as you can. Be loving, kind, and forgiving, even when it is hard.)

We have a special guest today. He knows a lot about forgiveness. David, king of Israel, will you please come and address the group now?"

Practice the interview ahead of time. Each pupil in the group should ask at least one question. Encourage the children to write other questions. Help them to write the questions. If David needs help with his answers, provide that also.

6. Prayer. This group will lead the group at prayer time. Provide paper, pencils, and the chalkboard.

We worship God because He always does what is right. And because He does what is right, we need to do what is right. Because He forgives, we need to forgive too. It's not always easy to forgive others, but we can ask God for help in forgiving.

Read Psalm 86:5. Ask pupils to write or dictate to you a prayer telling about God's forgiveness and asking for help to forgive others. You might suggest the following prayer and ask the pupils to fill in the words for the ones italicized.

If *I* do wrong, You will forgive me.

If *someone does wrong to me,* help me to forgive him completely.

The pupils will read their prayers in *Sharing in Worship.* Ask an adult to close in the prayer, praising God that He forgives us.

Sharing in Worship

(20-25 minutes)

Omit any of the following sections if you did not offer the corresponding activity.

Call to Worship (Group 1): **Today we will celebrate and worship God because He always does right, and He forgives us.**

Listen to these verses as students read Scriptures that tell about God's forgiveness for us. (Ask the designated students to read Psalm 103:11, 12 from the three different translations.)

How much do you think God loves us? Allow answers. **He loves us very much, especially in forgiving the wrong things we do. What do you think it means "as far as the east is from the west"?** Allow answers.**The east and west are two opposite directions. The east will never meet the west; that means the wrong things we do are gone forever when God forgives us.**

Scripture Review (Group 2): Ask Group 2 to show their wave bottles at this time and review the Bible story. **Jonah certainly started out doing wrong, didn't he? He wanted to do what HE wanted, not what God wanted. He was so stubborn that he tried to run away from God when God gave him a specific task to do. But can people really get away from God? No, God was with him every step of the way, including in the belly of the big fish. I think if I were in a big fish, I'd be praying too! And God was wonderful and generous and forgave Jonah. He gave Jonah a second chance by forgiving him. God wanted to give the people of Nineveh a second chance too; that's why He wanted to send Jonah.**

Lord's Supper: We want to remember that Jesus died on a cross for us. When He died, He made it possible for God to forgive us for the wrong things we do. We may not understand why Jesus had to die, but we know He did because He loves us. And praise God that He will forgive us. Think about that now as we take the Lord's Supper.

Offering (Group 3): If Group 3 is presenting information about missionaries your church supports, have them set up now while the offering is being taken. Or use the time while the offering is being taken to teach the first verse of "This Is My Father's World" and show the illustrated poster. Then ask a child from this group to lead in the offering prayer.

Special Music (Group 4): Ask Group 4 to sing the forgiveness song. Then let the small group be group A while the rest of the group will be group B. Sing it through again twice as a round.

Devotional (Group 5): **Today we will have a special guest. When we talk about God and His forgiveness, Jonah comes to mind. But there is another man in the Old Testament who also felt and understood God's forgiveness for himself because he did some awful things, including murder. Let's take this opportunity to welcome David, the shepherd boy who became king of Israel.**

(Do the interview now, and have students from this group ask the questions. If that's not possible, prerecord the the interview and play it now.)

David wrote some incredible things about God's forgiveness because He experienced it firsthand. We're going to take a few moments to look up a couple of those Scriptures and read them together. Provide Bibles to a few of your very good readers and let them look up the following Scriptures.

Would someone read Psalm 32:1, 2, and 5? David said that a man who is forgiven is blessed. And how do we obtain that forgiveness? Read verse 5 again. You have to confess your sin, and you have to ask for forgiveness. And after seeing how good and how gracious God is to forgive us, we need to remember that when others ask us for forgiveness. It isn't easy to give or ask for forgiveness, but it's essential that we do both.

Would someone else read Psalm 86:5? God is good and ready to forgive if we ask Him to. Also read Psalm 130:3, 4. Can you imagine that God knows every bad thing that you have ever done? But God doesn't want to remember that; He wants to forget that and help you keep going.

If you were going to write a psalm about God's forgiveness, what would you write? Take time now to write down suggestions from the large group. Give guidance and suggestions as needed. After you have three or four sentences, ask the entire group to read it together.

Prayer (Group 6): **Group 6 will read the prayers they wrote about forgiveness now. Then let's read our psalm together again as a prayer.** You or another adult should close the prayer time.

Closing Moments

(10-15 minutes)

Give each child a copy of activity page 21B. Provide crayons or markers and pencils. Let the children solve the rebus puzzle. The answer to the puzzle is "He forgives and forgets when you ask Him to!"

Forgiveness: It's for You!

Use an *NIV* Bible or the verses below to fill in the blanks in Psalm 103:11, 13, and the words in the puzzle.

"For as __6__ as the __7__ are __9__ the __2__, so great is his __8__ for those who __10__ him; as far as the __3__ is from the __1__, so far has he __5__ our __4__ from us."

Psalm 103:11, 12 *(KJV):* For as the heaven is high above the earth, so great is his mercy toward them that fear him. As far as the east is from the west, so far hath he removed our transgressions from us.

Psalm 103:11, 12 *(NIV):* For as high as the heavens are above the earth, so great is his love for those who fear him; as far as the east is from the west, so far has he removed our transgressions from us.

Psalm 103:11, 12 *(ICB):* As high as the sky is above the earth, so great is his love for those who respect him. He has taken our sins away from us as far as the east is from the west.

THE (-) T (+) 4
(+) LIVES (-) L (+)
G AND 4 (+) LETS
(-) L (+) G (+)
THEN (-) T (+) W
(+) U (+) ASK (+)
HIM (+) 2.

Hannah Keeps Her Promise

Worship Focus

Worship God because He always does what is right, and He keeps His promises.

Transition Time

(10-15 minutes)

Divide the class into two teams, seated in chairs, one behind another. Signal the first player on each team. He will stand, clap his hands twice, and say, "Hannah, Hannah" (team 1) or "Samuel, Samuel" (team 2). When he finishes, the next player repeats the action. When the last player finishes, he sits down and taps the player ahead, who repeats the claps and words, sits down, and touches the player ahead of him. When the action gets back to the first player, he claps, says the words, and stays standing. When both teams finish, go into *Launching the Theme.*

Launching the Theme

(10 minutes)

As the pupils come into the large-group area and sit down, take various objects (hair barrette, Bible, paper, purse, wallet) from several pupils. Promise them you will return them in one minute. Then continue with the introduction.

We want to worship God today because He always keeps His promises. Let's play a guessing game. I'm thinking of a promise God made to Noah. God still keeps this promise today. We see the sign of His promise in the sky after it rains. What is it? Let pupils respond. **I'm thinking of a promise God made to Abraham. God asked Abraham to leave his family and home to receive what God had promised. What did God promise Abraham?** He promised Abraham a new home and a land. **Oh, I forgot!** Give back the objects you took from the students. **I promised to give them back in one minute and I forgot. Isn't it great that God always remembers His promises and He keeps them? We may forget or decide not to keep our promises, but God always remembers to do what He says He will do.**

Building the Theme

(30 minutes)

1. Call to Worship. This group will prepare a rebus poster to help lead in the call to worship. Provide a sheet of poster board, markers, glue, and magazine pictures of different types of people, such as babies, adults, children, elderly, other ethnic groups.

Print the words "God Always Keeps His Promises" across the top of the poster. Then print the words "____________ can always count on God's promises" as many times as you have pictures. Make sure to leave space to insert students' pictures where the line is.

Ask each pupil in the group to glue his picture where the blank space is. One at a time, ask the pupils to read their rebus sentences aloud. Be sure to write "We can count on God's promises" at the bottom of the poster.

During *Sharing in Worship*, each student will read his rebus line aloud, and the whole group will answer back each time: "God keeps His promises." Then read Hebrews 10:23.

2. Scripture. You will need enough copies of activity page 22A for each child to have one. This group will act out a review of the events in the Scripture passage, 1 Samuel 1.

You will need at least four speaking parts and one part with no speaking involved. If you have more than five children in this group, each narration can be done by a different child. If you have fewer, a doll could be used for the part of Samuel and you could read the narration. If you have younger students, you read the script, using different voices for each person, and have the children act out the parts.

Practice the skit several times.

If you have materials (bath robes, towels, sashes, lengths of material) available, help the children fashion costumes for themselves.

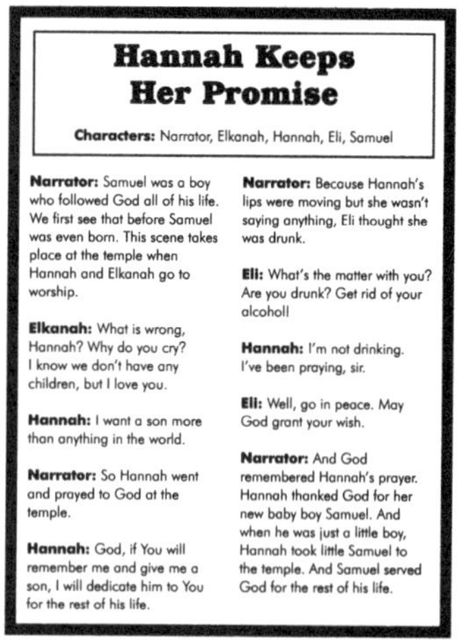

Hannah Keeps Her Promise

Characters: Narrator, Elkanah, Hannah, Eli, Samuel

Narrator: Samuel was a boy who followed God all of his life. We first see that before Samuel was even born. This scene takes place at the temple when Hannah and Elkanah go to worship.

Elkanah: What is wrong, Hannah? Why do you cry? I know we don't have any children, but I love you.

Hannah: I want a son more than anything in the world.

Narrator: So Hannah went and prayed to God at the temple.

Hannah: God, if You will remember me and give me a son, I will dedicate him to You for the rest of his life.

Narrator: Because Hannah's lips were moving but she wasn't saying anything, Eli thought she was drunk.

Eli: What's the matter with you? Are you drunk? Get rid of your alcohol!

Hannah: I'm not drinking. I've been praying, sir.

Eli: Well, go in peace. May God grant your wish.

Narrator: And God remembered Hannah's prayer. Hannah thanked God for her new baby boy Samuel. And when he was just a little boy, Hannah took little Samuel to the temple. And Samuel served God for the rest of his life.

During *Sharing in Worship,* the children will perform the skit.

3. Offering. This group will lead during the offering portion of *Sharing in Worship.* If you have had mission talks, conclude these today. If you have pictures, slides, or souvenirs from a missionary, make a bulletin board or display to remind the children of the missionaries and about the hard jobs that they do. Include a world map with missions locations marked.

Or do this activity for the offering. Provide a piece of poster board and markers. Write the word PROMISE straight down the poster board to create an acrostic. If you have older students, ask them to come up with words that start with the letters in PROMISE that mention things God has given or promised to us. If you have younger students, use these suggestions:

P – parents, people, peace
R – resurrection, rain
O – others
M – mothers, money
I – imagination
S – savior, seasons
E – everlasting life

Give the children markers and pieces of paper to illustrate each letter. Then ask the children to stand and practice how they will present the acrostic during the offering time. Also ask one student to be prepared to have the offering prayer.

4. Special Music. This group will prepare a song for special music. Have poster board and markers for the children to make a song chart.

Teach the song "He Promises Love." **God promises love, peace, and joy to us. When we know Jesus, we will have God's love, peace, and joy.**

Divide the children into two groups and sing the song. Group 1 will begin and Group 2 will do the echo. Sing the last phrase in unison as on the cassette tape.

To present this for *Sharing in Worship,* sing it once as practiced. Then ask the large group to sing the echo part.

5. Devotional. This group will make finger "Promise Puppets" to act out the situations for the devotional. Use the pattern on page 146 to make the puppets. Let the children add facial features. The puppet will slip on a student's finger after it has been cut out and taped together.

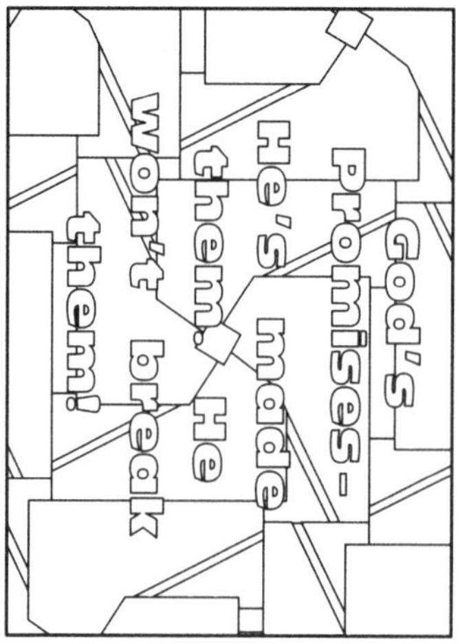

Divide the group into groups of three children each. Give each group one situation. (Some suggestions are below. Add others if you need to.) Ask the children to come up with dialogue and then practice it a few times.

Situation 1. Steven promised his little sister Kathy that he would play with her this afternoon. Then Steven's best friend Eric invited Steven over to play with his new video game. What should Steven say? How can Steven keep his promise?

Situation 2. Terri promised her dad that she would clean her room on Saturday. She forgot that she told her Bible-school teacher, Mrs. Crawford, that she could probably go on the class trip to the zoo. What should Terri tell her dad? What should Terri tell Mrs. Crawford?

Situation 3. Adam told his parents that he would start giving part of his allowance in the mission offering at church. But he saw a really great toy that he's been wanting for a long time, so he bought it at the store today. Now he doesn't have any money for the offering. His mother asked him how he could afford the new toy. What should Adam say to his mother and father? What should he say to God?

6. Prayer. This group will write prayers for *Sharing in Worship.*

Provide Bibles, pencils, and paper to students. Help students find Psalm 105.

Listen carefully while I read this psalm. This psalm tells about people to whom God made promises. It tells that God keeps His promises. After I have read the psalm, we will make a list of the people to whom God made promises.

Be sure to include Abraham, Isaac, God's people, Joseph, and Moses. If the children don't know the background of these people, fill in the gaps. After the children make their list, make another list of promises God has made and kept to us. Suggestions could be promises to meet needs, for food, clothing, care for us, answer our prayers, that seasons would continue.

Help children write or dictate prayers praising God for keeping His promises. Read Psalm 145:13 and model a prayer for students.

"Lord, You made a promise. We worship You for giving us __________."

The readers may read or say from memory their prayers during *Sharing in Worship.* If desired, have students record their prayers and then play the tape during the prayer time of *Sharing in Worship.*

Sharing in Worship

(20-25 minutes)

Omit any of the following sections if you did not offer the corresponding activity.

Call to Worship (Group 1): Ask Group 1 to share its rebus poster and lead the whole group in stating "God keeps His promises" after each individual student speaks. **We are here today to worship God and celebrate how He keeps His promises to us. God is dependable; we can always count on Him to keep His word.**

Scripture (Group 2): Ask Group 2 to perform its skit to review the story with the large group.

Lord's Supper: God promised many people that He would someday send a very special Person to earth. This Person would show us how to live and how to know and love God. He kept His promise when Jesus was born. Jesus showed us how much God loved us and died for us, so we could someday receive God's promise of Heaven. Let's remember Jesus now—He's God's best-kept promise to us.

Offering (Group 3): If you have made plans, ask this group to give its final missions presentation.

Or show the acrostic poster and ask each member of Group 3 to come up and show his picture and how he illustrated his letter. When all the students in the group have finished, lead the group in thanking God for keeping His promises to us. Ask two students to take up the offering.

Special Music (Group 4): **Group 4 will sing the song "He Promises Love."** After the group has sung the song, let Group 4 sing the song twice with the whole group.

Devotional (Group 5): **Group 5 will present some promise puppets at this time.** After the skits, encourage the whole group to participate in coming up with another appropriate ending for each skit or in suggesting other situations with the promisers' keeping their promises.

Then give the following talk.

Promises are very important things. There are many different kinds and forms of promises. But they all mean one thing: you will do what you said you would, and you keep your word.

There are legal promises, called contracts. These promises are down on paper and you have to sign your name to it. If you do not follow through and keep your promises, you could get in serious trouble with the law. You may have seen your parents or other adults sign for a new car or new house. People make promises to each other when they get married.

There are promises that you make to God. When you become a Christian, you promise God that you will put Him first in your life. This is a very serious promise that you should work hard to keep.

But God knows how we are. We aren't perfect. We try to do right, but we don't always succeed at it. He knows that we sin sometimes and that we break our promises to other people and to Him.

But the most wonderful part is first that God forgives us, and second He ALWAYS keeps His promises. Do you realize what that means? God will never let you down. It's not like making a promise to your best friend and then changing your mind. It's not like hearing a promise from your parent and then having him accidentally forget that he promised you anything.

God is dependable and faithful and true. It's reassuring to know that in a world where people forget and break their promises, God never does. And that's why we're here to worship Him today. We need to take time now to thank God for this wonderful gift or His promises to us.

Prayer (Group 6): **Group 6 will lead our group in prayer.** Ask each individual in Group 6 to read his prayer. The entire group should respond, "Thank You, God, for keeping Your promises," after each child has read his prayer.

Closing Moments

(10-15 minutes)

You will need crayons or markers and enough copies of activity page 22B for each child to have one. This is a doodle art poster that will take some time to color. The phrase says, "God's Promises—He's made them. He won't break them!"

Hannah Keeps Her Promise

Characters: Narrator, Elkanah, Hannah, Eli, Samuel

Narrator: Samuel was a boy who followed God all of his life. We first see that before Samuel was even born. This scene takes place at the temple when Hannah and Elkanah go to worship.

Elkanah: What is wrong, Hannah? Why do you cry? I know we don't have any children, but I love you.

Hannah: I want a son more than anything in the world.

Narrator: So Hannah went and prayed to God at the temple.

Hannah: God, if You will remember me and give me a son, I will dedicate him to You for the rest of his life.

Narrator: Because Hannah's lips were moving but she wasn't saying anything, Eli thought she was drunk.

Eli: What's the matter with you? Are you drunk? Get rid of your alcohol!

Hannah: I'm not drinking. I've been praying, sir.

Eli: Well, go in peace. May God grant your wish.

Narrator: And God remembered Hannah's prayer. Hannah thanked God for her new baby boy Samuel. And when he was just a little boy, Hannah took little Samuel to the temple. And Samuel served God for the rest of his life.

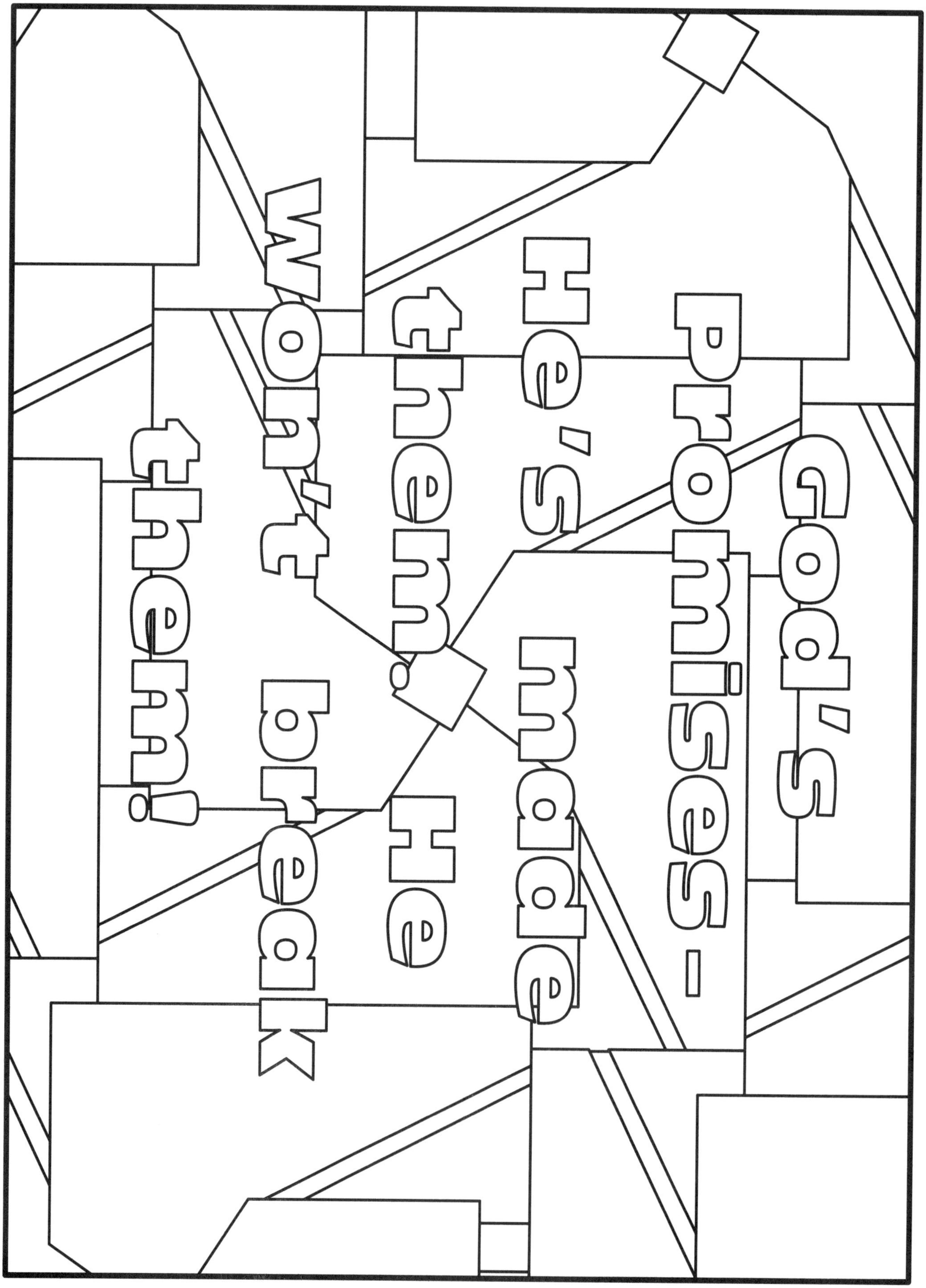
God's promises—
He's made them.
He won't break them!

Samuel Chooses to Do Right All of His Life

Worship Focus

Worship God because He does what is right and He is eternal—He has no beginning or end.

Transition Time

(10-15 minutes)

Send the pupils in small groups to the rest room and drinking fountains at this time. Welcome newcomers and involve everyone in the following activity.

I Am Here. Just as Samuel ran to Eli, let the pupils play this relay game. Before class, blow up and tie at least one balloon for each child you expect to attend. Put half of the balloons in one big box and the other half in another big box.

In class, have the children line up in two teams. The first player on each team takes a balloon from the team's box and puts it between his knees. At a signal, the race begins. The players walk as fast as they can to that team's adult player on the opposite side of the room. When the player gets to the adult, he must say, "I am here. You called me." The leader will say, "No. Go back." Then the player must walk around the leader and back to the team.

When the first player returns to the team, he gives the balloon to the next in line. If someone breaks a balloon, he takes another from the team's box and starts over. The race continues until everyone has had a turn.

Launching the Theme

(10 minutes)

What kinds of things help us keep track of time? Can you think of some things? List ideas on the board. Include digital and stop watch, calendar, sun dial, and others.

To do the first part of this exercise, you will need to have a stop watch. **Let's estimate the time on some things. How many seconds do you think it will take for you to jump up and down twenty times? Twenty seconds? Thirty seconds? One hundred seconds?** Write down their guesses and then have some of the children actually jump to see whether their guesses were close. **When you use a stop watch, you time things that have a beginning and an end. What are some other things that you time?** Races, spelling or math tests, baking cookies.

Let's make a list of events that have a beginning and an end. I'll describe something; you tell me what I'm describing.

It starts in the morning with the sound of a bell ringing. Children come together and sit in a room. They do different things all day. Then in the afternoon, another bell rings, and it is over (school).

This begins when someone yells, "Go!" Several people run as fast as they can to a finish line. The first person to cross the finish line wins. It is over when the last person crosses the finish line (race).

This begins when a lot of people yell, "Surprise!" One person opens packages wrapped in special paper, tied with bows. Everyone eats cake and ice cream. It is over when everyone goes home (a surprise birthday party).

This begins when one player on one team kicks a black and white ball down the field. Each of the two teams tries to move the ball down the field and score a goal. It is over when time has run out and a whistle is blown (a soccer game).

Do you know of other things that have beginnings and ends? Let's make a list of these now. List them on the chalkboard or on poster board.

There are many more things we could name that have a beginning and an end. Even people have a beginning. We begin marking time when a person is born. And we keep track of time until a person dies.

But there is someone who has no beginning and no end. He has always been, and He will always be. Listen. Read Psalm 102:25-27 from the *International Children's Bible.* **Whom are these verses describing? God has always been alive, and He will always be alive. That makes God very, very special. Today we will worship God because He is so special.**

Summarize the activities for *Building the Theme* and allow the children to choose the groups in which they would like to participate. Have an equal number of students in each group if possible.

Building the Theme

(30 minutes)

1. Call to Worship. This group will present the call to worship during *Sharing in Worship.*

Help the pupils find Psalm 90:1, 2 in their Bibles. Have the pupils listen as you read the verses from the *International Children's Bible.* Although God's eternal existence is difficult for even adults to comprehend, let the pupils put the verses in their own words. Ask questions to help pupils verbalize what these verses mean.

Was there ever a time when God was not there?

Will God ever die?

How long has God been alive?

Demonstrate the motions illustrated on activity page 23A or make up your own motions with the children's help. If you use the motions on the activity page, make enough copies of the page for each child to have one. Let them look at the page and practice doing the motions while thinking the words. When the children are familiar with the motions, practice saying the verses with the motions. Practice many times until the children can recite the verses and do the motions.

2. Scripture. This group will present a review of the Scripture story. You will need Bibles, copies of activity page 23B, and pencils for the children.

Help the children find 1 Samuel 2:18, 21, 26; 3:1-10, 19, 20; 4:1; 7:15-17 in their Bibles. Read the passage aloud to the children.

Let's pretend we are the boy Samuel. We are at the temple with Eli. What do you think we might write to our parents about the events that happened the night we just read about? Write a letter to your family describing what happened and how you felt.

Assist the children in their letters. Give help with spelling, with accuracy in recorded events, and with suggestions about how they might have felt—especially when they found out the one calling them was the Lord. Volunteers will read their letters during the Scripture time of *Sharing in Worship.* You will conclude the Scripture review by pointing out that Samuel chose to do right all his life, that he served God all his life.

3. Offering. This group will present examples of how offering money is used for God's work. Provide a cover from an old activity book, a *Weekly Bible Reader* take-home paper, pictures of missionaries your church supports, several labels from food cans, material scraps, small pieces of poster board (4" x 11"), crayons, yarn, tape or stapler, LEGO™ building bricks, and a Bible.

These children will be making posters and labels to represent materials that offering money helps to buy: Bible-school materials; clothing and food for needy people; items for people that the church supports, such as missionaries and the preacher.

Let the children choose the area that they would like to illustrate. The Bible-school papers and activity book pages can be taped or stapled to one piece of poster board. The food labels and clothing scraps can be attached to another sheet of poster board (or have children cut out pictures of food and clothing from newspapers, magazines, and catalogs). The preacher can be represented by one student holding a Bible. The pupils can use the building bricks to build a simple building to represent the church. Have each group make a label for its items. Cover the labels until the indicated time.

During *Sharing in Worship,* the pupils will hold their posters and the block building. The "preacher" should also stand in front of the large group. Ask for volunteers from the large group to tell what things offering money is used for. As the responses are given, the pupils will uncover the labels. Give assistance so that each group is mentioned.

4. Special Music. This group will present the special music during *Sharing in Worship.*

Use the song "It's Time to Praise the Lord" from the song section and also "I Want to Praise You, Lord" from a chorus book. Ask the children to list things God does for them or some attributes of God. Give assistance as needed to help the children get started.

You will use these suggestions in the first song where there are asterisks. Write the suggestions on the chalkboard or on a sheet of poster board, making them fit the rhythm of the phrases in the song. For example: God tells the truth; God helps us; God helps us do hard jobs. Choose three different phrases to use in the song.

For the remaining time practice singing the songs. To help pupils learn the first song, divide the song into small sections (about eight measures) and practice these small sections several times. Then sing the song through until the pupils feel comfortable.

5. Devotional. This activity would probably be good for older or more advanced students. If you have younger students, provide plenty of guidance and structure the activity very carefully. This group will present a television commercial for the devotional during *Sharing in Worship*. You may do the commercials live during worship or, if possible, have video equipment available and record the commercial for playback at the appropriate time.

Begin by asking students to name attributes of God, such as He has no beginning or end (is eternal), He is loving, He forgives, He hears and answers prayers, He is perfect, He is powerful. List their suggestions on the chalkboard or a piece of poster board.

Also have the children list things that God has provided for or given them, such as parents, food, home, air, water, the Bible, Jesus. Also list these on the chalkboard or poster board.

Then have the children list the responses they should have toward God, such as worship, thankfulness, obedience to God and parents, prayers, choosing to do right, telling others about Jesus.

Structure a commercial (more than one if possible) to show how great God is and what our response should be. **You see commercials on television all the time. We want to use a commercial to convince first- and second-graders that God has no beginning or end and that He is greater and more powerful than anyone or anything we could ever imagine. How would you present the commercial? How can you get them to listen to you, be convinced, and respond in one of the ways we listed?**

A possible format would be for a narrator to present a situation where a Primary child is talking about God to one or more of his friends. The child should tell a few attributes of God (or things He has done) and what a child's response to God should be. The listening child could ask questions and at the end should decide to worship God and respond in a way that he is told. At the end of the commercial, the narrator should respond with a short statement, such as, "God has always been and always will be—worship Him!" or "God always does what is right—try to be like Him!"

This group could be divided into groups of two or three with more than one commercial being presented.

Practice several times. Videotape the commercial if possible. If not, it will be performed live during the devotional part of *Sharing in Worship*.

6. Prayer. This group of students will sing the song "Thank You, Lord" for the closing prayer.

Sing the song through once or twice. (Practice it more if your children are not familiar with it.) **Let's think of some other reason we can thank God. These can be things God has given us or done for us, such as food, shelter, or love, or things that we know about God, such as that He has no beginning or end, that He always does what is right, and that He hears our prayers.** Use the chalkboard or poster board to list what the children suggest. Then write new words for the song using the children's suggestions. Come up with at least a second stanza for the chorus.

Practice the chorus with the group's additions. Remind the children that this song is a prayer. Encourage them to sing reverently and thoughtfully.

Sharing in Worship

(20-25 minutes)

Omit any of the following sections if you did not offer the corresponding activity.

Prior to this session, prepare slips of paper with one of the following Scripture references on each slip of paper: Genesis 1:1; Job 38:1-7; Psalm 33:11; Psalm 39:4; Psalm 90:1-4; Psalm 107:1; Isaiah 43:10-12; Isaiah 46:9, 10.

At this time, distribute the slips of paper among volunteers who are willing to read Scripture aloud. Explain that you will call on the children to read these Scriptures during the devotional. Provide Bibles for children who volunteer but do not have Bibles with them. Have another adult assist the children as needed in looking up the Scriptures.

Call to Worship (Group 1): Ask Group 1 to recite Psalm 90:1, 2 and present their motions. **God has existed throughout all of time. He has always been and will always be. We praise Him today because He does what is right, and He is eternal—He has no beginning or end.**

Special Music (Group 4): Group 4 should present its two songs at this time. Then have Group 4 lead the large group in singing the songs.

Scripture (Group 2): Have volunteers from Group 2 read their letters from Samuel to his parents. After they are done, fill in any details they might have missed. **Samuel is a good example for each one of you. He was just about your age when he started ministering in the temple. He knew how important it was to do the right thing. He did the right thing, even when some of the adults didn't. He was a good example to everyone.**

Lord's Supper: God always does what is right. But you and I

don't always do what is right. Jesus died on the cross so that you and I could go to Heaven and live with God even though we sometimes do wrong things. Can you see how much God loves each of us? Can you see how much God you loves you?

Offering (Group 3): Group 3 will present the display at this time. Enlist ideas from the large group of things that the offering goes for, and have the groups turn their labels over as they are mentioned. Give appropriate hints as needed so that all groups are mentioned.

Devotional (Group 5): Group 5 will present its commercial at this time. Have a chalkboard or poster board available to write down the characteristics of God.

This commercial was a different way to remind us that God is very special to us. There is no one else just like Him. So we're going to take a few minutes to review some interesting facts about God just now. We'll discover that no one else in the world is quite like Him!

Have the volunteers read Genesis 1:1 and Job 38:1-7. **It's hard to imagine that God was here before the world and before time began. He created everything in the world and no one else could do that. I wonder what it would have been like before the world was created.**

Have the volunteer read Psalm 33:11. **God's plans are forever—He is here to guide you, your children, your grandchildren, and your great grandchildren! Isn't that hard to understand? God does not age as we do; He does not have birthdays and get older each time.**

Have the volunteer read Psalm 39:4. **God knows everything about you, even the stuff you don't think your parents or teachers know about you. He knows when you were born and how many years you will live. He'll be there through all of those years.**

Have the volunteers read Psalm 90:1-4 and Psalm 107:1. **I can't even imagine what one thousand years would be like. It just seems like it goes on forever. And there are many other places in the Bible that mention God's lasting forever.**

Have the volunteers read Isaiah 43:10-12 and Isaiah 46:9, 10. **Only God himself understands what His capabilities are. God knows what He can do—everything! Isn't it awesome to know that the God we worship is that powerful? It is hard for us to understand, but we can praise Him even for what we don't understand.**

Because of all these reasons, and for many more than this, we worship, honor, and praise God by choosing—of our own will—to live the right kind of life for Him. We choose to do right because we WANT to honor our wonderful God in that way.

Prayer (Group 6): **Group 6 will sing our prayer for us now. Listen carefully and in a prayerful attitude while Group 6 leads us in prayer.**

Closing Moments

(10-15 minutes)

Our God is great! Today we will make reminders of that fact and how we should respond to God.

Brainstorm ideas about ways that God is great. Then brainstorm responses the children should have. Many of these attributes and responses will have been discussed earlier. Record the children's suggestions on the chalkboard or poster board.

Distribute index cards and markers or pencils. Encourage the children to choose an attribute of God and something reasonable which they can do this week in response to that. Ask the children to put the cards in their Bibles to keep as a reminder for the rest of the week.

Lord 1

home 2

mountains 3

earth 4

you always have been, 5

and you will always be. 6

Dear Mom and Dad,

Love,
Samuel

Samuel Chooses to Obey God

Worship Focus

We worship God because He always does what is right and He is king of everything.

Transition Time

(10-15 minutes)

Allow the children to go to the rest room and get a drink. Greet each child by name.

King Do This! Use this game to provide movement and relaxation. Divide the class into teams of five or six students. Have them sit together in teams. Tell each pupil to sit up straight in the seat and form a circle with his hands by touching thumbs together and pointer fingers together. Then he should put this crown on top of his head. Now the pupils will look like kings. The adult leader will tell the pupils to do something and he will say "Kings do this!" The pupils must then do what the leader says as quickly as possible and then resume their king positions again. If a team player moves before the leader says, "Kings do this!" one point is lost for the team.

Following is a list of instructions for the kings: Touch your right foot. Clap twice behind your back. Stand up. Touch the floor. Stand up and turn around. (Add more of your own ideas.)

Launching the Theme

(10 minutes)

Use the following pretend situation to help give the pupils some understanding of what a king is. Designate one male leader (or ask a special guest) to be the king. Put a paper crown on his head and have him sit in a chair labeled "throne."

Then introduce the activity with this: **Hear ye! Hear ye! You have just become loyal subjects of the king of Primaryland. You must do whatever the king says. He is the ruler over all Primaryland. If you do not do what the king says, you will be banished to the far part of Primaryland and you will be required to wear a bag on your head** (or stand in the corner) **to show your disobedience to the king.**

King: "Everyone must stand up. You must never speak unless I call on you. You must bow three times and say, 'Yes, Your Majesty!' when I call on you. Everyone who wears glasses will be given a treat. Everyone who has blue eyes must stick his fingers in his ears."

Be sure to enforce these laws. The king should ask several pupils what they would do if they were king. The king should adopt several of the suggestions, if possible, and not allow other suggestions that are given. Then the king leaves the room. After the king leaves, lead the group in a discussion with the following questions.

How did it feel to be ruled by a king? Allow responses. **Which of the king's rules did you like? Which of the rules did you dislike? What does a king really do?** He decides everything that happens in his kingdom. **Do you think the king of Primaryland was fair? Why or why not?** Allow responses.

The Bible tells us we have a very special King. Our King is always fair and He always does what is right. Listen to what the Bible says: "I praise your greatness, my God the king. I will praise you for ever and ever. Everything the Lord does is right. With love he takes care of all he has made" (Psalm 145:1, 17, ICB). **Today we are going to spend time worshiping God, our very special King.**

Explain the worship choices today. Work so that there is an equal number of students in each group. Today you will be making Communion bread, so you will need to have access to a kitchen or bring in all necessary ingredients, utensils, and a toaster oven.

Building the Theme

(30 minutes)

1. Call to Worship. This group will present the call to worship during *Sharing in Worship.* You can carry this out two ways. You may want to provide different slides of landscapes and people and have these students decide which slides to show to illustrate the Scripture being read.

If you do not have access to a slide projector or slides and the students are having trouble deciding what to draw, show them how to draw stick figures to illustrate the verses. If your students are drawing, you'll need to provide drawing paper, crayons or markers, Bibles, and pencils.

Help the children find Psalm 95:1-7 in their Bibles. If possible, have the students listen as you read the verses from the *International Children's Bible.* Then divide the verses up so that each students gets one or two verses to illustrate. Also take time to practice so that the children feel comfortable reading the verses aloud. Give help as needed so students draw appropriate pictures to illustrate their verses. After students have finished drawing, rehearse the Scripture verses again, and have students hold up their pictures as they read.

You may even want to write the Scripture verses on the back of the pictures, especially if you have younger readers. Or if you have younger students, you may want to read each of the Scriptures aloud while the students hold up their pictures.

2. Scripture. Before the session, assemble the following materials: copies of activity page 24A, markers or crayons, pencils, and Bibles. This activity will probably work best for older or more advanced students.

This group will make a "wanted poster" to help review the Bible story during *Sharing in Worship.* To help find characteristics to put on the poster, review the Bible story's main ideas. Have students go to the Scripture (1 Samuel 8:1—10:1) for ideas. Give an example of what a wanted poster is and what kinds of things would need to be included on it if the Israelites were looking for a king.

Let's pretend that we were part of the Israelite group looking for a king. If we were going to put up a sign to publicize our search, what kind of information would we put on a poster for people to see?

Use the following verses: 1 Samuel 8:19, 20; 9:2, 21; 10:24. Brainstorm ideas about what the Israelites were looking for in a king. Include such characteristics as smart, intelligent, tall, impressive, can lead people.

Distribute copies of the activity page and writing and drawing utensils. The children may work individually or together. The activity page has the following copy for the children to fill in the blanks:

Wanted:
A man who is _______________,
_______________________, and
______________________ to lead
_______________ of Israel. He
must be able to _______________,
______________________, and
______________________. All
interested parties must talk to the prophet Samuel.

During *Sharing in Worship*, the students from the group will show the poster (posters) and tell the highlights of the Bible story.

3. Lord's Supper. This group will prepare the bread to be used for the Lord's Supper during *Sharing in Worship.* They will also sing "According to Thy Gracious Word" from a hymnal to prepare the worshipers for the Lord's Supper. If possible, have an instrumentalist record the tune to "According to Thy Gracious Word."

Show the students in this group a picture of any famous monument or statue, such as the Lincoln Memorial. Or refer to a monument or statue in your city or nearby. **People today build monuments to help us remember important people who have died. When we see the monument, it reminds us of the famous person and what he did. Instead of asking His followers to build a statue to remember Him, Jesus asked His followers to do something to remember Him and what He did.** As the pupils make bread, use some of the following ideas to keep the conversation purposeful. If you have tape recorded the hymn, play that as background music to your conversation.

What do Jesus' followers do to remember Him?

What do we remember? Why do we do this?

Why do we use bread and grape juice? What does it represent?

RECIPE
1 1/2 cups flour
1/2 teaspoon salt
1/2 cup shortening
4 to 5 tablespoons water

Mix ingredients in the order given. Give each pupil a small piece of dough to flatten into a thin circle. Place flattened dough on ungreased baking sheets and bake at 450° for 10 to 12 minutes.

If your church kitchen is not available, mix the dough before the session. Allow the children to flatten the dough. Bring a toaster oven to class for the baking.

While the dough is baking, rehearse the first three stanzas of "According to Thy Gracious Word." If you wish, use this as a poem, having the children practice reading it together. You may also assign parts of the poem to individual children rather than having them read it as a chorus.

Also choose two people from this group to take up the offering during *Sharing in Worship.*

4. Special Music. This group will sing antiphonally with the large group during *Sharing in Worship.*

This group will sing the song "Praise Ye the Lord" (also known as "Hallelu"), but the phrase "Praise Ye the Lord" will be replaced with sentences that tell things God does. The large group will sing all the phrases of "Hallelu" and Hallelujah" as well as joining together to sing the final phrase of the song.

Write on a chalkboard or poster board as the pupils dictate things that God does or is (God is eternal, God is our King). An example of one stanza follows:

Large group: Hallelu, hallelu, hallelu, hallelujah!
Small group: God always does what's right.
(Repeat the first two lines.)
Small group: God does what's right.
Large group: Hallelujah!
(Repeat last two lines twice.)
All: Praise ye the Lord!

Practice the song with any new phrases that your pupils have suggested.

5. Devotional. This group will present pantomimes during the devotional part of *Sharing in Worship.*

Present each of the following problems to the group. Let the pupils make up the story about the problem. Write down the story as the pupils dictate it. Then have the pupils make up the main character's thoughts as he contemplates doing the right thing. End the story with the main character's choosing to do right. Include the thought that God is King over all and that it is right to obey the King.

After each situation has been completed, assign pupils to the characters in each situation. Have the pupils practice pantomiming as you read each story. When the main character is contemplating what choice to make, have the pupil pantomiming that part step to the side of the scene and make facial expressions corresponding to his thoughts.

Problem 1. Jenny's mother told her to clean her room before she goes out to play with her friends. But Jenny's friend Michelle has to go home in thirty minutes.

Problem 2. Brian is in Bible school. He has just been kicked under the table for the third time by Jason.

Problem 3. Philip's friend Michael found a magazine with bad pictures in it. Michael wants Philip to look at it with him.

Problem 4. Melissa's friend Suzanne wants her to walk to the store with her. Melissa's mother told her not to leave the yard.

6. Prayer. For this activity, you'll need large sheets of paper or poster board, crayons or markers, and pencils.

Begin the activity by asking the students to name areas or places where they spend time and where it is important to obey God, the King over everything and everyone. Write the suggestions on the chalkboard or on another piece of poster board. Areas that should be included or mentioned: home, relatives' or friends' homes, school, playground, mall, sports activities.

Label each sheet of poster board or paper with one of these areas. Then the students will draw a picture of the area underneath the title. They should try to include areas in their drawings where children will need to make decisions about obeying God.

During *Sharing in Worship,* these students will lead the prayer time with the large group. Each student should show his poster, name the situation, and ask the large group to name other times in that area where it is important to obey God. Then the student who has the poster should lead a sentence prayer asking God for help and strength to obey Him in that situation. (Example: "God, please give us the strength to obey You, even when we're at school and our friends are watching us.")

Sharing in Worship

(20-25 minutes)

Omit any of the following sections if you did not offer the corresponding activity.

Call to Worship (Group 1): Group 1 will present their illustrated Scripture verses at this time. (If you're using the slides, have the slide projector set up and ready to go before the students come into worship.) **God is great and He is our King. We, as His children, come together today to worship and praise Him.**

Scripture (Group 2): Group 2 will present the wanted posters at this time and review the highlights of the Bible story. Include important facts about Samuel's needing to find a king, why Saul was chosen king, and how Saul was chosen king.

Lord's Supper (Group 3): Group 3 will read or sing "According to Thy Gracious Word." Members of this group will participate in serving Communion and collecting the offering.

Offering: One way we worship God our King is by bringing our offerings to Him.

Special Music (Group 4): Group 4 will lead the large group in singing "Praise Ye the Lord" ("Hallelu") with the new words they have written. Be sure to have the words of the verses displayed prominently so all children can see them.

Devotional (Group 5): Group 5 will present their pantomimes at this time. After each pantomime, stop and discuss the character's decisions. Discuss the consequences for students if they had not obeyed God. Then stress the following thoughts.

Jenny, Brian, Philip, and Melissa had important decisions to make. They had to choose what they thought God wanted

them to do or what someone else wanted them to do or they themselves wanted to do. And it made it even tougher because in most situations it involved making choices that included friends.

If a friend wants you to do something, it makes the decision harder because you want the friend to like you. So you might think twice about what they are asking you to do, especially if you know it is wrong. Or maybe you might say, "Why would disobeying one time hurt anything?" BUT DON'T! Disobeying God always has consequences. God knew that when He created us, and when He created certain rules.

Remember Samuel. He followed through on God's decision to make Saul king, even though Samuel didn't agree with God at first. And it wasn't an easy decision to make either.

Doing what God asks is not always easy. Sometimes your friends and family may not understand. They may ask you questions or may tease you. Or maybe your friends just don't want to be around you. Or they might try to get you in trouble—think of Philip and Brian!

Think back again to how we started the session today. Did you like having to obey our "king"? How did you feel about having to do whatever that king suggested? Some of his rules and orders did not make much sense. They seemed rather silly. It is hard to obey silly rules. It's not always easy to obey a king when you don't exactly know how he feels or what he thinks about you. Why obey someone if you don't know whether he cares about you or not?

But that's what is so wonderful about God—He does love and care about you. It makes it easier to obey someone when you know that he really is concerned about you. And obeying God's rules will bring joy. We've come together to celebrate and worship our mighty King. And because He's a King who loves us and cares about us and wants the best for us, we will always try to do the right thing in obeying His commands.

Prayer (Group 6): Group 6 will lead the prayers at this time. One at a time each group member should stand, show his poster, and ask for ideas about times when the children need to obey in that area. Then he should offer a sentence prayer, asking God for help and strength to obey in that situation.

Closing Moments

(10-15 minutes)

Distribute copies of activity page 24B and pencils. Show the children how to solve the secret code puzzle that reads, "Jesus is king of everything!" If you have time left, play "Kings Do This!" until closing time.

Wanted:

A man who is ______________________,

______________________________, and

____________________________ to lead

________________________ of Israel. He

must be able to ____________________,

_________________________________,

and _______________________________.

All interested parties must talk to the

prophet Samuel.

Use this code to solve the puzzle. You will find a special message about a special king.

Unit Six
We Choose to Do What God Says Is Right

Session 25

Saul Chooses to Disobey God

Worship Focus

Worship God because He always does right.

Transition Time

(10-15 minutes)

Animal Roundup. Play this game to give the children time to stretch and relax in between sessions. If you can, you might want to play this game outside. One player is one of Saul's soldiers. He is blindfolded. The other players choose to be cows or sheep. The soldier stands apart from the animals and calls out, "Baa, baa. Moo, moo. Come here." Then everyone skips and runs around the soldier making noises like cows or sheep. The soldier tries to tag any animal that comes close to him. The first animal the soldier tags becomes the next soldier.

Launching the Theme

(10 minutes)

Present the following puppet skit. Prior to the session, make two paper bag puppets. Use a table turned on its side as a stage. Two leaders could do this skit or one leader could use a different voice for each puppet.

Joel: Timothy, will you please help me put away these toys we've been playing with?

Timothy: No. I'm too tired to help you, Joel.

Joel: Then will you sing a song to cheer me up?

Timothy (in a raspy voice): No. I feel a sore throat coming on. I can't

Joel: Well, how about whistling a tune so I'll get done in a jiffy.

Timothy: No, my lips are chapped, and I can't pucker.

Joel: I know. Just clap your hands. It will sound like a drum in a band.

Timothy: No. I have a cut on my baby finger, and I can't clap.

Joel: All right. Just tap your toes then.

Timothy: No. I've got an ingrown toe nail, and it hurts too much.

Joel: Well, you sure have a lot of reasons for not helping me. Let's see if I can remember them: your baby finger is too tired, your throat has a cut, your toes are chapped, and your lips have an ingrown nail. Is that right?

Timothy: No, no, NO! You see, I'm too tired, my throat is sore, my lips are chapped, my. . . .

Joel (interrupting): I know, Timothy. My point is that you are just making up excuses not to do what is right. I'm sure glad that God is not like that.

Timothy: What do you mean?

Joel: I mean that God always does what is right. Always, always, ALWAYS. He doesn't get tired or make up excuses.

Timothy (in a small voice): Joel, I . . . I . . . I'm feeling quite a bit better. Let me help you with those toys.

Use these questions to focus a short discussion:

Name times when you don't want to do what's right. When you're tired, when friends do what is wrong, when you don't feel good, when you're grouchy or in a bad mood.

How do we know that God always does what is right? We can read in the Bible. **Listen while I read Psalm 71:14-16.** Do so.

Explain the choices of activities. Allow the children to choose the groups, but try to make sure that all groups have about the same number of students.

Building the Theme

(30 minutes)

1. Call to Worship. This group will present illustrations for the call to worship during *Sharing in Worship.* Provide powdered tempera paint, liquid starch, butcher or shelf paper, paint smocks (old large shirts and clothespins work well), newspaper to cover the tables, sponges or paper towels, and water for cleaning up.

Help the children find Psalm 69:30, 31 in their Bibles. Have the children listen as you read the verses from the *International Children's Bible.* Help the students put the verses in their own words by asking the following questions:

What does it mean to praise God?

What do we give to God today instead of cattle?

Write the paraphrase the pupils dictate on poster board or on the chalkboard. Both the verses and the paraphrase will be read during *Sharing in Worship.*

Ask the pupils to name things for which they are thankful or things they praise God for. Write down their responses. Let each child draw one thing for which he is thankful or for which he praises God. He should then cut it out.

When the children are done with that, have them put on paint smocks. Pour one or two tablespoons of liquid starch on the shelf or butcher paper. Sprinkle the undiluted tempera paint over it. Let the pupils finger paint designs on their part of the mural. Then have each child place his drawing on the wet paint. If possible, place the finished mural in a warm place to dry while you and the children clean up. You may wish to hang it from a string suspended across the front of the worship area. That way, no one need touch it again while it is damp, but all the children will see it for the call to worship.

2. Scripture. For this activity, you will need copies of activity page 25A, crayons or markers, scissors, glue, construction paper or shelf paper cut to 5" x 24", pencils, Bibles, and rulers.

Distribute activity page 25A. This has six different events from the Bible story, but they are not in the proper sequence. Work as a group to review the story from 1 Samuel 15:1-22 and put the pictures in the proper sequence by writing the correct number in the corner. When all have finished ordering the events of the Bible story, encourage the children to color the pictures and cut the picture boxes out.

Give each child the longer sheet of paper. Have him measure and mark the paper at 3" intervals and fold along these lines, accordion style. (See illustration on page 168.) Then show the children how to glue each picture to the longer paper in order, so they will have an accordion-style book. Have the children write the title and Scripture reference on the first section: Saul Chooses to Disobey, 1 Samuel 15:1-22. On the last section, the children can write, "It is better to obey God than to offer a sacrifice (1 Samuel 15:22, ICB)."

During *Sharing in Worship,* these children will show their accordion-style books and review the different events in the Bible story.

3. Offering. This activity is a challenge activity. This group will need pencils, paper, and Bibles. Have these references listed on the chalkboard or on a piece of poster board: Psalm 96:8; Deuteronomy 16:17; 2 Corinthians 9:7; and 1 Corinthians 2:12.

Have this group of children look up these Scripture references and read them aloud. They need to decide what these verses say about God or about giving in general. Then help the children work as a group to write a modern-day paraphrase of these verses or write what they think these verses mean. If time permits, you may want to work with this group to show them how to use a concordance to look up other references about giving and offering.

During *Sharing in Worship,* introduce the offering by saying, **This is some of what God said about himself and about offerings.** Then have one student read each verse aloud and then read the paraphrase of that verse.

Designate two children to collect the offering.

4. Special Music. This group will play rhythm instruments while singing "Give the Lord Some Praise" during *Sharing in Worship.* Provide already-made instruments or allow the children to make some of their own. Obtain empty plastic containers, unpopped popcorn, wooden dowels sawed into eight-inch pieces, empty oatmeal boxes or coffee cans, blocks of scrap wood, sandpaper, an old sock, and pop bottle lids.

Show the children how to make the instruments. Fill the empty containers with the unpopped corn to make maracas. The wooden dowels can be rhythm or drum sticks. The empty coffee cans or oatmeal boxes can serve as drums. Bang blocks of wood together for cymbals. Glue sandpaper to blocks of wood and rub together for an unusual sound. Place the pop bottle lids in the sock to make a tambourine.

While the students are making the instruments, read Psalm 92:1-5 from the *International Children's Bible.* Ask the students to name things that God has done and things that God does. Help them review what they have learned about God in recent sessions. Then teach the children the song "Give the Lord Some Praise." If the pupils do not know the song well, spend time learning the song without the instruments. Practice several times with the pupils singing and playing the instruments too.

5. Devotional. This group will present tape-recorded stories for the devotional time of *Sharing in Worship*. You will need paper and writing utensils. Also prepare a poster with Deuteronomy 6:17, 18 (ICB) written so the large group will be able to read it.

Have students dictate to you their stories about children who have to choose between doing the right things or the wrong thing. Or have students work in a cooperative group together; give help or begin a situation as needed to get them started thinking. Direct the children's thoughts with questions or statements, such as **Tell us about a time you did something wrong,** to help them get ideas for stories. Make sure that the character in one of the stories chooses to do wrong. Let that story have a negative consequence because of choosing to do wrong.

Write the stories in first person, as if the character is telling the story aloud. At the point in the story when the character is contemplating the choice, have the character say, "What should I do?" When presenting the tape-recorded stories during *Sharing in Worship,* you will stop the recording at this time and the large group will respond by reading or reciting Deuteronomy 6:17, 18. Then you will release the button and the tape will continue, playing the conclusion of the story, and the large group will learn what the character chooses to do.

In small-group time beforehand, let different pupils read the stories into the tape recorder after the stories have been written. If you have beginning readers, read the stories into the tape recorder for them.

6. Prayer. This group will present its illustrated prayers during *Sharing in Worship.* Provide copies of activity page 25B and markers or crayons.

Brainstorm with the children about situations when it is very hard for them to choose to do right. Let each situation begin, "When. . . ." Write their ideas on chalkboard or poster board. Let each pupil choose one situation to illustrate.

During *Sharing in Worship,* you will begin the prayer, "Dear God. . . ." Each pupil will show his illustration and say, "When. . . ." and tell what the illustration depicts. For example, one student may have drawn a picture of two children on the playground. One child is calling the other child a name. During *Sharing in Worship,* this pupil would say, "When I'm playing and someone calls me a name, . . ." After each pupil shows his drawing and tells his situation, the large group should respond, "God help me choose to do the right thing." When all the drawings have been shown, you will close with, "In Jesus' name, amen."

Sharing in Worship

(20-25 minutes)

Omit any of the following sections if you did not offer the corresponding activity.

Call to Worship (Group 1): Group 1 will present its mural and the paraphrase of Psalm 69:30, 31 at this time. **We take this time now to praise and glorify God who always does what is right. We need to focus our attention, our minds, and our hearts on God to worship Him now.**

Scripture (Group 2): Group 2 will show the accordion-fold books at this time. Be sure to ask the children to highlight the main points of the Bible story: God told Saul to destroy the Amalekites; Saul disobeyed God; and Samuel chastised (scolded) Saul.

Lord's Supper: God is perfect and always does what is right. Man sinned and was separated from God. But God who loves us so much, sent His Son to earth so He could make things wrong and we could be close to God again. Think about how much God loves us during this Communion time.

Offering (Group 3): Ask children from Group 3 to read the offering verses and paraphrases at this time. Then have two of these children collect the offering.

Special Music (Group 4): Group 4 will use the rhythm instruments to accompany "Give the Lord Some Praise." Have Group 4 sing the song once without instruments, and then once with instruments. If there is time, sing it again and ask the large group to sing along.

Devotional (Group 5): Play the tape-recorded stories at this time. When all stories have been played, and you have discussed each one, take time to stress the following thoughts.

(You will need to have a clock with moveable hands to use during your talk.)

There is a book that came out a long time ago. The name of the book is *In His Steps* and it was written by Charles Sheldon. The main idea of this book is that each person started making decisions by asking himself the question, "What would Jesus do?"

Think about that for a moment—how would your day be different if at every big decision you made, you would ask the question, "What would Jesus do?"

Set the clock at 7 AM. **What are you doing at this time of day? What kind of mood do you wake up in every morning? How could you honor Jesus and do the right thing in the morning as you begin the day?** (or get ready for school?) If the children have a hard time getting started thinking about their activities, you can begin by telling about what you're doing at that time of the morning.

Go through each hour or half hour through dinner time and have the children practice telling time while you're discussing activities. If time is limited, choose certain important times of the day, such as 10 AM, 12 noon, 3 PM, 6 PM, and 9 PM.

Ask the children to tell what they would be doing at those times of the day and how they could honor Jesus in the activities they do at those times.

If you can get a copy of *In His Steps*, show it to the children at this time. **This book talks mainly about adults who obeyed God. But think about how different school would be or the playground would be if children asked themselves, "What would Jesus do?"**

By obeying God, you are pleasing Him. You feel better about yourself for doing the right thing. Other students may see your example and see you taking a stand for Jesus. Maybe some adults would see you take a stand too.

Since God always does what is right, let's work hard to obey Him at all times, even when it is difficult.

Prayer (Group 6): Have students from Group 6 show their poster pictures. Begin the prayer, "Dear God. . . ." Then, one by one, each pupil will show his illustration and say, "When. . . ." and tell what the illustration depicts, such as "When I'm playing and someone calls me a name, . . ." Then the large group should respond, "God help me choose to do the right thing." When all the drawings have been shown, you will close with, **In Jesus' name, amen.**

Closing Moments

(10-15 minutes)

Have chalkboard and chalk or a large pad of drawing paper and markers available. The children will take turns drawing (with stick figures) situations where they need to make a decision to do what is right. The other children will guess what that situation is and suggest the decision that would be most pleasing to God. The child who is drawing should not use letters or numbers, gesture with his hands, or talk while the children are trying to guess what he is drawing.

Be prepared with ideas for the children to draw in case some are having trouble coming up with situations. Include ideas such as when friends want him to do something his parents have told him not to, when he is being laughed at, when the rest of the class is doing wrong.

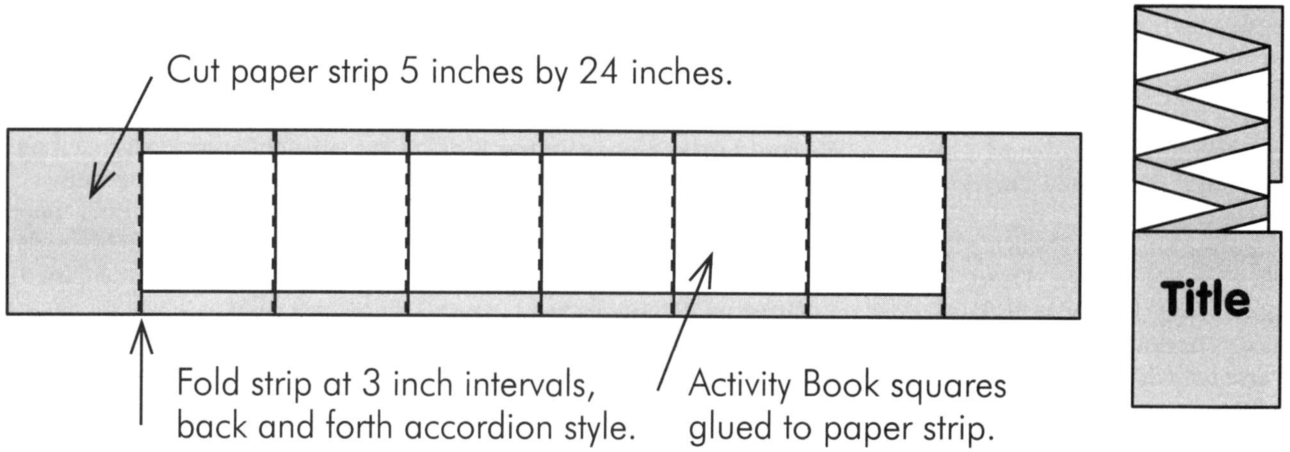

Saul and his men attack the Amalekites.

Samuel tells Saul to go attack the Amalekites.

Samuel confronts Saul.

God talks to Samuel.

Saul spares Agag and animals.

Saul summons men.

Dear God,

God help me choose to do the right thing.

Samuel Chooses to Do Right

Worship Focus

Worship God because He always does right.

Transition Time

(10-15 minutes)

Anoint King David. Play the game to help pupils relax and stretch. The game is played the same way as "Pin the Tail on the Donkey." You will need a blindfold, a picture of David, a ram's horn cut from construction paper, and Plasti-Tak. Mount the picture of David on the wall or chalkboard at the pupils' eye level. Place Plasti-Tak on the back of the horn. Blindfold a child. The blindfolded pupil will try to place the horn above David's head. Allow each child a turn.

Launching the Theme

(10 minutes)

The children will review what they have learned about God in previous worship sessions by learning new words to the tune of "The Twelve Days of Christmas." The large group will learn the refrain together. Then divide the pupils into at least three smaller groups. The repeated phrases of the song will be divided among the small groups.

Oh, I praise the Lord in Heaven,
And tell Him He is great!
Yes, the Lord always does the right thing.

Oh, I praise the Lord in Heaven,
And tell Him He is great!
He is very special. *(sung by one small group)*
Yes, the Lord always does the right thing.

Oh, I praise the Lord in Heaven,
And tell Him He is great!
He tells the truth. *(sung by second small group)*
He is very special. *(sung by first small group)*
Yes, the Lord always does the right thing.

Continue in this manner, adding the following phrases, one each stanza:

He gives instructions.
He does good things.
He helps us do hard jobs.
He helps us to be brave.
He can do all things.
He forgives us.
He keeps His promises.
He lives forever.
He is king of all.

Spend time in the large group learning the refrain. Then break into small groups with an adult to lead each one. After each small group is comfortable with its phrases, practice putting the song together. When everyone is comfortable singing the song, sing it one more time, and this time record it on the tape recorder. Ask the pupils to listen for their group singing as you play back the recording.

Explain the choices for worship today. Try to arrange it so that each group has about the same number of students as the other groups.

Building the Theme

(30 minutes)

1. Call to Worship. This group will present the call to worship during *Sharing in Worship*. You will need poster board and markers or crayons.

Pupils will write sentences that review some things that God does. Use the attributes of God for the song that was sung during *Launching the Theme*. The large group will respond to each sentence by reading or reciting Psalm 7:17 (ICB): "I praise the Lord because he does what is right."

Write out the responsive reading on poster board as the students dictate, using large lettering to facilitate reading at a distance. After this is completed, let the pupils decorate the poster board with a border.

Your responsive reading might look something like this:

Pupil: God always does what is right.

Large Group: I praise the Lord because he does what is right.

Pupil: God always tells the truth.

Large Group: I praise the Lord because he does what is right.

Pupil: God gives His instructions in the Bible.

Large Group: I praise the Lord because he does what is right.

2. Scripture. This will be a good way to review the Bible stories but will take some extra time to complete. Keep that in mind as you plan your worship time.

This group will be making a story quilt to show during *Sharing in Worship* to review the Bible stories for the past quarter. You will need to provide: 12 squares of muslin 1′ x 1′, crayons, fusible bonding strips (1″ wide) or needle and thread, iron, and newspaper. You will also need to draw a 1″ border with pencil around each muslin square. Students should keep the border blank for attaching the squares together. (If you do not want to use material to do this, use paper squares 1′ x 1′ and attach the squares together with glue.)

Take a few moments to review the stories from the past quarter. (They are listed below.) Try to get students to tell the main characters and the final outcome of the story. Be sure that they understand how the characters did right in each instance. Assign one or two stories to each child in the group. They will need to draw a picture to illustrate each story, and then label each story with a title and the Scripture reference.

After the students have colored their squares, set the color by placing the square face down on newspaper and ironing over it with a warm (not hot) iron. Then attach the squares in order with the fusible bonding or a needle and thread. While you are attaching the squares together, help the children practice what they will say when they show the quilt.

Here are the review stories:

Joshua Chooses to Obey God
Deuteronomy 31:1-8, 14-23; 34:1-9; Joshua 1

Joshua and Caleb Tell the Truth
Numbers 13; 14:5-9, 30, 34, 36

Joshua Follows God's Instructions
Joshua 5:13—6:20

God's People Choose to Do Right
Joshua 24:1-7

Deborah Helps Barak Do a Hard Job
Judges 4:1-16, 23, 24

Gideon Chooses to Be Brave
Judges 6:1-16; 7:1-22

Ruth Works Hard
Ruth 1, 2

Jonah Changes His Mind
Jonah 1—2:1, 10; 3:1-3

Hannah Keeps Her Promise
1 Samuel 1

Samuel Chooses to Do Right All His Life
1 Samuel 2:18, 21, 26; 3:1-10, 19, 20; 4:1; 7:15-17

Samuel Chooses to Obey God
1 Samuel 8:1—10:1

Saul Chooses to Disobey God
1 Samuel 15:1-22

Samuel Chooses to Do Right
1 Samuel 16:1-13

During *Sharing in Worship*, each student will explain his quilt pieces and tell a little bit about each Bible story.

3. Offering. The students in this group will help lead the group in thanking God for different things He gives us. You will need poster board; old catalogs, magazines, activity papers, and take-home papers; scissors; glue; and markers.

Have this group brainstorm a list of things that they are thankful to God for. After you make a list of about twenty items, ask the group to categorize the items into the following: creation/nature; families; friends and other people; toys and possessions; God and His church.

Write each one of these categories at the top of a sheet of poster board. Then ask students to look through old magazines, papers, and so on to find pictures that would illustrate these main groups. Show them how to glue the pictures down on the appropriate category poster.

During *Sharing in Worship*, these students will hold up each poster and direct prayers to God, thanking Him for the things in each category. After the prayer time, ask two children to collect the offering.

4. Special Music. Help the pupils find the following verses in their Bibles. Read the verses aloud and together decide what each verse has to say about what God does. List these characteristics on poster board or on the chalkboard. The verses are Psalm 7:17 (does what is right); Psalm 105:8 (keeps His promises); Psalm 86:5 (forgives us); and Psalm 10:16 (is King).

Sing the chorus "God Is So Good" with the students. Ask them to suggest other stanzas about God from the list of characteristics that you have made. Practice singing the new stanzas until the pupils are comfortable.

5. Devotional. This group will present a puppet story for the devotional during *Sharing in Worship*. Older or more advanced students would do better at this center. Try to have extra adult help also.

You will need activity page 26A, paper, pencils, crayons or markers, scissors, tape, and craft sticks. Students will be able to make their own puppets to take with them. The puppets on activity page 26A can be designed by each child to represent either boys or girls.

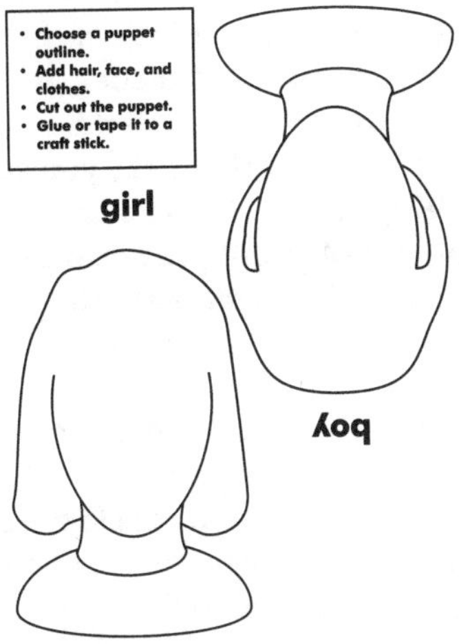

Pupils write a story about two children to illustrate choices that one of the children has to make. The story should contain at least four choices for one child to make that are neither right or wrong. For example, one can choose what color shirt to put on, what to eat for a shack, which friend to go see, and what toy to play with. These choices should always be between two things, such as whether to wear a red or yellow shirt. The pupils will draw a picture of each choice the child has to make, so help pupils use things for the choices that can be drawn rather easily.

The climax of the story is a final choice the child has to make. This choice must be between doing the right thing and doing the wrong thing. Help the pupils make up two endings: one ending where the child chooses to do right, and the other ending where the child chooses to do wrong. Each of these choices will also be illustrated.

After the story has been dictated to you, let the pupils decide among themselves the illustrations to be drawn. Allow enough time so that each student will have a chance to make his own puppets. Have the children color the puppets, cut them out, and attach each of them to a craft stick with tape.

During *Sharing in Worship*, you (or an able reader) will read the story. Pupils from the large group will choose what the child does at each point of choice in the story, including the final outcome.

As the story is read, pupils from this group will hold up the corresponding illustrations when the child is presented with a choice. They can also hold up their puppets when it is their time to illustrate the story. The pupils from the large group will select which choice the child makes. The pupil holding the unchosen illustration will lay that illustration face down.

6. Prayer. This group will lead the closing prayer during *Sharing in Worship*. Provide coloring paper and crayons or markers.

Help the pupils make conclusions between what God did in the following Bible stories and what He does for us today. Write these conclusions on the chalkboard or on poster board.

Session 3: Joshua led the people in the battle of Jericho. (God gave Joshua instructions for what to do. God gives us instructions in the Bible.)

Session 5: Deborah helped Barak by going with him to battle. (God helped Deborah do a hard job. God will help us do hard jobs.)

Session 8: Jonah finally goes to Nineveh. (God forgave Jonah for disobeying Him at first. God forgives us when we do wrong.)

Session 9: Hannah prayed and asked God for a son. (God heard her prayer. God hears our prayers.)

Have the children discuss how to illustrate the ways God helps us today. Let the pupils choose what they will illustrate. A picture of each Bible story and a picture of the corresponding way God helps us today are needed. Use fewer stories if the group is small.

During *Sharing in Worship*, have each pupil say a sentence prayer thanking God for what He did or for what He does, as illustrated in his picture. For example, "Thank You, God, for giving Joshua instructions how to beat Jericho. Thank You, God, for giving me instructions on how to live in the Bible."

Sharing in Worship

(20-25 minutes)

Omit any of the following sections if you did not offer the corresponding activity.

Before the session cut apart the seven sentence strips from activity page 26B. You will need to put up a sentence strip with the appropriate words as you introduce each concept during the devotional. You might want to ask different students either to come put up the strip or to read it aloud.

Call to Worship (Group 1): Group 1 will present their responsive reading at this time. Be sure the large group knows what they are to say, and when they are to say it. You might want to practice one or two lines together first before you put the whole thing together.

Scripture (Group 2): Group 2 will show their quilt at this time. This will take some time, so encourage students to keep their remarks brief. Make sure they mention the main characters of the story and the eventual outcome of the Bible person's obedience or disobedience of God. (Find a place to display the quilt for the next few weeks.)

Lord's Supper: Did you know there was a time that Jesus asked God whether He had to do what God had said? Think about Jesus' prayer in the Garden of Gethsemane. Even Jesus thought about the hard thing God had asked Him to do, and He went ahead anyway. Jesus knew that His death would be very painful, but He obeyed God. He knew how important it was, even to us today. If Jesus had not obeyed God, His Father, we would not have the opportunity to communicate with God today.

Offering (Group 3): Group 3 will hold up its category posters at this time. Each child who holds up a poster can lead a sentence prayer, thanking God for those items. Then ask two students to collect the offering.

Devotional (Group 5): Group 5 will present the puppet story at this time. After the story is finished, take time to talk about the consequences of obeying or not obeying God.

At this time, you will need to remind your volunteers with the sentence strips to be ready when you call on them. The phrases on the strips are in all capital letters.

For most of this summer, we've been talking about doing right. Today, we want to review what doing right means. Can you tell me the definition of doing right for God? Ask for the children's responses. Write their ideas on the chalkboard or on a piece of poster board. **These are all good ideas. Let's take time to review some ideas now.**

Put up the first strip: DOING RIGHT MEANS HONORING AND WORSHIPING GOD. **Each Sunday we do right by coming together. All of the activities we do together—praying, singing, giving, reading, listening—honor God for who He is and what He has done for us. Since God is so great and wonderful, we want to praise and thank Him. It is right to do that.**

Put up the second strip: DOING RIGHT MEANS DOING WHAT GOD ASKS. **God has told us what He wants us to do. We can read and find out what His instructions are in the Bible. That's our guidebook to know what to do. That's why we take time to read and study it here in church. That's why we want you to take time to read and study it at home.**

Put up the third strip: DOING RIGHT MEANS TELLING THE TRUTH. **That means telling the truth even when it's hard or even when you know you might or will get in trouble. It may mean that some people or a friend may be angry with you. But Jesus is our example. He always told the truth.**

Put up the fourth strip: DOING RIGHT MEANS DOING HARD JOBS. **Doing the right thing isn't always the easiest thing to do. Look at our example, Jesus. He died on the cross for us. And that was an extremely hard thing to do. But when we have to do hard jobs, we remember that we don't have to do them alone. Jesus is our friend who is with us all the way, helping and guiding us.**

Put up the fifth sentence strip: DOING RIGHT MEANS BEING BRAVE. **Being brave means speaking up. It means telling the truth. It's being honest with your family, your teachers, and your friends. Being brave doesn't mean you might not feel scared sometimes, but you know you're not alone. And you trust Jesus to be right there with you.**

Put up the sixth sentence strip: DOING RIGHT MEANS FORGIVING AS HE FORGIVES. **This is hard, even for adults. When we've been hurt, it takes some time to forgive someone. When we forgive someone, we are acting as Jesus does when He forgives us.**

Put up the last sentence strip: DOING RIGHT MEANS KEEPING OUR PROMISES. **This shows the kind of person you are. People will trust you and respect you if they know you keep your word and don't break your promises. And it means asking for forgiveness if you do accidentally break a promise.**

As you read through these sentence strips, think about how you can do these things each day, whether you are at school, at home, or with your friends. Choose one of the ideas you see here right now. Let's have a moment of silent prayer to ask God to help us do that thing in a particular situation we have to face. Do that now.

Prayer (Group 6): Ask Group 6 to offer sentence prayers, thanking God for what He does or what He did, depending on what they have drawn in their pictures.

Closing Moments

(10-15 minutes)

Spend time reviewing what has been learned about God during this quarter by singing again the song learned during today's *Launching the Theme.* Point to the different stanzas as you sing them together.

If time allows, have the children make puppets from activity page 26A and act out situations of making right choices.

Be sure the children have all their papers and activity pages from this past quarter to take home with them.

- **Choose a puppet outline.**
- **Add hair, face, and clothes.**
- **Cut out the puppet.**
- **Glue or tape it to a craft stick.**

girl

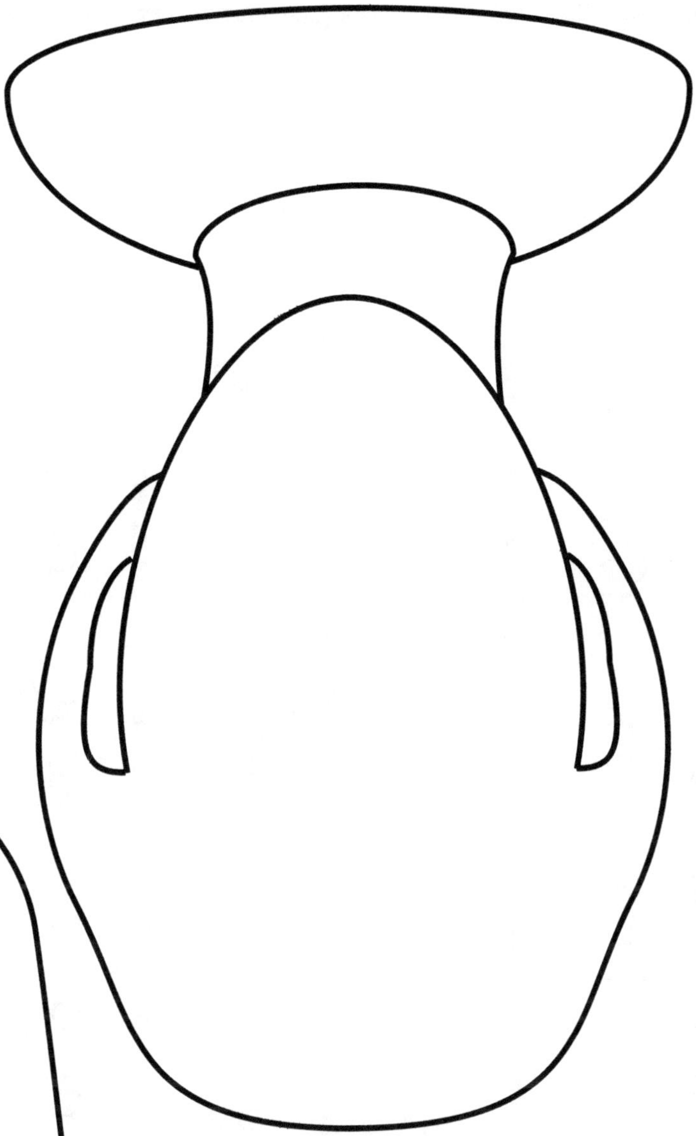

boy

1. Doing right means honoring and worshiping God. ★

2. Doing right means doing what God asks. ★

3. Doing right means telling the truth. ★

4. Doing right means doing hard jobs. ★

5. Doing right means being brave. ★

6. Doing right means forgiving as He forgives. ★

7. Doing right means keeping our promises. ★

WORSHIP SONGS

If You Got Good News, Tell It Brother

N. L. S. NORMAN L. STARKS

My Offering

J. E. C. Janis E. Combs

I Can Tell

Janis E. Combs | Janis E. Combs

It's Time to Praise the Lord

Janis E. Combs

Janis E. Combs

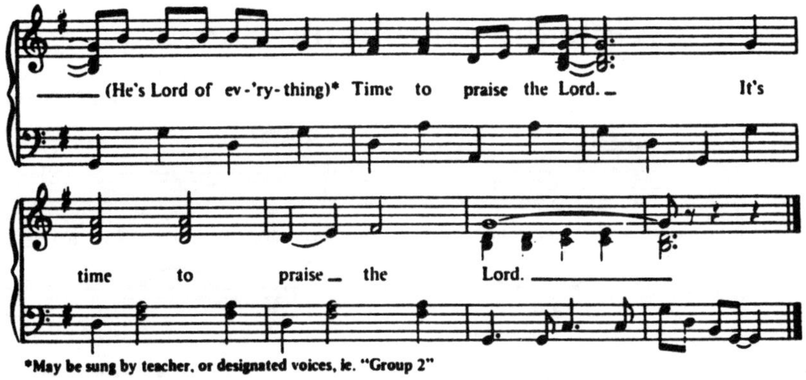

*May be sung by teacher, or designated voices, ie. "Group 2"

I Will Sing

Janis E. Combs Janis E. Combs

v.2—I will learn about the Lord today.
v.3—We will sing about God's word today.
v.4—We will praise God for His word today.

Give the Lord Some Praise

J. E. C. | Janis E. Combs

*May be sung by teacher or designated voices.

All the World Was Made by God

Heather Smith Turner **Heather Smith Turner**

Ev'-ry-thing God does is right.
Ev'-ry-thing God does is right.
Ev'-ry-thing God does is right,
so praise His name.

All God's words are true, true, true.
All God's words are true, true, true.
All God's words are true, true, true,
so praise His name.

Jesus, I Love You

M.K.B. Mary Kay Bottens

x = Clap hands.

Shout the Word

Cindy Tamplin | Cindy Tamplin

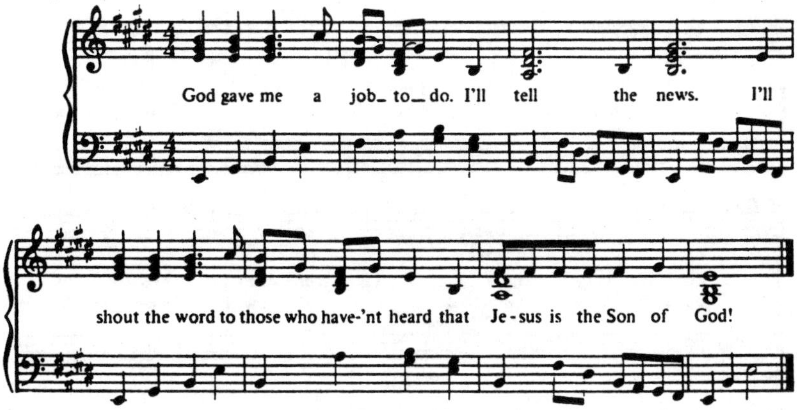

Go Everywhere!

Cindy Tamplin | Cindy Tamplin

I Love to Tell About Jesus

D.W. | Don Whitman

Who Can I Tell?

Brent Little | Brent Little

He Promises Love

D.O. | Doris Owens

I'll Tell the Good News

M.K.B. Mary Kay Bottens

Jesus, Teach Me

D.W. Don Whitman

I Will Bring a Friend to Jesus

M.F. Mark Fessler

Communion Hymn

CHARLES McMILLAN

J. C. BLAKER

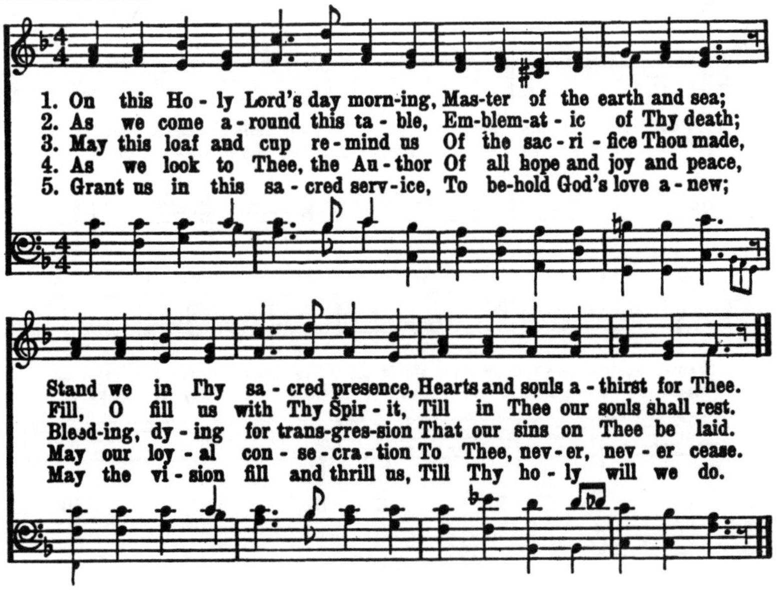

God Wants Me to Do Right

D.C.

Dot Cachiaras

Arranged by Michelle Pittinger

Paul and Silas

M. K. B.

Mary Kay Bottens

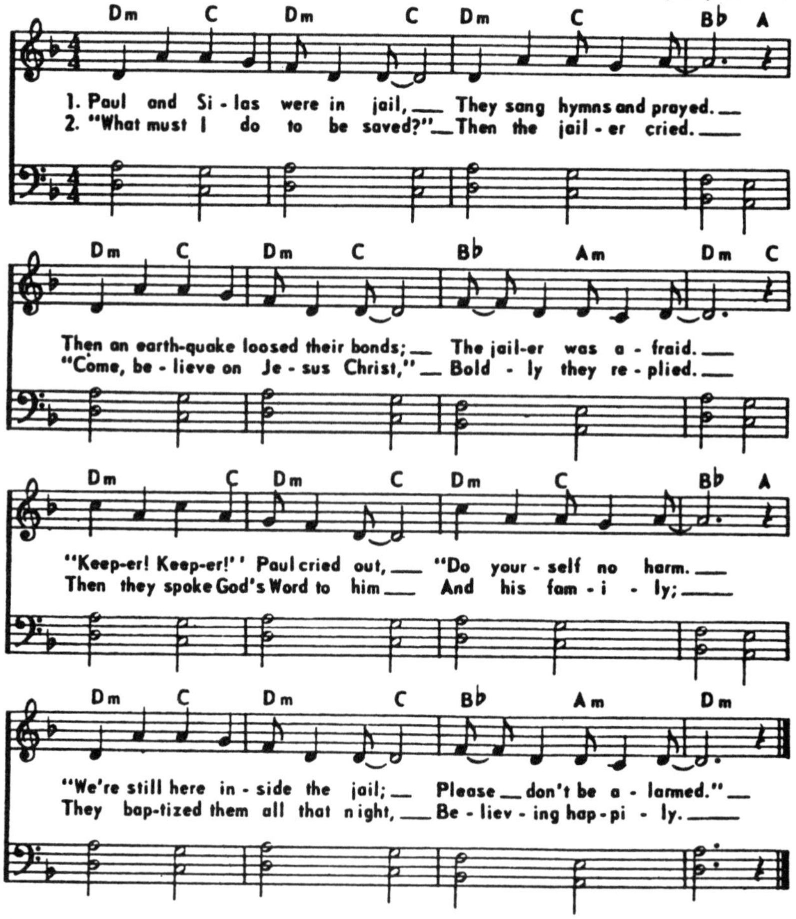

Samuel Pleased the Lord

D. C.

Dot Cachiaras
Arr. by Michelle Pittinger

Samuel did what was right always.
Samuel did what was right always.
Samuel did what was right always.
He wanted to please the Lord.

He did right even when it was hard.
He did right even when it was hard.
He did right even when it was hard.
He wanted to please the Lord.

Oh, Be Careful